"Mark and David present the key challenges facing the healthcare system and provide a comprehensive solution that is easy to understand for the general public while challenging the status quo among healthcare leaders. The book is very timely given the disruptive changes taking place in healthcare and definitely contributes to the current discourse regarding our industry's future!"

Céu Cirne-Neves, MPA, CPHQ, FACHE
Vice President—Physician and Patient Services
Saint Barnabas Medical Center
RWJBarnabas Health

"The book's patient-centered, resource management view of the U.S. healthcare system offers a unique perspective that will resonate with and generate fresh discussions among policy makers, healthcare payers, physician leaders, and hospital executives alike. The book provides a fresh understanding of the healthcare delivery system that would be useful in healthcare–business academic degree programs as well as in educational sessions for healthcare managers and executives. This book motivates a new conversation, focused on a highly integrative, comprehensive approach to improving healthcare delivery."

Jeffrey P. Gold, MD
Chancellor
University of Nebraska Medical Center

"*A Healthcare Solution* is a comprehensive and timely resource that is presented in a way that is understandable and engaging. The examples that are given are great insights into current healthcare problems and their root causes. The true intent of the authors is to improve health. Bravo."

Rene Zipper, MBA, FACHE
Vice President Mid-Market
Press Ganey Associates

"Vonderembse and Dobrzykowski provide a future-thinking, grounded, holistic approach to health care reform. A welcome addition to the health care leadership toolbox and a must read."

Juan Manuel Tovar, MD
Medical Director Quality, Performance Improvement, and Utilization Management
Scripps Mercy Hospital

"Vonderembse and Dobrzykowski provide meaningful insight into the challenges we face with healthcare delivery and the solutions all stakeholders should reflect in our strategies and business models. This book should be mandatory reading for provider executives, supply chain leaders, product and services company representatives, and anyone involved with healthcare services—physicians, clinicians, providers, suppliers, consultants, and patients. It offers a comprehensive tool for helping us all achieve higher quality and more cost-effective patient care and wellness."

David Myers
EVP & Chief Customer Officer
Concordance Healthcare Solutions
Past Chairman, Healthcare Industry Distributors Association

A Healthcare Solution

A Patient-Centered, Resource Management Perspective

Series on Resource Management

A Healthcare Solution

A Patient-Centered, Resource Management Perspective

Mark A. Vonderembse

David D. Dobrzykowski

Foreword by Randy Oostra, President & CEO, ProMedica

CRC Press
Taylor & Francis Group
Boca Raton London New York

CRC Press is an imprint of the
Taylor & Francis Group, an **informa** business

CRC Press
Taylor & Francis Group
6000 Broken Sound Parkway NW, Suite 300
Boca Raton, FL 33487-2742

© 2017 by Taylor & Francis Group, LLC
CRC Press is an imprint of Taylor & Francis Group, an Informa business

No claim to original U.S. Government works

ISBN-13: 978-1-4987-5875-8 (hbk)

Visit the Taylor & Francis Web site at
http://www.taylorandfrancis.com

and the CRC Press Web site at
http://www.crcpress.com

To my wonderful wife, life companion, and best friend, Gayle.

In memory of our loving parents: Paul Edward Vonderembse, Ruth Mary Vonderembse, Robert L. Bauer, and Pauline M. Bauer.

To our children and their spouses and significant others: Leisje and Dan, Tosje and Ted, Anthony and Lindsey, Vanessa and Don, Talia and Jake, Elaine and Greg, and Maryke and Jeremy.

To our grandchildren: Perry, Koen, Milo, Aubriella, Stella, Trevor, Logan, Lillia, Ava, and Jack.

Love to all.

To my loving and brilliant wife, Sarah. You are an amazing partner in this wild ride we call life.

To my parents: Patricia A. and Daniel S. Dobrzykowski, for their guidance as I grew into adulthood and their unwavering support throughout my career(s) and academic development.

To my in-laws: Catherine M. and Dr. Joseph F. Tomashefski for their kindness and understanding.

To our sons: David D. and Adam J. Dobrzykowski. As Papa Dobie told me, there is no love like the love of a father for his sons.

I appreciate and love you all.

Contents

Foreword

This book by Mark Vonderembse and David Dobrzykowski is ambitious. They develop and describe a comprehensive and integrated solution that addresses the root causes and underlying problems in the healthcare delivery system. They focus on how to implement the solution and describe the most important stakeholders in driving change.

They indicate that the solution depends on three key elements: implementing patient-centered care so that patients are better served, enhancing wellness so that less care is needed, and finding ways to use resources so that outcomes improve and costs decline. As part of the solution, they discuss shifting the value proposition for healthcare because it is a critical influencer in decision making. As patients focus primarily on the benefit side of the value proposition and, to a lesser extent, on the cost side because a third party pays most of the bill, patients tend to overconsume care and hospitals and providers have less incentive to focus on productivity, efficiency, and reducing costs. Patients should be more aware of the total cost of services they receive so that they can make more informed decisions about their care. In addition, hospitals and physicians need to change their focus and primary responsibilities from diagnoses and treatment to health and well-being. These are dramatic changes as each of these key constituencies in the value chain potentially has something important to lose, and as Vonderembse and Dobrzykowski point out, the gains are not necessarily well defined.

This is an important book for the C-level suite at any healthcare organization to read. But this book takes a broad view that would also appeal to graduate students and others interested in learning about healthcare administration and leadership or anyone interested in helping shape the future of healthcare, including the general public. It is a book with thoughtful and thought-provoking ideas written in a practical, common-sense manner.

The role of healthcare systems and how and when they care for individuals and communities is irrevocably changing. As healthcare leaders and professionals, we can no longer afford to think inwardly; we must take the broader view in driving industry change as we strive to achieve the triple aim of improving health outcomes, enhancing the care experience, and reducing costs.

Innovation can take many forms, including new and better approaches to clinical care, new models of care, and going beyond the traditional role of healthcare organizations to have a greater, longer-lasting impact on the health of the people we are privileged to care for and for our communities.

This book will make you think. And it will give you meaningful, actionable ideas in furthering the path to a patient-centered, resource management solution to our current healthcare environment.

Randy Oostra, DM, FACHE
President and CEO
ProMedica

ProMedica is a community-based, mission-driven, not-for-profit health system serving 27 counties in northwest Ohio and southeast Michigan and seeing more than 4.7 million patient encounters annually. ProMedica is a fully integrated health system comprised of 12 hospitals, six ambulatory surgery centers, continuum services, a provider network with more than 800 employed physicians and providers, and a comprehensive health insurance services organization. ProMedica has more than 15,000 employees and nearly 2300 physicians. Learn more at https://www.promedica.org/Pages/about-us/default.aspx.

Acknowledgments

There are many people to thank for their superb contributions to the creation of this book, including our teachers, mentors, and colleagues who, over the years, have helped to prepare us to write this book. There are simply too many to mention by name.

We owe special thanks to the following people. William T. Walker, CFPIM, CIRM, CSCP, is a Resource Management Series Editor for CRC Press/Taylor & Francis Group. He has guided us through the writing and creative processes, giving us valuable comments as well as reading the manuscript and providing excellent feedback. Lara Zoble, Editor for CRC Press/Taylor & Francis Group, believed in the project early on and acted quickly to clear the path so our project could move forward. Kristine Mednansky, Senior Editor for Business Improvement—Healthcare for CRC Press/Taylor & Francis Group, has been instrumental in the success of the book including the development and execution of its marketing plan. Amy Blalock, Supervisor for Editorial Project Development for CRC Press/Taylor & Francis Group, has been very helpful in creating and presenting the book. Jay Margolis, Project Editor for CRC Press/Taylor & Francis Group, guided us through the final steps to publication. We appreciate their efforts very much.

Dr. Thomas Gutteridge, former dean of the College of Business and Innovation at the University of Toledo, provided us with an opportunity to investigate and work extensively on healthcare projects. He was an important influence in putting us on a path to write this book. Brian Hinch, MD, provided us the opportunities to examine the implementation of electronic health records (EHR) and the "meaningful use" of EHR at the University of Toledo Medical Center (UTMC). We wish to thank Thomas Schwann, MD, Chief of Staff, Interim Chair of Surgery, and a leading Cardio-Thoracic Surgeon at UTMC, for his support for our initiatives and passion for improving healthcare delivery. While at the University of Toledo, Jeffrey Gold, MD, Chancellor, Dean of the College of Medicine, led efforts to form the School of Healthcare Innovation and Excellence, which provided opportunities for interdisciplinary collaboration among the Colleges of Medicine and Business. These interactions were essential in forming key ideas that are part of this book. David would like to thank Dr. Lei Lei, Dean of Rutgers Business School, for her stout interest in and support of research and academic programing at the intersection of healthcare and business. Thank you to Karen Culler and Arden Brion, David's former colleagues at Mercy Health, who opened his eyes to the complicated inter-dependencies that exist among hospitals and physicians and ignited in him a life-long passion for improving coordination in healthcare delivery. We would also like to thank Dr. Mahmud Hassan, professor of finance and economics and director of the MBA in pharmaceutical management program at Rutgers Business School, for his thoughtful contributions to the book.

Finally, we want to express our thanks and love to our wives, Gayle Vonderembse and Sarah Dobrzykowski, who graciously took on additional responsibilities so we could focus on the book. We always appreciate what they do for us.

About the Authors

Mark A. Vonderembse earned a PhD in business administration from the University of Michigan, an MBA from the Wharton Graduate Division of the University of Pennsylvania, and a BS in civil engineering from the University of Toledo. In addition to holding the rank of professor at the University of Toledo (UT), he has held important leadership positions, including founding director of the School of Healthcare Innovation and Excellence and founding director of the Intermodal Transportation Institute. In addition, he served six years as chair of the information operations and technology management department and three years as chair of the finance department.

He has taught courses in Germany, India, and China and traveled extensively, making presentations on operations and supply chain management in China, Hong Kong, Japan, Korea, Singapore, India, Morocco, South Africa, Spain, England, Germany, Greece, and Canada. He and another faculty member led efforts to design and build UT's PhD program in manufacturing and technology management, and he served as its director for nine years. He chaired or cochaired 22 PhD dissertations at UT and served as a member of 19 other dissertations, including 11 from outside the United States.

He has more than 160 publications, including 13 articles in the *Journal of Operations Management*, which is widely regarded as the best journal in the field. In a 2009 study, he was ranked third in publications in this prestigious journal. He has also published in *Management Science, Decision Sciences, International Journal of Production Research, European Journal of Operational Research*, among others. He has nearly two dozen awards for his research, including Outstanding Researcher at UT. He has more than 40 research grants from various sources, including the U.S. Department of Transportation, U.S. Department of Education, and the National Science Foundation. He has received more than $4 million in grants as the principal investigator and another $10 million as coinvestigator.

David D. Dobrzykowski served in a variety of management and leadership roles in the healthcare sector during a 12-year career with companies including Mercy Health (formerly Catholic Health Partners) and United Healthcare. He has worked in hospital tertiary care, physician–hospital, diagnostic imaging, emergency department contract management, managed care, and employee benefits organizations. In the provider vertical, Dr. Dobrzykowski served as regional CEO of BIDON Companies, a national diagnostic imaging provider, at which he managed all aspects of strategic planning and operations, including physician contracting, managed care contracting, medical billing, capital equipment purchasing, day-to-day operations (staff management), and physician marketing. He led the turn-around of a distressed facility and launched three start-ups, securing more than $3 million in funding. In the insurance vertical, he served as VP of strategy for Corporate One Benefits, an employee benefits firm, consulting with fully insured and self-funded employer groups to develop and implement healthcare cost management and patient/employee engagement strategies.

Dr. Dobrzykowski earned four degrees and certificates from the University of Toledo: a PhD in manufacturing and technology management from the College of Business, a graduate certificate in public health epidemiology from the College of Medicine, an executive MBA, and a BBA in marketing. He is an associate professor with tenure in the department of supply chain management at Rutgers Business School–Newark and New Brunswick at Rutgers, The State University of New Jersey. He teaches graduate level courses in healthcare services management, operations analysis, and project management and serves as program director of the masters of science in healthcare services management degree program.

His research has been presented in seven countries on three continents, and he is a frequent presenter at the American College of Healthcare Executives (ACHE) Leadership Congress. He has published more than 20 refereed articles in top journals, such as *Journal of Operations Management, Decision Sciences, Journal of Supply Chain Management*, among others. As an academic, he has worked with a variety of industry partners, including the U.S. Department of Veterans Affairs (Veterans Health Administration), New Jersey Department of Health, Henry Ford Health System, RWJBarnabus Health System, McLaren Health System, Sisters of St. Francis Continuing Care Retirement Community (CCRC), Wesleyan Senior Living CCRC, Seneca Medical, and the healthcare vertical of UPS. Learn more at dobrzykowski.wordpress.com.

Prologue: About the Book

The evidence is undeniable. By any measure, the United States spends more on healthcare than any other country in the world, yet its health outcomes as measured by longevity are in the bottom half among developed countries, and its health-related quality of life has remained constant or declined since 1998. In addition to high costs and lower-than-expected outcomes, the healthcare delivery system is plagued by treatment delays as it can take weeks to see a specialist, and many people have limited or no access to care because they do not have health insurance. It is essential to address these problems so that quality and access improve and costs are under control.

Part of the challenge is that the healthcare delivery system is a large, complex, and sophisticated value creation chain. Successfully changing this highly intercon-nected system is difficult and time-consuming because the underlying problems are difficult to comprehend; the root causes are many; the solution is unclear; and the relationships among problems, causes, and solutions are complex and inter-connected. To address these issues, this book explains the *underlying problems*; examines their *root causes* using information, data, and logic; and presents a *comprehensive and integrated solution* that addresses these causes. These three steps are the methodological backbone of this book.

In addition to these challenges, implementation is difficult because there are many participants in the healthcare delivery value chain, including a wide variety of healthcare professionals, such as physicians, nurses, and medical technicians as well as many provider organizations, such as hospitals, clinics, physicians' offices, and labs. Further up the value chain, there are pharmaceutical companies, equip-ment providers, and other suppliers. These participants have diverse and sometimes conflicting goals, but they must work in a coordinated manner to achieve the desired outcome for the healthcare delivery system to be effective. If the prob-lems with healthcare are systemic and there are many participants with conflict-ing goals and a solution should be comprehensive and integrated, then a solution should not be implemented piecemeal. This makes implementation challenging and time-consuming.

This book makes two important overarching contributions to address these challenges:

1. It develops and describes a comprehensive and integrated solution that addresses the root causes and the underlying problems in the healthcare delivery system.
2. It discusses how to implement the solution, including insights about who are the important participants that drive change.

The following sections provide high-level insights about the solution and its implementation.

A Comprehensive Solution

The solution is comprehensive because it considers both the demand side and supply side of healthcare, which are the essential ingredients for making a market for any service or good. The demand side includes the factors that drive patients to consume healthcare, and the supply side consists of the resources that providers assemble to create the services patients want as well as how they organize and manage those resources. The value proposition for healthcare or other goods or services is determined as patients evaluate the trade-off between what they pay for services and the benefits they receive from them. For many people with insurance, the trade-off is biased toward having care because a third party pays for insurance that covers all or most of the costs. For patients to make good decisions about healthcare, they should consider the full cost, even the portion of the cost paid by third parties.

With respect to supply, service providers respond to patients' desire for value. When patients focus on the benefit side of a trade-off and pay limited attention to the cost side of the value proposition, providers sense this and act accordingly. This means providers focus on the quality of care intently while expending far less effort to increase productivity and efficiency, which would allow them to reduce costs. It is a reaction that many people and organizations would have. For example, how would a car dealer react if customer after customer came into the dealership to buy a vehicle and asked about the vehicle's capabilities and performance but never asked the price? Many patients—maybe even most patients—are unaware of the cost of healthcare services as they decide to have or not to have them.

Once healthcare service providers understand and actually see patients looking for value, they are more likely to pay attention to the cost of care. Hospitals will alter their actions to reduce costs and improve the quality of care. They will restructure the hospital, rationalize demand and capacity, examine the size and scope of middle management, outsource services, and build capabilities to improve processes in order to increase quality and lower costs. Physicians will embrace information technology and work effectively with physician assistants and nurse practitioners to serve patients better and more efficiently.

A comprehensive solution that touches so many participants is, by its nature, complex. Because of this complexity, some people suggest that the best and possibly only way to fix the problem is to pass laws so that government can plan and control the system and act as the single payer. The effect of central planning and government control is like placing a huge hierarchy on top of the value creation chain for healthcare. The cost of doing so would be staggering. High cost, slow response to customers, and overall poor performance is why many large companies have reduced their hierarchies dramatically, divested large parts of their businesses, and opted to create supply chains for goods and services that are not core competencies—that is, they are not critical factors for success. It is faster and more efficient for markets to manage and coordinate relationships among firms than it is for hierarchies to plan and control these relationships. But government still has a role. It can bring key participants to the table, eliminate regulations that limit competition or that add cost but have little benefit, work to establish protocols and standards so that access to electronic health information is fast and effective, and assist in creating nationwide health information exchanges.

An Integrated Solution

Healthcare delivery is a multifaceted, complex, and far-reaching segment of the economy. It is multifaceted because there are many different professionals, provider organizations, insurers, and suppliers that must work together to discover and solve problems. It is complex because there are many different ailments, technologies, complications, risks, and working relationships that must be examined, understood, and addressed to attain success. Healthcare delivery is far-reaching because it impacts two critical health outcomes: longevity and quality of life. It has economic impacts as well because when healthcare spending increases faster than the rate of inflation, the country is forced to spend less on other parts of the economy, such as highway safety and entertainment, or go deeper into debt. In addition, businesses that compete in global markets are burdened with high health insurance costs for their employees, putting them at a disadvantage against foreign competitors.

As a result of the complexity and interconnectedness of healthcare, the solution must be integrated. The root causes that impact the underlying problems have multiple dimensions and points of interaction, which the solution must address. Chapter 1 examines the current status of the healthcare delivery system and explains the underlying problem. Chapter 2 discusses the root causes and their impact on the underlying problems, and it summarizes these relationships in Figure 2.2. A review of this table shows that each root cause impacts several of the underlying problems. For example, poor lifestyle choices increase cost, reduce quality of life, amplify delays, and limit access to care for those without health insurance. These factors, in turn, reduce patient satisfaction. There are also relationships among the root causes. For example, when people make poor lifestyle choices, they place more demand on healthcare resources, which exacerbates the physician shortage.

Chapter 3 describes the *patient-centered, resource management* approach that frames the solution with patient issues being the demand side and resources being the supply side. Chapter 4 presents an overview of the comprehensive and integrated solution, including brief discussions of the nine elements that make up the solution. Chapter 4 describes the relationships between the elements in the solution and the root causes, and it provides an indicator of these relationships in Figure 4.1. Once again, the elements of the solution typically address more than one root cause. For example, emphasizing wellness and personal responsibility allows people to make better lifestyle choices, reduce the demand for healthcare facilities and equipment as well as physicians, cut back on the use of prescription drugs, and reduce the risk of malpractice liability. The elements of the solution are also closely connected as patient-centered care, the personal health plan, and wellness reinforce and support each other. The combination of Chapters 1 through 4, Figure 2.2, and Figure 4.1 provides a roadmap for the comprehensive and integrated solution.

Approach to Implementation

No matter how good the solution, implementation is the key to success. Each of the nine pillars in the solution, which are described in Chapters 5 through 13, discusses three important ideas that are essential for successful implementation:

1. Factors that propel change: The sections in these nine chapters titled "Driving Forces for Change" describe important problems that must be overcome as well as identify key groups who need to be at the table so that change can happen. As readers progress through the book, they see a pattern of who should be involved, including government, third-party payers, hospitals, healthcare professionals, and insurers. Knowing the pitfalls and the participants is essential for successful implementation. National attention and strong leadership are required as well.
2. Review impact of a solution element: These sections describe the "Impact of…" a particular element of the solution "…on Healthcare Outcomes," and they discuss how this element impacts the root causes of the underlying healthcare problems. Understanding these relationships as well as recognizing that the elements of the solution are interrelated requires implementation to move forward on a broad front rather than one element at a time.
3. Summary of actions: The "Summary of Recommendations" sections list the action items that should be addressed when implementing the solution. A compilation of these summary sections is available in Appendix A.

Although these are useful tools that help with implementation, there will be resistance to change that is reinforced by the fact that the proposed solution is complex and touches every corner of the healthcare delivery system. Even though the current system may have significant problems and may be financially unsustainable, many patients, healthcare professionals, and healthcare organizations have dealt with and compensated for these problems for decades. They have found ways to make the system work, at least from a short-term and narrow self-interest perspective. Part of this coping mechanism can be explained by the analogy of a frog in a pot of water on a stove; when heat is applied slowly, the frog's body adjusts to the slowly increasing temperature until catastrophe happens.

Because the new solution touches every part of healthcare delivery, all participants are affected in some way, usually both negatively and positively. Maybe it is human nature, part of people's resistance to change, but participants easily see the negative aspects of the new approach. They may also anticipate problems with the new way of doing things that simply do not exist. On the other hand, they are reluctant to believe that the expected positive changes will actually occur and that the new approach on balance will be better. This is further support for an implementation effort that is all-inclusive rather than piecemeal because participants see that everyone has to take some risks for the system to improve. Here are brief discussions of these concerns for some key participants:

1. Patients: Patients, especially those with employer-based insurance or Medicare, may feel they have the most to lose because much of their healthcare cost is covered by a third party. Any changes to health insurance may not be viewed positively, and the opportunity to have patient-centered care (PCC) may be seen as requiring more effort on their part, effort they are reluctant to expend. The benefits of PCC and wellness, which are better quality of life, greater longevity, and lower healthcare costs, seem abstract, far in the future, and difficult to understand.

2. Primary care physicians: They face very big changes as their primary role and responsibility shift from diagnoses and treatment to health and wellness, which requires them to expand their knowledge base. They may also be required to embrace new ways to use information technology. In addition, the basis of their compensation shifts from turning ailments into cures to keeping patients healthy and well. Although the job may offer more satisfaction because patients have a better quality of life and live longer, it takes a long time before physicians see these benefits.

3. Hospitals: They face substantial reorganization in order to build economies of scale that are able to spread rising fixed costs over more patients, provide top-quality care for people living in rural areas, and implement process improvements to enhance quality and reduce cost. This is done with the hope that at some future time hospitals will have strong revenue streams, more appropriate levels of reimbursements, and long-term financial stability.

These examples support the claim that implementation will be challenging because there is uncertainty, everyone has something important to lose, and gains are not well defined and take place at some unspecified future date. To overcome these problems, strong national leadership is needed to get the attention and support from the people and organizations involved in healthcare and to make the comprehensive changes that will lower healthcare costs, improve healthcare quality, eliminate delays, increase access, and enhance patient satisfaction.

This begins with the federal government, which has the clout to bring other key players to the table including third-party payers, insurers, the American Medical Association representing physicians, the American Hospital Association representing hospitals, the states regulating insurers and operating the Medicaid programs, and others. Plus, the federal government controls Medicare and Medicaid, which accounts for about 35% of healthcare expenses. There must be a meeting of the minds among these participants that leads to better outcomes for patients and for the country.

Third-party payers and healthcare providers, with a push from government, must be willing to develop and implement new ideas. The Center for Medicare and Medicaid Services can use its status as a third-party payer to encourage appropriate behavior from participants. States can use their rules and regulatory power over insurers to encourage participation. The new healthcare plan should come about by compelling and logical persuasion and some measured arm-twisting with legislation as the last resort.

This requires leadership from three important members of government: the president, the speaker of the house, and the majority leader of the senate. They do not have to agree on all of the details in the solution, but they must be willing to consider new ideas and compromise so that a workable solution can be formed. This is the type of leadership and behavior that the American people deserve.

The clock is running; now is the time to address the healthcare problems in the United States. We must start before the problems overwhelm the economy and cannot be fixed without severe dislocations. We cannot wait until the 11th hour as we have on many budget bills and debt crisis legislation and then kick the can down the road for a few weeks, months, or years. This is the time to craft a long-term solution to our healthcare problems before they consume us. Making the changes will take time, but the outcomes will be worth the effort.

Chapter 1

Healthcare: Where Do We Stand?

Healthcare in the United States is like *A Tale of Two Cities*. What people see depends on where they look and what they are looking for. With respect to creating new medical devices and procedures, doing research on deoxyribonucleic acid (DNA), developing pharmaceutical drugs, and other technical innovations, the United States leads the world. But in the execution and delivery of healthcare services, the United States has the highest cost in the world by far, and its health outcomes, such as longevity, are middle of the pack at best. This narrative examines the problems that explain this dichotomy between spending and outcomes. More importantly, it offers a comprehensive solution that should improve people's health, ensure healthcare dollars are spent wisely, and enhance the performance of the healthcare delivery system. Before getting started, some definitions are appropriate:

1. *Health* is the overall condition of a person's body and mind, and good health is a state of physical and mental well-being. It is not simply the absence of disease or infirmity. Someone in good health would have a good quality of life and longevity.
2. *Healthcare* is a set of actions or services that promote healthy living, prevent disease and infirmity, and diagnose and treat medical problems.
3. *Healthcare delivery system* is the people and organizations that must work in harmony to provide healthcare.

Try to imagine how health would suffer and how much healthcare would cost if advances in medical technology had not taken place, such as laparoscopic surgeries that are less invasive and stents used in arteries to keep blood flowing to the heart. Laparoscopic surgeries decrease surgical time, reduce complications, shorten or eliminate hospital stays, and shrink recovery time. Stents can be inserted in 30 minutes or less and have dramatically reduced the need for coronary bypass surgery, which is more complex, more costly, and has greater risks. Table 1.1 contains a set of activities that are part of medical technology, where the United States excels, as well as a list of important participants in delivering healthcare, which is the focus of this book.

Improving health and healthcare delivery begins by understanding the underlying problems and their root causes. With this knowledge, it is possible to develop and implement a solution that make a difference—a big difference—in the quality, availability, and cost of healthcare. The solution requires a focus on being healthy; rethinking how to organize, manage, and pay for healthcare; and understanding what adds value for patients and what does not. The solution is not a single idea, technique, or process change. It is a group of common-sense, easy-to-understand actions that address different aspects of healthcare, and are discussed in detail in subsequent chapters.

If there is an overriding theme to the changes, it is to put patients in charge, commonly call patient-centered care, which is more than asking patients how they feel. It is about placing them in a position to make informed decisions, that is, putting them in control. It is about personal responsibility, when patients, supported by their physicians, become custodians of their health and their healthcare.

The intent of the book is to present a comprehensive set of changes that will drive dramatic improvement in the health of the U.S. population and the performance of the healthcare delivery system. If these two goals can be achieved, it should be possible to extend high-quality care to those who currently do not have it while spending the same total amount on healthcare, possibly less.

Table 1.1 Elements of Medical Technology and Healthcare Delivery

Medical Technology Includes	*Healthcare Delivery Includes*
• Medical device design • Surgical procedure innovations • Pharmaceuticals development • Applied research, such as human genome • Medical simulation for diagnosis and treatment • Medical education advances	• Patients • Primary care physicians and physician specialists • Other medical and health professionals • Pharmacists and pharmacies • Hospitals and clinics • Testing and lab facilities • Information services providers • Third-party payer, insurers and employers

1.1 The Healthcare Problem

A perception held by many is that healthcare in the United States is not working—costs are too high, and outcomes are less than they should be. It often takes too long to have a health problem diagnosed and treated, and people, even some who have health insurance, do not have access to the care they need.[1] There are several important benefits to be had from achieving better health and improving the healthcare delivery system:

1. People should need less care, have a better quality of life, and enjoy greater longevity.
2. More resources should be available to treat people who currently have limited access to care and to invest in other worthwhile activities, such as cancer research or safer automobiles.
3. When healthcare costs are lower, U.S. businesses become more competitive globally because their healthcare costs are in line with their international competitors.

1.1.1 Healthcare Costs

The scope of the problem is enormous. According to the Center for Medicare and Medicaid Services (CMS), the United States spent about 17.2% of its gross domestic product (GDP) on healthcare in 2012,[2] making it the largest sector in the U.S. economy. This is much higher, more than 50% higher, than other developed countries as reported by the Organisation for Economic Co-operation and Development (OECD), including France (10.8% of GDP), Germany (10.8%), Canada (10.2%), Japan (10.1%), and the United Kingdom (8.5%). Israel and Korea spent only 7.4% and 6.7% of the GDP on healthcare, respectively, so the United States spent more than twice the rate for these developed countries. Tied for second place were the Netherlands and Switzerland at 11.0%. As a percentage of the GDP, the United States spent at nearly twice the rate as the overall average for OECD countries, which was 8.9%.[3] For more details, see the data in Table 1.2.

When healthcare spending is examined on a per capita basis, the United States spent $8917 per person in 2012 ($2.8 trillion in medical expenses[2] with a U.S. population of 314 million[4]). That is more than 2.5 times the OECD average, which was $3389.30 measured in U.S. dollars (USD). In USD, France spent $4045.14, Germany spent $4693.27, Canada spent $4304.44, Japan spent $3591.81, and the United Kingdom spent $3175.48. Switzerland was second in per capita spending at $6140.46. See Table 1.2 for more data.[3] Caveats about data used in the book, including different numbers reported by different sources, are described in Appendix B.

Spending more on healthcare should be a good thing if health outcomes, such as life expectancy, are better. This is not the case. OECD lists the "at-birth"

Table 1.2 OECD Health-Related Data from 2012

Country	Healthcare Spending (% of GDP)	Per Capita Healthcare Spending (USD)	Life Expectancy at Birth (Years)	Daily Smoker (% Population 15+ Years[a])	Alcohol (Liters/Capita 15+ Years[a])	% Population 15+ Years with BMI > 25[a,b]
Australia	8.8	$3865.72	82.1		9.9	
Austria	10.1	$4528.05	81.0			
Belgium	10.2	$4224.69	80.5		9.8	50.9
Canada	10.2	$4304.44	81.5	16.1	8.1	
Chile	7.0	$1475.89	78.7			
Czech Republic	7.1	$2021.46	78.2	22.9	11.6	
Denmark	10.4	$4512.35	80.1		9.3	
Estonia	5.8	$1442.81	76.5	26.0	12.2	48.9
Finland	8.5	$3402.73	80.7	17.0	9.3	49.4
France	10.8	$4045.14	82.1	24.1	11.7	44.4
Germany	10.8	$4693.27	81.0		11.2	60.0
Greece	9.1	$2328.73	80.7			
Hungary	7.5	$1696.97	75.2		11.1	
Iceland	8.7	$3525.54	83.0			

(Continued)

Table 1.2 (Continued)   OECD Health-Related Data from 2012

Country	Healthcare Spending (% of GDP)	Per Capita Healthcare Spending (USD)	Life Expectancy at Birth (Years)	Daily Smoker (% Population 15+ Years[a])	Alcohol (Liters/Capita 15+ Years[a])	% Population 15+ Years with BMI > 25[a,b]
Ireland	8.1	$3662.97	81.0		11.5	
Israel	7.4	$2329.68	81.8	13.8		63.3
Italy	8.8	$3137.48	82.3	22.1		46.0
Japan	10.1	$3591.81	83.2	20.7	7.2	23.7
Korea	6.7	$2142.09	81.3	21.6	9.1	31.8
Luxembourg	6.6	$4370.79	81.5	16.8	11.3	59.2
Mexico	6.1	$1026.26	74.4	11.8	5.7	71.3
Netherlands	11.0	$5081.31	81.2	18.4	9.1	47.9
New Zealand	9.8	$3213.71	81.2	16.5	9.2	63.8
Norway	8.8	$5823.03	81.5	16.0	6.2	46.0
Poland	6.3	$1447.69	76.9		10.2	
Portugal	9.3	$2522.69	80.5			
Slovak Republic	7.7	$1977.42	76.2		10.1	
Slovenia	8.7	$2482.62	80.2	20.5	11.0	56.9

(Continued)

Table 1.2 (Continued) OECD Health-Related Data from 2012

Country	Healthcare Spending (% of GDP)	Per Capita Healthcare Spending (USD)	Life Expectancy at Birth (Years)	Daily Smoker (% Population 15+ Years[a])	Alcohol (Liters/Capita 15+ Years[a])	% Population 15+ Years with BMI > 25[a,b]
Spain	9.0	$2956.80	82.5			
Sweden	10.8	$4743.23	81.8	12.8	7.3	47.1
Switzerland	11.0	$6140.46	82.8	20.4	9.9	41.0
Turkey	5.0	$889.78	74.6	23.8	1.6	52.0
United Kingdom	8.5	$3175.48	81.0	20.0	9.7	61.9
United States[c]	16.4	$8454.41	78.8	14.2	8.8	68.6
Overall average	8.9	$3389.30	80.2	18.8	9.3	51.7

Source: Organisation for Economic Co-operation and Development (OECD). 2012. Health resources. https://data.oecd.org /healthres/health-spending.htm (accessed November 27, 2015).

[a] Blank indicates that the data were not reported by the country.
[b] In some cases, a measured and a self-reported value were available. The measured value is listed here.
[c] United States data for per capita healthcare spending as reported by the OECD is different from the data reported by the Center for Medicare and Medicaid Services in the United States.

longevity of the U.S. population at 78.8 years in 2012, which is 1.4 years less than the OECD average. The United States is behind Slovenia (80.2 years), which spent $2482.62 per person—about 75% less than the United States. U.S. longevity is slightly better than that of Chile (78.7 years) and the Czech Republic (78.2 years), which spent $1475.89 and $2021.46 per person, respectively. The only other countries in the OECD report that are behind the United States are Estonia (76.5 years), Hungary (75.2 years), Mexico (74.4 years), Poland (76.9 years), the Slovak Republic (76.2 years), and Turkey (74.6 years).[5] All spent much less per capita on healthcare than the United States. More information is available in Table 1.2.

1.1.2 Healthcare Quality and Outcomes

The Centers for Disease Control and Prevention (CDC) has defined and is attempting to assess health-related quality of life (HRQOL), which is a multidimensional measure of physical and mental health, including health conditions and risks, functional status, social support, and socioeconomic status.[6] A study by Salomon et al. (2009) used four national U.S. health surveys to assess HRQOL: (a) Behavioral Risk Factor Surveillance System (BRFSS), (b) the Current Population Survey (CPS), (c) the National Health Interview Survey (NHIS), and (d) the National Health and Nutrition Examination Survey (NHANES). For the three surveys with annual data (BRFSS, CPS, and NHIS), the following results were found in the United States for the period 1998 to 2007 using a five-point scale to rate HRQOL (excellent, very good, good, fair, or poor).

1. For men and women, there were declines in excellent ratings for all three surveys.
2. For men, there were significant increases in the number of fair or poor ratings in the BRFSS, but there were significant declines in fair and poor ratings in the CPS. The increase in the number of fair or poor ratings for the NHIS was not statistically significant.
3. For women, there were significant increases in fair and poor ratings for BRFSS and CPS.

The data from the different surveys offer some useful insights. Over time fewer people, both men and women, believe that their HRQOL is excellent. More women feel that their HRQOL is fair or poor. For men, these results were mixed. Overall, it seems that the HRQOL in the United States declined from 1998 to 2007.[7]

Another aspect of healthcare quality is the frequency of hospital-acquired infections or nosocomial infections. As reported by the CDC, the United States had approximately 722,000 nosocomial infections in 2011, which resulted in about 75,000 deaths.[8] Not only do nosocomial infections impact longevity and quality of care, they cost billions of dollars to treat, thereby driving up healthcare costs.

It is most likely that the underperformances in longevity and quality of life are not caused by differences in tobacco use or alcohol consumption because the United States is a below-average user of these substances when compared to other countries in the OECD. Table 1.2 shows that only 14.2% of the United States' population 15 years and older are daily tobacco users compared to 18.8% in OECD countries who have reported these data.[9] The annual per capita consumption of alcohol per persons 15 years and older is 8.8 liters compared to 9.3 liters for OECD countries.[10]

However, the United States is near the top in obesity as measured by the body mass index (BMI). According to the OECD data in Table 1.2, 68.6% of the U.S. population is either overweight (a BMI of more than 25) or obese (a BMI of more than 30).[11] This is the second highest percentage among countries reporting the data, behind only Mexico at 71.3%. Without digging too deeply into statistics, it is useful to note that Mexico has the highest percentage of overweight people and the shortest longevity at 74.4 years. Japan, with the lowest percentage of overweight people at 23.7% has the greatest longevity at 83.2 years. The United States, which spends the most on healthcare by far, has the second highest percentage of overweight people and a longevity that is 1.4 years below the average.

As many people are aware, health in the United States is in serious danger from obesity and its resulting diseases. The negative impacts of obesity on healthcare costs as well as longevity and quality of life are substantial—reaching epidemic proportions. Left unchecked, this epidemic is likely to lead to more negative consequences than smoking, drug abuse, or alcohol consumption.

The United States spends more on healthcare, by a wide margin both as a percentage of GDP and per capita, than other developed countries, and U.S. health-related outcomes are middle of the pack or less. Although this discrepancy between spending and outcomes is caused, in part, by lifestyle choices, the discrepancy also indicates that the U.S. healthcare delivery system may be inefficient and prone to error. As the root causes and solutions to the underlying healthcare problems are discussed in future chapters, these possibilities are examined.

1.1.3 Delays and Limits to Access

There are delays in the healthcare delivery system that prevent patients from getting problems diagnosed and treated in a timely manner. How would U.S. consumers react if they had to wait several days to get an appointment with a specialist to have their transmission checked or their smartphone problem diagnosed and then have to wait two or three weeks to have it repaired? This is often the case with healthcare; it can take weeks to get an appointment with a specialist and an additional delay for the diagnosis and treatment. Delays occur for various reasons including the following:

1. Insufficient number of primary care and physician specialists, such as cardiologists and endocrinologists, so patients must wait for an appointment.

2. Insurers have an insufficient number of physicians on their panels of doctors, so patients have a difficult time finding qualified physicians.
3. Reimbursement levels are so low that few qualified physicians are willing to participate.

In addition to delays, some people do not have access to care. Patients without insurance may obtain some care through emergency room visits, but they do not get the routine care they need, so small problems become big ones. Even those with employer-based insurance may have limited coverage because of high deductibles. People who buy insurance in the private market may opt for insurance with high deductibles and copayments as well as other restrictions to save money. Limiting access is also caused by low reimbursement amounts, so physicians and hospitals find ways not to treat certain patients or to treat only a limited number of them. Regardless of the cause, delays and limits to access are mechanisms to ration healthcare.

If the goal is to provide better healthcare to more people, the United States must have a healthier population that needs less care, improve the efficiency of the current system so more people can be treated, and address overuse. Overuse is consuming healthcare resources that provide minimal benefit to patients. Overuse is caused by a number of factors, but the most important one is poor decision making by patients with insurance. These individuals pay little if any of the cost of care, so their decisions about using healthcare are biased in favor of using more. This is a critical topic that is discussed in detail in Chapters 2 and 3.

1.1.4 Patient Satisfaction

As shown in Figure 1.1, patient satisfaction is a function of receiving a good value for their healthcare dollar, meaning that if patients pay a fair price, receive

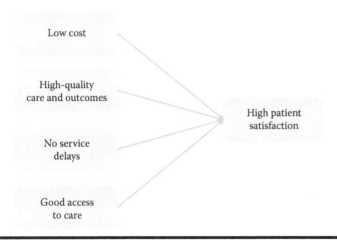

Figure 1.1 Determinant of patient satisfaction in healthcare delivery.

high-quality service and outcomes, have no delays in getting service, and have access to the services they need, their satisfaction will be high. As with any service, when the cost is too high, quality is less than it should be, there are long delays in getting service, and some people are without access, customer satisfaction suffers. What would happen if an oil change cost $150 rather than $30, oil was splattered on the engine, it took three weeks to get an appointment, and some people were denied service? New competitors would open businesses to change oil, more customers would change oil at home, and, ultimately, existing businesses would have to reform or close.

What makes the current healthcare delivery system tolerable for many patients is that a third party pays most of the bill. If a third party paid all or most of the cost for an oil change, customers might accept the other problems. What makes the healthcare problem more difficult is that creating new competitors, such as physicians and hospitals, is challenging. It takes more than a decade after graduating from high school to become a physician, and there are already too many hospitals, so building more carries big risks. In some ways, patients are in a box. They don't get the service they want and deserve, yet for many of them, someone else pays the bills, so the current system limps along even though patients are not fully satisfied. At some future time when patients pay a bigger percentage of their healthcare costs, this problem will reach a tipping point, and patients will demand better care. Future shocks to healthcare, which are on the horizon, are likely to exacerbate the problems and accelerate the need for change.

1.2 Future Shocks

Looking forward, there are shocks to the healthcare delivery system that will make matters much worse if significant changes are not made. Increases in demand for healthcare will stress the system, increasing costs, reducing availability, and lengthening delays. This will ultimately impact the quality of care.

1. Demand will increase as the U.S. population ages and consumes more care. There were 76.4 million births from 1946 to 1964, the baby boom years. When deaths so far and immigration are considered, the net result is about the same, 76 million baby boomers, nearly one quarter of the U.S. population.[12] An average of 10,000 baby boomers qualify for Medicare each day.[13]
2. The intent of the ACA is to extend coverage to the roughly 45 million U.S. residents[14] who do not have health insurance, thereby increasing the amount of healthcare consumed and the associated costs of providing the care.
3. If the level of immigration continues, the demand for healthcare is likely to increase further. These events will strain a healthcare system that already has significant problems.

4. Medical research and technology development is likely to find new diagnostic and treatment techniques. Some of these will reduce the cost of care and may even eliminate the need for some tests and treatments. On the other hand, some innovations will lead to more expensive diagnostic tests and treatments to tackle cancer, heart disease, diabetes, and other problems.

Can the U.S. healthcare delivery system find a way to satisfy these additional demands and keep total healthcare cost at the same level or lower? Can the United States actually reduce healthcare costs while increasing the quality of care and eliminating delays? Can the United States increase the HRQOF and longevity while doing this? It seems clear that the answers must be yes. The solutions discussed in this book describe the things that should be done and explain how these actions address the underlying problems.

1.3 Look Back at a Fundamental Cause: Disrupted Decision Making

What must be done so the U.S. population gets value for their healthcare dollars? To begin to answer the question, it is essential to understand how healthcare in the United States reached its current state. Factors, some driven by the human condition and others as unintended consequences of decisions made to solve different problems, have combined to create the current situation: an environment in which costs are out of control, quality of care is less than it should be, and coverage is uneven.

Health and healthcare are intensely personal, and they impact people's ability to live productive and meaningful lives or to live at all. Everyday activities, including the ability to see, hear, think, feel, and move about, are impacted by a person's health. In addition, having access to healthcare is a powerful force that stirs a deep emotional response. When people look at their spouse, significant other, parents, siblings, children, grandchildren, grandparents, or friends who are dying, they often expect all possible actions to be taken to cure their loved one regardless of the cost or the likelihood of success.

These conditions and the associated strong feelings disrupt decision making about healthcare, and they cause healthcare decision making to be different from purchasing an automobile, farm implement, lawn care services, or even life insurance. These decisions are typically made by balancing the cost to purchase the good or service against the benefits of acquiring it. For example, consumers might assess the advantages of buying lawn service as having more free time and avoiding the costs to buy, maintain, and operate lawn equipment. They will weigh the cost to purchase the service against the benefits of the service to see if the purchase is a "good deal." A good deal is one in which the benefits exceed the cost by a significant amount. How much excess benefit is needed to trigger the purchase depends on other uses that consumers have for their funds, such as a vacation, investing for retirement, or dining out. In theory, a similar analysis should take place for a decision about healthcare. However, as people consider the healthcare decision, the benefit side of the decision usually overwhelms the cost side because quality of life and life itself are judged to be very important, even infinitely valuable.

This decision is further impacted by employer-sponsored health insurance plans, which expanded greatly during World War II. Then, companies could not increase salaries to attract and retain workers because of government-imposed wage and price controls. However, when the Labor Board declared that fringe benefits, such as health insurance, were not subject to wage and price controls, companies responded by increasing these fringe benefits. As a result of this emphasis on fringe benefits, by the mid-1950s, approximately 75% of the population in the United States had health insurance.[15] After the war and the elimination of wage and price controls, employers would often add benefits to these health insurance plans because these plans were not subject to federal income tax, thereby giving the employees a tax-free pay increase. These fringe benefits were usually not subject to state or local income taxes, further expanding the tax-free gain. Many of these plans did not require the employee to pay any part of the premium. These plans usually had no deductibles and no coinsurance payment. The entire bill was paid by the insurance company, and the employer paid the entire premium. In essence, for many people, healthcare had zero cost. This further disrupted decision making about healthcare, skewing the decision toward consumption because there was no out-of-pocket cost to the patient.

Medicare, implemented in 1965, was the logical extension of health insurance to those 65 and over. Medicare is mandated by federal law, and it disconnects the payments for Medicare, which occur, for the most part, during an individual's working life, from the consumption of healthcare services. Once again, healthcare decisions are disrupted because the consumer sees the full benefits from treatment against a copayment of only 20% of the costs or less. Medicare does require a small annual payment, which is currently about $100 for most people. This annual payment is taken from their social security check, and the amount does not increase as more healthcare services are consumed. To further disrupt this decision, many who enroll in Medicare have supplemental insurance that pays most of the remaining 20% copayment.[16] Often this supplemental insurance is paid in whole or in part by former employers as a retirement benefit. Once again, the Medicare enrollee gets the full benefit of the healthcare service but incurs only a small part of the cost.

So when the benefit side of the healthcare decision is very large and the cost side is zero or close to it, the natural outcome is to consume more. This tends to increase both the usage and the price paid for services. Over time, usage increased because consumers viewed healthcare as a free or nearly free service. The price increased because, even if patients knew the price, they consumed the service because a third party paid the bill. As a result, there was little incentive for healthcare providers to carefully manage their resources or make investments to improve efficiency and workforce productivity. Providers simply passed along cost increases to third-party payers. As time passed, controlling costs became less and less important because the benefit side of the cost–benefit trade-off dominated decision making. In fact, this inattentiveness to the price for healthcare services on the part of the consumer granted providers the opportunity to raise prices without pushback. These increases in usage and price had a multiplicative effect on the rate of increase in healthcare costs. This is evident by the fact that healthcare costs have, for many years, increased much faster than the rate of inflation.

1.4 Building Excess Capacity: Responding to Growing Demand

The push to consume healthcare without regard to its price led healthcare providers to invest and, in many cases, to overinvest in facilities and equipment. During the period after World War II, providers saw a need to expand capacity, and most did so based on optimistic assumptions about demand, so expansions were often larger than needed. In addition, adding capacity in small increments is more expensive than adding it in large ones because there are economies of scale in construction. For example, it costs less per room to add eight surgery rooms than it does to add only four, so larger expansions have lower costs per room. As hospital administrators faced what they believed was unending growth in demand, they opted for more rather than less capacity, so they were not caught short and forced to send patients to their competitors. Furthermore, as population sprawled from dense urban to more suburban geographies, the hospitals chased this sprawl, adding capacity in the suburbs by opening new facilities. In many cases, this left urban facilities with low patient volumes, substantial over capacity, and expensive, underutilized inpatient infrastructure.

As a result of this growth, hospitals tend to have excess or unused capacity as measured by the number of beds available minus the number of beds used. In other industries, having excess capacity leads to price reductions and the closing of inefficient and outdated facilities to bring demand and supply into balance. Generally, these things did not happen in healthcare in the 1970s through the 1990s because the healthcare consumer did not make decisions based on the price of services. They continued to consume more healthcare, and third-party payers paid ever-increasing prices for these services. As a result, there was no effective pushback on prices and only a modest number of hospital closings. Eventually, these conditions led to a revolt by the third-party payers.

1.5 Healthcare Payer Revolt

In reaction to these conditions, which have evolved since World War II, employers and insurance companies who paid the bills began to push back by setting limits on reimbursements for healthcare providers and requiring premium sharing, deductibles, and coinsurance payments from individuals. The government, which funds Medicare and Medicaid, also cut reimbursements to hospitals and doctors in an effort to contain healthcare spending. These changes have been implemented to reduce the costs to the employers, insurers, and the government but have had only a limited impact on changing the behavior of consumers. Many consumers still see their out-of-pocket costs as low and the benefit from treatment as high. This leads to poor decision making by consumers and higher medical costs.

Putting pressure on the level of reimbursement without taking action to address the fundamental causes of these escalating costs is not an effective way to reduce costs and improve the quality and availability of healthcare. Consumers still demand services because the cost impact on them is low. So healthcare providers are squeezed between declining reimbursement levels and consumers with high service expectations.

1.6 Framing the Healthcare Solution

The bottom line for healthcare is that regardless of the size of the U.S. economy there is a limit on the amount of healthcare a country can afford. As mentioned earlier, the United States already spends substantially more on healthcare as a percentage of both the GDP and per capita than any other country in the OECD study. Even this very high level of spending is insufficient to cover all residents in the United States for all of their needs or at least their perceived needs. As with all spending problems, there are two basic ways to address them:

1. Increase the revenue to pay the ever-increasing healthcare costs by
   a. Making third-party payers and those with insurance pay more for insurance premiums
   b. Having people with insurance pay higher deductibles and copayments
2. Reduce the costs of the services by
   a. Cutting the price paid for healthcare services
   b. Consuming fewer healthcare services

Most employers and third-party payers have asked their employees to pay a bigger share of the ever-increasing insurance premiums, which provides additional revenue to pay for rising healthcare costs. They have added deductibles and copayments, which, in effect, increase revenue. These revenue increases have taken place over the last 30–40 years and appear to have had little or no effect on slowing the rise of healthcare costs or improving healthcare quality. Increasing revenue is also the approach used in the ACA, which has several tax increases as well as a requirement that everyone purchase health insurance or pay a penalty/tax collected by the Internal Revenue Service.[17] When raising revenue is the primary way to deal with a high level of spending, the implied assumption is that the cost of the service is reasonable and the usage level of service is appropriate. In other words, the United States is consuming the right amount of healthcare and is paying a fair price. Both of these assumptions appear to be incorrect.

To reduce healthcare costs, it is critical to differentiate between the price paid for individual services, such as the cost of an office visit or a sonogram of the carotid artery, and total healthcare costs. Total healthcare cost is a function of the price of each service and the service's level of use. Many would argue the costs of individual healthcare services are higher than they should be for a variety of reasons, and this contributes to the problem with total healthcare costs. They would go further and suggest that it is possible to reduce the cost to deliver specific services by eliminating wasted efforts, such as mountains of paperwork and excessive reporting requirements, and by increasing the productivity of the workforce. When costs for patient visits, testing, and/or treatment are reduced, even if usage remains the same, total healthcare costs decline. Some healthcare providers have had great success in reducing healthcare costs and improving quality by improving healthcare processes and procedures. These efforts are in their infancy, and the potential for further improvement may be substantial.

As an example, consider how the Mayo Clinic chose to deal with an important safety issue, retained surgical items (RSI), which are items, such as sponges, needles, or instruments, that are left inside the patient after surgery. Although this is an infrequent event, patient safety and complications as well as the economic consequences can be substantial. The national numbers for RSI are not precise, but estimates range from one occurrence in 1500 surgeries to one in 18,000. Over several years, the Mayo Clinic had 34 occurrences in more than 190,000 surgeries, and 23 of the RSIs were sponges. The Mayo Clinic's Systems Engineering and Operations Research Group was tasked with studying the problem and making improvements. The focus was sponges because sponges were more than two thirds of the RSIs. The team reviewed counting policies and practices, and they did direct observation, which showed marked variations in counting procedures. The initial recommendation was to create clear definitions, protocols, and performance expectations for counting sponges. The team implemented a series of actions, including white board posting to focus attention, policy clarification and standardization of practice, a conscientious count campaign that involved double counting, daily count reminders, and posters with days since the last RSI event, among other actions. The number of incidents dropped by about two thirds, and sponges remained the primary problem. To address the last one third, the team recommended RFID with which each sponge has a unique ID number and is scanned into and out of surgery. For the three years following the RFID implementation, there were no RSIs involving sponges in more than 150,000 procedures. As a by-product of these efforts, RSI involving other items also declined. The additional cost per case for the RFID implementation is only a few dollars, and the time to scan the sponges in and out does not increase surgery time. This increases patient safety, reduces complications and liability, and improves Mayo's already superior reputation. Everyone at Mayo owns part of the problem and is part of the solution.[18]

It is also important to address the level of use. The prior discussion about considering both the benefits and costs of using healthcare services suggests that the level of consumption may be too high. When a third party pays most of the cost and patients have the benefits, the decision is biased in favor of using more care. It is essential for patients to evaluate the benefits and cost and make good choices.

> The following example illustrates this important point. Four years ago, Sally had surgery on her right shoulder to repair her rotator cuff. After the surgery, Sally was advised by her doctor to have physical therapy at the rehab center to improve her range of motion. After the initial evaluation by the therapist, Sally was shown a series of exercises that she should do at least three days a week. She was given the option of coming to the center for therapy or doing the exercises on her own and returning in three weeks for a final evaluation. Sally had healthcare insurance at her job and so did her husband, so the out-of-pocket cost for the therapy was zero. Sally opted for the therapy at the center, which was three days per week for three weeks, including the initial evaluation and the final assessment. Doing the therapy at home was not really considered because the out-of-pocket cost was zero. Recently, Sally had the same surgery on her left shoulder and was given the same options for therapy. The cost per therapy session was approximately $150. Once again, Sally chose to use the center for therapy. If Sally had to pay this cost, would she select a different option? She could do the therapy at home and save $1350 (nine sessions times $150). She could opt for the initial and final evaluation sessions and do seven therapy sessions at home and save $1050 (seven sessions times $150).

There is another and potentially more powerful way to reduce the consumption of healthcare. People can adopt good nutrition, increase exercise, control their weight, eliminate smoking and harmful drugs, and lower alcohol consumption. Wellness is a combination of these lifestyle changes and appropriate health screenings that provide early warning for problems. Early warnings lead to faster, easier, and less expensive treatments. Specific actions and programs that are needed to successfully implement wellness are discussed later. Wellness is not a quick fix because it requires education, establishing and reinforcing good practice, providing good role models, and giving positive feedback. These efforts may be most effective when begun at an early age but should be rolled out for all. Wellness is an essential and effective way to reduce healthcare costs, improve quality of life, and increase longevity. The following is an example of how wellness enhances health and reduces healthcare costs.

> For most of her adult life, Marion's total cholesterol fluctuated between 200 and 240. Over time, her weight had crept higher until her body mass index was approaching 30. As she passed 50, she saw the first signs of high blood pressure. Her doctor wanted her to take a diuretic to lower her blood pressure and a statin to reduce her cholesterol. After having significant side effects from the statin, Marion decided to take herself off both drugs and change her lifestyle. Her doctor was not supportive, but Marion did it anyway. Marion had stopped eating meat several years earlier. She decided to eliminate fish and all dairy except for small amounts of cheese and ice cream at times of celebration. She replaced cow's milk with almond milk. She cooked without salt, didn't add salt at the table, and went out of her way to find canned foods that had no added salt. She ate whole grains and brown rice. Marion had exercised for years, but she increased the frequency and the intensity of her workouts. After 18 months, Marion's cholesterol was 170, and her blood pressure was normal. She had lost weight, so her BMI was 25. She felt better and had more energy. She increased her quality of life and likely increased her life span, which should be reason enough to make these lifestyle changes. In addition, she reduced healthcare costs by the annual cost of the diuretic and the statin. She also made fewer trips to the doctor and required less testing, which saved additional money and time. Her fewer trips to the doctor freed medical staff and facilities to treat other patients. Everyone wins!

The points raised in these examples are the foundation for creating an effective solution to the healthcare problem faced by the United States, a solution that improves quality, lowers costs, and increases access.

1. *Patient-centered care* puts patients supported by their primary care physicians in charge of their healthcare. Patients must be the focal point and the decision makers if healthcare reform is to succeed.
2. *Wellness and prevention* must be the cornerstone of an effective solution.
3. *Better decision making* is needed about how much healthcare to consume.
4. *Careful examination and reform of the healthcare delivery system* to improve quality, efficiency, and productivity are essential.

These ideas form the core of the solution that leads to the desired results: a healthier population and a healthcare delivery system that is more efficient, has higher quality, has few delays, and is more accessible. The purpose of this book is to discuss these underlying problems and their root causes and to frame a comprehensive solution.

This chapter described the underlying problems in healthcare, and the next chapter describes the root causes for these underlying problems. Chapter 3 discusses the patient-centered resource management approach that provides a framework for the solution. Chapter 4 flows from this discussion and gives an overview of the solution and links the solution to the root causes. By the end of Chapter 4, the reader sees the link *from solution to root causes to underlying problems* within a *patient-centered, resource management perspective*. One by one, the chapters that follow discuss each element of the solution and important implementation issues. The intent is to create a comprehensive solution to improve healthcare and, more importantly, health.

References

1. Binder, L. 2013. The five biggest problems in health care today. *Forbes*, (February 21). http://www.forbes.com/sites/leahbinder/2013/02/21/the-five-biggest-problems-in-health-care-today/ (accessed November 24, 2015).
2. Center for Medicare and Medicaid Services. 2012. National health expenditure highlights. http://www.cms.gov/Research-Statistics-Data-and-Systems/Statistics-Trends-and-Reports/NationalHealthExpendData/downloads/highlights.pdf (accessed February 20, 2014).
3. Organisation for Economic Co-operation and Development (OECD). 2012. Health resources. https://data.oecd.org/healthres/health-spending.htm (accessed November 27, 2015).
4. Multpl.com. 2015. US population by year. http://www.multpl.com/united-states-population/table (accessed November 27, 2015); United States Census Bureau. 2015. U.S. census quick facts. http://www.census.gov/quickfacts/table/PST045214/00 (accessed November 27, 2015).
5. Organisation for Economic Co-operation and Development (OECD). 2012. Health status. https://data.oecd.org/healthstat/life-expectancy-at-birth.htm (accessed November 27, 2015).
6. Centers for Disease Control and Prevention. 2015. Health-related quality of life. http://www.cdc.gov/hrqol/concept.htm (accessed November 29, 2015).
7. Salomon J. A., Nordhagen S., Oza S., and Murray C. J. 2009. Are Americans feeling less healthy? The puzzle of trends in self-rated health. *Am J Epidemiology*, 170(3) (August 1): 343–351. http://www.ncbi.nlm.nih.gov/pmc/articles/PMC2714952/ (accessed November 29, 2015).
8. Centers for Disease Control and Prevention. 2011. Healthcare-associated infections. http://www.cdc.gov/HAI/surveillance/index.html (accessed November 29, 2015).
9. Organisation for Economic Co-operation and Development (OECD). 2012. Health risk: Daily smokers. https://data.oecd.org/healthrisk/daily-smokers.htm#indicator-chart (accessed November 29, 2015).
10. Organisation for Economic Co-operation and Development (OECD). 2012. Health risk: Alcohol consumption. https://data.oecd.org/healthrisk/alcohol-consumption.htm#indicator-chart (accessed November 29, 2015).

11. Organisation for Economic Co-operation and Development (OECD). 2012. Health risk: Overweight or obese population. https://data.oecd.org/healthrisk/overweight -or-obese-population.htm#indicator-chart (accessed November 29, 2015).
12. Pollard, K., and Scommegna, P. 2014. Just how many baby boomers are there? *Population Reference Bureau*, (April). http://www.prb.org/Publications/Articles/2002 /JustHowManyBabyBoomersAreThere.aspx (accessed September 14, 2015).
13. Ellison, A. 25 things to know about Medicare spending. Becker's: Hospital CFO (January 25). http://www.beckershospitalreview.com/finance/25-things-to-know -about-medicare-spending-january25.html (accessed January 26, 2016).
14. Young, J. 2013. Uninsured Americans 2012: More than 45 million lacked health insurance last year, CDC reports. Huffington Post (April 23). http://www.huffingtonpost .com/2013/03/21/uninsured-americans-2012_n_2918705.html (accessed November 29, 2015).
15. Texas Association of Health Plans. 2008. Health insurance in Texas. https://www .web.archive.org/web/20111223193910/http://tahp.org/documents/THS/2008 /FINAL_FINAL_Health_Ins_in_Texas.pdf (accessed November 29, 2015).
16. Center for Medicare and Medicaid Services. 2015. Medicare coverage. https://www .cms.gov/ (accessed November 29, 2015).
17. Healthcare.gov. 2015. Read the Affordable Care Act. https://www.healthcare.gov /where-can-i-read-the-affordable-care-act/ (accessed January 8, 2016).
18. Cima, R. R. 2011. Application of safety technology in the operating room. Power Point presentation, Mayo Clinic Conference on Systems Engineering and Operations Research (June 11); Berry, L. L. and Seltman, K. D. 2008. *Management Lessons from Mayo Clinic*. New York: McGraw Hill.

Chapter 2

Making Healthcare Work: Understanding Root Causes

Many people accept as true the notion that health and healthcare are things that happen to them rather than things they control, things, in fact, that can be impacted substantially by their actions. They often believe health is controlled by God, fate, genes, or other factors. They also believe they cannot play a major role in decision making about healthcare because healthcare is complex, difficult to understand, and best left to the experts. Ultimately, too many people believe they don't know enough or are not smart enough to play a meaningful role in making healthcare decisions.

There are elements of truth in each claim because genetics impact health, and some elements of healthcare require special knowledge, training, and skill. But these are small truths, and subscribing to them is misleading and dangerous. Learning the basics about health and healthcare is important, so people can participate effectively in diagnosing and treating aliments. Learning is not only worth their time; it is part of their responsibility to themselves, to their loved ones, and to society in general. Learning enables patients to be better judges of whether healthcare is delivered effectively and efficiently and whether outcomes are high quality.

Although there are genetic factors that may predispose people to one ailment or another, the more important determinants of health and healthcare needs are environmental factors, such as nutrition and exercise, which people control. People make the decision to smoke, take drugs, or drink alcohol in excess. Don't get caught in the trap that usually begins like this: "...well, my Uncle Bill lived to be 90 and he smoked cigarettes since he was 14, never exercised, and ate whatever he wanted." These anecdotes, even if truthful, were fulfilled because Uncle Bill was the "last man standing." What is unseen are the many people who followed Uncle Bill's regimen and died in their 40s, 50s, 60s, and 70s. In fact, Uncle Bill was exceptional. Uncle Bill may have had "really good genes," had a high metabolic rate, kept his weight under control, did physical labor so he was physically fit, and/or was just plain lucky. He beat the odds! He might have reach 100 years or more and had a better quality of life if he followed a healthier lifestyle. And, of course, the contrasting example that confirms that Uncle Bill's approach was right is "…my friend Edith never smoked or drank a day in her life, a picture of health, but she got cancer and died before she turned 50." There are always exceptions or what statisticians call outliers. Don't be trapped by these stories and make lifestyle choices hoping to be an outlier like Uncle Bill.

It is best to recognize that good life choices give people the best chance to live a long and high-quality life—much better than having good genes. When considering what is important, quality of life should be at the top of the list, so people can avoid being bedridden with limited opportunities to interact with friends and family. Being stockpiled in a nursing home or tied to medical devices and a feeding tube for life support substantially reduces the quality of life.

Even for those with a genetic predisposition to a disease, hope is not lost. Genome tests have been and are being developed to determine if a person carries the gene that increases the likelihood of suffering from cancer, heart attack, diabetes, or other disease. Armed with this information, it is possible to take actions to increase the chances of avoiding or at least postponing these diseases. Knowledge allows people to make good decisions.

Even people who make all the right lifestyle choices will, at some point, need healthcare services, so it is essential to improve the healthcare delivery system. This began by describing the underlying problems, which occurred in the previous chapter. As shown by the curved arrows moving from right to left in Figure 2.1, understanding the healthcare problems helps to identify their root causes, and knowing the root causes helps to shape a comprehensive and integrated solution. When the solution is properly formulated and successfully implemented, the causal impact moves from left to right as seen in Figure 2.1; the solution addresses the root causes,

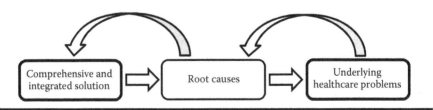

Figure 2.1 Relationships among comprehensive and integrated solution, root causes, and underlying healthcare problems.

which, in turn, resolves the underlying problems. The balance of this chapter offers a brief summary of the underlying problems and a detailed discussion of their root causes.

2.1 Review of the Fundamental Problems with Healthcare

The fundamental problems with healthcare are well known, have been discussed at length in other forums, and are described in the first chapter. These problems are summarized here and listed as the rows in Figure 2.2.

1. Healthcare *costs* are too high: It is documented here and in other places that the United States spends about 17.2% of its GDP (2012 data)[1] and nearly $9000 per person on healthcare (about $2.8 trillion in medical expenses[1] with a U.S. population of 314 million[2]), which is much higher than other developed countries. It appears that high expenditures are driven by both the rate at which U.S. consumers use healthcare services and the price paid for those services.

2. *Quality* is lagging other developed countries: In the United States, longevity is middle of the pack among developed countries, quality of life is flat or declining, and the rate of hospital-acquired infections is much too high. These factors indicate that the United States lags other developed countries even though the United States outspends them substantially. Poor healthcare policies, procedures, and practices, which are discussed later, may reduce the quality of care that patients receive.

3. *Delays* in treatment: Although delays are currently visible in certain medical specialties for which it takes weeks or months to get appointments, it is likely to become a bigger problem as some physicians leave the profession for different careers. Others take early retirement to avoid increasing regulations and paperwork, declining reimbursement rates, and a litigious environment with high malpractice costs. On top of these circumstances, there is more demand for healthcare services caused by an aging population, among other things, so the current physician shortage will likely get worse and delays will increase.

4. Limited *access*: Prior to the Affordable Care Act, approximately 45 million people in the United States do not have health insurance,[3] which limits their access to care. Improving access depends on either finding additional healthcare resources and a means to pay for them or finding enough cost savings in the current system to reduce delays and extend coverage to those with limited or no access. This must be done while improving healthcare quality. The goal should be to extend access and eliminate delays while spending the same amount or less on healthcare, adjusted for inflation.

Root Causes / Problems	1. Poor Lifestyle Choices	2. Biased Trade-Offs	3. Unused Facilities and Equipment	4. Poorly Design Policies and Processes	5. Limited and Ineffective Information Technology	6. High Drug Costs	7. Excessive Legal Liability and Malpractice Insurance Cost	8. Shortage of Healthcare Professionals
Cost	Increase: More usage, long-term care, and serious complications drive up costs	Increase: Poor decision making leads to more use and limits pushback from patients about service price	Increase: These spaces must be maintained and managed; operating costs and fixed costs are rolled into service costs	Increase: Services are delivered inefficiently with low productivity	Increase: Inefficient information processing, duplicative tests, and poor decisions add costs	Increase: Price and use drive up costs	Increase: High legal fees, settlement costs, tests to protect against lawsuits, and more physician time to prepare	Decrease: Shortage may lead to rationing, which may lower costs
Quality	Decrease: Lesser quality of life and longevity	Decrease: High demand leads to poor or no care for people without health insurance		Decrease: Poor processes cause errors and mistakes	Decrease: Limited and inaccurate information lead to poor outcomes	Decrease: People with limited ability to pay do not receive needed medications	Decrease: Defensive medical tests expose patient to dangers such as radiation in X-rays	Decrease: If physicians not available, service quality will suffer

Figure 2.2 Linking root causes to the underlying healthcare problems. The first word in each cell describes whether cost, quality, delays, access, and patient satisfaction increases or decreases. *(Continued)*

Root Causes / Problems	1. Poor Lifestyle Choices	2. Biased Trade-Offs	3. Unused Facilities and Equipment	4. Poorly Design Policies and Processes	5. Limited and Ineffective Information Technology	6. High Drug Costs	7. Excessive Legal Liability and Malpractice Insurance Cost	8. Shortage of Healthcare Professionals
Delays	Increase: More healthcare services are needed, so the system is clogged	Increase: More services are demanded, so more patients clog the system		Increase: Services take longer to deliver, and waiting time increases	Increase: Duplicate tests and limited information increase waiting time	Increase: Research and development and clinical trials delay access to drugs	Increase: Physician is not available, so appointments are delayed or canceled	Increase: Fewer physicians lead to longer wait times for appointments
Access	Decrease: Any activity that increases healthcare cost and/or demand will ultimately reduce access, in particular to the patients who are least able to pay for services. This becomes a method for rationing limited healthcare resources.							
Patient Satisfaction	Decrease: High costs, poor prognosis, delays, and limited access lead to dissatisfaction	Decrease: High costs, delays, and limited access cause dissatisfaction	Decrease: High costs and limited access lead to dissatisfaction	Decrease: Low quality, delays, and poor access cause dissatisfaction even when a third party pays the bills	Decrease: Limited access to information, lower quality, long delays, and high costs lead to lower satisfaction	Decrease: High costs, limited access, and delays lead to lower satisfaction	Decrease: High costs, delays, and limited access lead to dissatisfaction	Decrease: Delays for appointments, limited access, and lower quality contribute to dissatisfaction

Figure 2.2 (Continued) Linking root causes to the underlying healthcare problems. The first word in each cell describes whether cost, quality, delays, access, and patient satisfaction increases or decreases.

5. Low *patient satisfaction*: As expected, high cost, lagging quality, delays, and limited access contribute to low patient satisfaction. Satisfaction will improve when patients are at the center of the healthcare delivery process; that is, patients control their care. Patient-centered care, by its nature, focuses on cost, quality, and timing—problems that currently plague the system.

2.2 Root Causes of U.S. Healthcare Problems

Even if these problems are well understood, the United States cannot snap its collective fingers and resolve them. Determining an effective solution begins by identifying the root causes of these underlying problems and understanding how these causes created the problems. Figure 2.2 is a visual mechanism to organize the root causes, which are the column headings, and relate them to the underlying problem, which are the row headings. The individual cells at the intersection of the rows (problems) and columns (root causes) indicate how a root cause influences a problem. Ultimately, the solution must be comprehensive and integrated because there is not a simple one-to-one relationship between root causes and underlying problems. The root causes and relationships are discussed in the following sections. Some of the root causes are mentioned in Chapter 1 in an attempt to understand and explain the problems.

2.2.1 Poor Lifestyle Choices

Many people make poor lifestyle choices involving nutrition, exercise, smoking, drug use, and alcohol consumption that lead to high incidents of disease, which increases the use of healthcare services and total healthcare costs. It seems clear that changes are needed to encourage better choices. For example, a few companies that offer healthcare to their employees have put policies in place that prohibit the hiring of individuals who smoke, and many more workplaces are nicotine free.[4] The logic is that smoking increases healthcare costs and the amount of sick time used, plus it reduces worker productivity. Other companies offer lower health insurance premiums to their nonsmoking workforce. Smokers pay more for life insurance; should they pay more for health insurance as well?

These actions lead to a number of interesting questions, including should people who are obese, as defined by BMI or other criteria, pay more for healthcare? Should an extreme snowboarder, who has a very high risk of injury, pay more? Is society responsible for providing care for someone like Roger Craig Knievel, better known as Evel Knievel, who attempted more than 75 motorcycle jumps and broke dozens of bones?[5] Although the snowboarder and daredevils like Evel are few in number and therefore have a small impact on healthcare costs, there are millions of people who smoke, take drugs, and are obese. Should they pay more for healthcare because their lifestyle choices are likely to have a much higher incident of disease than the general population? Who should pay these costs? These are challenging and interesting questions for which there are no easy answers. Insights may be gained by turning to other types of insurance that have addressed similar concerns, such as life insurance where providing products to high-risk individuals may require a higher premium differential.

As described in Figure 2.2, poor lifestyle choices often lead to diseases requiring extensive, long-term care, which significantly increases costs. These patients are also likely to have costly, serious, and life-threatening complications. Declining health ultimately leads to a lower quality of life and less longevity. As these patients consume more healthcare resources, patients with no or limited healthcare insurance lose access as they are priced out of the market, and patients with health insurance experience delays. As a result, the quality of care declines, and patients are less satisfied. Limited access, which is a form of rationing, is an unintended consequence of an inefficient and wasteful healthcare system that uses its scarce resources to provide care that should not be needed. Even the richest countries in the world have limits on what they can spend on healthcare.

2.2.2 Biased Trade-Offs

When people consider decisions about healthcare, they often face an unbalanced trade-off between its benefits and costs. Through health insurance, they receive all the benefits from healthcare but pay little or none of its costs. In most cases, patients do not even know the costs of the medical services they receive. As a result, they tend to have services that could be postponed to see if the problem gets better with rest, could be treated with less expensive remedies, or may not be needed at all. There may be a less costly treatment, such as therapy or prescription drugs, instead of surgery. There may be simple, low-cost treatments, such as over-the-counter medicines or icing a sore joint, that can be applied.

As described in Figure 2.2, healthcare costs tend to increase because the trade-off between costs and benefits is biased in favor of having care. In addition, there is little pushback from patients that would help to control the price for healthcare services. As both the use of and the price for services accelerate, healthcare costs rise faster than the rate of inflation. Companies in other segments of the economy, such as automotive, banking, and air travel, feel pressure from consumers to manage their resources better and lower costs while keeping quality and service high. This should be the case for healthcare, but it is not. In addition, as the demand for healthcare increases, the delivery system becomes clogged, which limits access and creates delayed services. This drives down quality and reduces patient satisfaction.

2.2.3 Unused Facility and Equipment

According to an analysis by GE Healthcare Performance Solution, about 70% of U.S. hospitals do not make the best use of key resources, including facilities, equipment, and people.[6] Even when facilities appear to be busy, it is often because they are poorly planned and scheduled and have unexpected delays, such as late surgery starts that steal capacity. Poor utilization of these expensive resources makes it difficult for hospitals to cover their costs because most of their costs are fixed, meaning these costs must be incurred regardless of the patient load. Plus, revenue is less than it should be when resources are not fully utilized. This revenue shortfall is exacerbated by reimbursements from third-party payers, such as Medicare, that have been and will continue to decline. This puts substantial pressure on hospital budgets. There may be opportunities to treat more patients and better use facilities, equipment, and staff by eliminating non–value added activities and increasing productivity.

As described in Figure 2.2, when hospitals or other healthcare entities have unused or underused resources, society pays these costs. Medical, clerical, and administrative staff must be paid whether they are fully utilized or not. Non–value added work, poor planning, and delays are costly. Facilities and equipment must be cleaned, maintained, and managed. Facilities must also be heated and cooled, and equipment must be stored whether these resources are used or not. Facilities and equipment are part of the fixed costs of the hospital, which are rolled into the costs for services. In effect, when people pay their healthcare bills, they are paying for all facilities and equipment whether they are used or not.

2.2.4 Poorly Designed Policies and Processes

The goal of healthcare has always been to provide the best care for patients. After all, society places great value on human life and goes to great lengths to preserve it. When patients paid directly from their pockets for healthcare, the natural limit on spending was the patients' ability to pay. With the advent of health insurance paid for by employers, the bill was paid from the "deep pockets" of these companies. The natural responses to removing this limit have been more demand, increasing efforts to develop new healthcare technologies and services, and less emphasis on finding ways to deliver healthcare more efficiently. As a result, the productivity of healthcare workers and the efficient use of facilities and equipment became a much less important consideration. Policies that governed how facilities operated and the processes and procedures used to deliver care did not consider efficiency in a meaningful way.

As described in Figure 2.2, when policies and processes ignore efficiency and productivity and focus solely on providing healthcare, costs rise quickly—in the case of healthcare, much faster than the rate of inflation. With limited incentives and efforts to improve processes, quality and access to care decrease, and mistakes and delays increase. These conditions cause patient dissatisfaction.

2.2.5 Limited and Ineffective Information Technology

In part because of insulation from pressures to reduce costs and the natural resistance to change, healthcare has lagged behind nearly all other industries in adopting state-of-the-art information technology (IT). The most obvious deficiency, and the one that is beginning to change, is implementing electronic health records (EHRs), which allow physicians to search and access patient information quickly and accurately. Why does the local auto repair shop with a dozen locations have a service record for each vehicle its customers own, yet physicians do not have this technology or are just now getting this capability for their patients? Without EHRs, physicians must rely on their memories, their patients' memories, or their ability to thumb through a two-inch stack of paper records with speed and precision. On the other hand, the repair shop can quickly inform the customer when the tires were last rotated or the air filter was last changed regardless of which shop did the work.

There are other IT tools that physicians can use effectively, such as iPads or smartphones, to provide access to the latest treatment information, such as available antibiotics for treating specific infections. These tools can be used to consult with other physicians about patient status and treatment options.

As described in Figure 2.2, EHRs, health information exchanges, and other IT tools provide ways to cut costs, improve patient care, and reduce delays. Without these tools, the cost of capturing, organizing, and processing information increases significantly. Also, duplicative testing is often done because results from prior tests cannot be found, so healthcare costs go up, and decisions are delayed. Limited access to information leads to poor decisions and outcomes, which increase costs, create delays, and reduce quality, which leads to lower patient satisfaction. With EHRs, updates can be seamlessly added to patients' personal health record, enabling fast and easy access to their health information, which helps patients manage their health and increases their satisfaction.

2.2.6 High Drug Costs

The high cost of pharmaceutical drugs is driven by both usage and price. There certainly are positive reasons why drug use is rising. Many exciting new drugs are being developed to treat serious health problems, and in some cases, drugs are the only treatment option. Also, drug therapy may have a lower cost and better outcomes than surgery or other treatments. On the other hand, drug use may be high because patients want a quick fix. For example, patients may want medication to lower cholesterol rather than make lifestyle changes to deal with the problem. In addition, physicians are knowledgeable about drugs, are trained to prescribe drugs, and feel a sense of accomplishment when a prescription is given. This desire from patients for a "fast and easy" fix and the physician's training and attitude may be increasing drug use. Drug use is also influenced by the biased trade-off discussed previously because in many instances the lion's share of drug costs is paid by health insurance.

Two other important factors increase total spending on drugs. Research and development costs as well as advertising costs, which are substantial, must be recouped, so the price for new drugs is usually very high. Once a drug is no longer patent-protected, other companies can copy the drug, creating what are commonly called generic drugs. Generic drug makers charge much lower prices because they did not incur expenses to develop the drug or market it to build up demand.

As described in Figure 2.2, the high cost of drugs increases healthcare costs. Plus, creating new drugs can take 10 years or more, so patients must wait years to get access to effective treatments. When costs are high and delays are substantial, the quality of care suffers, and patients are less satisfied.

2.2.7 Excessive Legal Liabilities and Malpractice Insurance

The United States is one of the most litigious countries in the world, and healthcare is no exception with malpractice lawsuits impacting healthcare in at least three ways:

1. Regardless of the outcome, malpractice lawsuits drive up the cost of insurance because the insurer, hospital, and physician have legal expenses. In the case of a pretrial settlement or a successful prosecution by the plaintiff, there is a payout in addition to these legal fees. Many times, cases are settled even when the insurer believes it could win the case at trial because the legal fees will be significant, and if the insurer loses, the award may be substantial. Settlements allow the insurer to pay a small amount to avoid this possibility.
2. Second, as a protection against lawsuits, many physicians and hospitals have established processes for diagnosing and treating patients that are elaborate not for medical reasons, but to protect themselves in a lawsuit. This security blanket, sometimes referred to as defensive medicine, leads to unnecessary testing and higher medical costs.
3. Third, dealing with lawsuits takes the physicians' and hospital managers' time as they help prepare the case and testify in court. This leads to canceled appointments, delayed treatment, and missed opportunities to design and implement new policies and procedures to provide better care for patients and improve hospital performance.

As described in Figure 2.2, malpractice lawsuits drive up the cost of healthcare. In addition, when the threat of a lawsuit is high, physicians may avoid complex cases or treatments that are high risk. Stress on the system and physicians may lead to errors or to physicians' dissatisfaction with their profession, which may result in early retirement or career change.

2.2.8 Shortage of Healthcare Professionals

Healthcare is facing a number of staffing challenges, and the current physician shortage may be the most significant. The shortage is exacerbated by growing demand form baby boomers, who will consume more care and the ACA as it expands coverage to many who currently do not have health insurance. At the same time, many physicians are approaching retirement, and others are taking early retirement or are switching careers. On the opportunity side there are factors that may partially offset this shortage. If healthcare is more efficient, facilities are better used, and staff becomes more productive, the healthcare delivery system can do more with the existing resources. If the U.S. population is healthier, demand for healthcare may decline. Plus, the number of nurse practitioners and physician assistants is increasing, so they may be able to fulfill part of the shortfall.

As described in Figure 2.2, the impact of a shortage of healthcare professionals creates uncertainty for patients. This shortage will ration care, which could lead to lower costs. It is almost certain that a shortage of physicians will have a negative impact on quality because of restricted access and delays for diagnosis and treatment. This would lead to lower patient satisfaction.

References

1. Center for Medicare and Medicaid Services. 2012. National health expenditure highlights. http://www.cms.gov/Research-Statistics-Data-and-Systems/Statistics-Trends-and-Reports/NationalHealthExpendData/downloads/highlights.pdf (accessed February 20, 2014).
2. Multpl.com. 2015. US population by year. http://www.multpl.com/united-states-population/table (accessed November 27, 2015); United States Census Bureau. 2015. U.S. census quick facts. http://www.census.gov/quickfacts/table/PST045214/00 (accessed November 27, 2015).
3. Young, J. 2013. Uninsured Americans 2012: More than 45 million lacked health insurance last year, CDC reports. Huffington Post (April 23). http://www.huffingtonpost.com/2013/03/21/uninsured-americans-2012_n_2918705.html (accessed November 29, 2015).
4. Koch, W. 2012. Workplaces ban not only smoking, but smokers themselves. *USA Today*, (January 6). http://usatoday30.usatoday.com/money/industries/health/story/2012-01-03/health-care-jobs-no-smoking/52394782/1 (accessed December 9, 2015).
5. Evel Knievel. 2015. Legendary Evel. http://evelknievel.com/the-man/ (accessed December 9, 2015).
6. Terry, J., Donoghue, M., and Butz, D. 2011. Management 201: A new era of tight capacity. GE Healthcare. http://nextlevel.gehealthcare.com/WP_PCCM_MGMNT%20201_2011_final.pdf (accessed December 17, 2015).

Chapter 3

A Patient-Centered Resource Management Approach: Balancing Demand and Supply

It is difficult to read a news feed or watch the nightly news and not see a story about national concerns over cost, quality, delays, access, or patient satisfaction in healthcare.[1] These are serious and real concerns that are often showcased in the media by stories covering families forced to file for bankruptcy because of medical bills, deaths caused by medical errors or a diagnosis that came too late in a patient's disease progression, or an elderly person dissatisfied because of the physical or logistical and intellectual challenges in navigating a healthcare appointment at a large multispecialty clinic.[1] These issues are receiving substantial attention from a variety of key stakeholders, including the following:

1. Politicians who incorporate healthcare reform as a major aspect of their platform, calling for more accountability on the part of healthcare providers
2. Insurance executives who assert the value of competition and their role in coordinating care
3. Hospital leaders who see their revenues being linked to quality and satisfaction for the first time

4. Physicians trying to operate in an increasingly financially integrated system while lacking much of the operational infrastructure (i.e., information technologies) necessary for success
5. Patients who are poorly prepared to navigate the complex and costly healthcare system and are ultimately dissatisfied with their access to high-quality care[2]

The final group, patients, plays a particularly important role in the system given the comprehensive way in which they influence other stakeholders and the system in general. More specifically, patients serve as constituents of politicians influencing their perspectives through lobbying and, of course, directly at the polls during election time. Patients influence the performance of insurance companies when (a) selecting health plans if multiple plans and perhaps several insurance companies are offered as alternatives by employers; (b) accessing care because patients determine how much care and where to have it; and (c) managing paperwork and billing, following care delivery as engaged patients verify their charges. This latter practice is beneficial for insurers and third-party payers because some industry experts estimate that as many as 8 out of 10 hospital bills contain errors.[3]

Perhaps most clearly, patients have the opportunity to influence the performance of hospitals and physicians not only by picking the right providers, but also by fully engaging with these providers and complying with treatment plans that emerge from these engagements. Unfortunately, studies show that many patients do not fully participate in their health and well-being and are not vigilant healthcare consumers because they do not believe they have the information or ability to participate.[4] This is easy to understand given the complexity and fragmentation apparent in healthcare delivery. As an example, information sharing among providers is often suboptimal, leaving patients with an inadequate understanding of their health status, ways to improve their health, and actions needed to cope with their medical conditions.[5] Given patients' key roles and generally sluggish engagement, it is not surprising that many discussions about fixing the healthcare delivery system embrace a patient-centered approach.

3.1 What Is a Patient-Centered Approach?

Although multiple and varying definitions exist, patient-centeredness generally involves engaging patients as active participants in their health, well-being, and consumption of care as well as effectively coordinating providers who deliver the care. For example, the Agency for Healthcare Research and Quality's (AHRQ) National Healthcare Disparities Report (2010) links the healthcare delivery system to patient preferences when discussing patient-centeredness.[6] This report builds on a definition established by the Institute of Medicine, stating that patient-centered care (PCC) is "healthcare that establishes a partnership among practitioners, patients, and their families (when appropriate) to ensure that decisions respect patients' wants, needs, and preferences and that patients have the education and support they need to make decisions and participate in their own care."[7] Large-scale studies support these ideas by showing that improving partnerships and coordination among providers and involving patients in the process enhances patient satisfaction.[8]

In its Declaration on Patient-Centered Healthcare, the International Alliance of Patients' Organizations (IAPO) points out responsibilities for patients as well as providers. It describes a patient-centered approach as one in which the healthcare system is designed and care is delivered to address the needs and preferences of individual patients so that healthcare is appropriate and cost-effective. The declaration sets out five principles of a patient-centered approach to healthcare. Patients should have the following:

1. Involvement in health policy
2. Support and information
3. Choice and empowerment
4. Access
5. Respect[9]

The IAPO calls for patient engagement to drive the development of a healthcare system that provides the information and resources patients need to manage their health and well-being and make informed choices when seeking care. Such a healthcare system would offer patients the appropriate access to care that matches their needs and would deliver care in a respectful, collaborative way. In other words, the healthcare system would integrate patients and providers, thus linking the demand side of healthcare with the supply side. In order to provide access to effective PCC, the providers and resources on the supply side cannot be fragmented or suffer from misalignments and information disconnects.

Summarizing, patient-centeredness has two important themes:

1. *A demand-side* dimension related to patients' level of engagement in their health and their role as consumers of healthcare services
2. *A supply-side* dimension related to the coordination (or service system design) among the providers involved in caring for the patient

3.2 Key Demand and Supply Issues

The notion that there are demand and supply elements in PCC is consistent with the underlying problems facing healthcare: the needs to reduce cost, increase quality, limit delays, improve access, and enhance patient satisfaction. Although the pressures to address these problems seem, and frankly are, daunting for industry leaders, the healthcare system is not alone in experiencing these challenges, so it may be possible to learn from other industries.

During the 1970s, 1980s, 1990s, and 2000s, U.S. manufacturers, especially auto-makers, faced similar challenges that required a dramatic rethinking of how value is created for and with customers. This propagated new and innovative methods for product design and increased manufacturer's interest in outsourcing non-critical, valued-added activities to suppliers. The new approach to product design began with efforts to gather more and better information about customers, the demand side, so design teams could create safe, high-quality cars that provided good value and met the needs of consumers *more precisely*. At the time, this was called "listening to the voice of the customer." For similar reasoning, healthcare needs to get closer to its customers/patients, and PCC is the way to do that. More outsourcing created a need for manufacturers to effectively organize and manage suppliers, so supply chain man-agement, the supply side, emerged as an important tool to do so. Supply chain man-agement enables organizations to focus more intently on what they do best (their core competency) and allowed them to tap into core competencies of partners/suppliers, even product design capabilities, in order to work together and deliver value to cus-tomers. Similarly, healthcare providers should examine how they manage and use resources to achieve the best possible outcomes.

This signaled a major shift away from the use of "hierarchies" that con-trol actions and make decisions along the value creation process. An example is Henry Ford's centralized and vertically integrated production system for cars. Centralization means that most decisions are made by top management. High ver-tical integration means that one firm owns all the assets used in value creation from raw materials to car dealerships. Like a *Titanic*-sized ship, these immense hierarchies are expensive and difficult to maneuver, and they move slowly and inef-ficiently in response to changing customer needs. Instead, a more decentralized approach is needed in which decisions are made quickly and well by qualified peo-ple who are closer to the customer, thereby reducing management costs and increas-ing responsiveness. These supply chains, which create value for final customers, use "markets" and market forces rather than hierarchies to manage and control transac-tions among participants. In this environment, organizations become decentralized and work closely with key partners/suppliers who focus on what they do best in order to collectively provide high value goods and services.

Consider the question: "What does Apple manufacture?" The answer: nothing. When customers pick up their iPhone or iPad, they may think of Apple as one of the most innovative manufacturers in the world, but in reality, this statement is only half true. Apple is innovative, so much so that it considers designing its prod-ucts to be a core competency, but it leaves manufacturing to partners who specialize in this.[10] Today, it's hard to argue with Apple's outcomes in terms of quality or cus-tomer satisfaction. The use of market forces to manage the value creation process is changing an organization's cost structure substantially, reducing fixed cost obliga-tions, and leading to volume flexibility.

Prior to the "great recession" of the late 2000s, domestic automobile manufacturers differed in how they were organized: centralized versus decentralized and high versus low vertical integration. More centralization and vertical integration meant top-down decision making and owning most of the facilities, infrastructure, and other resources needed to make cars. General Motors (GM) was the most centralized and vertically integrated of the big three U.S. automakers. On the other hand, Chrysler was the most decentralized and least vertically integrated, in part a result of efforts to divest assets and generate cash to avoid liquidation in the 1970s. Ford was in the middle.

GM suffered most from the drop in demand because of its high fixed costs, a result of high centralization and a high level of vertical integration, and it needed a larger government subsidy. Chrysler, which used market forces and was less centralized and less vertically integrated, needed a much lower subsidy. The government recouped $39 billion of the $49.5 billion it lent to GM (a negative return of $10.5 billion or about a 21% loss), and it recovered $11.13 billion of the $12.3 billion it lent to Chrysler (a negative return of $1.2 billion or a bit less than a 10% loss).[11] Ford, the only one to survive without a subsidy or bankruptcy, made a fortuitous decision a couple of years prior to the downturn in demand when it borrowed more than $20 billion from banks and other sources, using its plants and equipment as collateral. Because of these loans and Ford's efforts to outsource non–core business activities to suppliers, it emerged from the steep decline in demand as a strong and profitable company.

This incident supports a claim that a decentralized "market" approach can outperform vertically integrated hierarchies, especially when products are complex and many suppliers/participants are needed to address customers'/patients' needs. Although this statement is true, it is predicated on effectively managing the complex relationships in the value creation process as well as reliance on participants to respond to "markets." It requires participants to be financially aligned and have adequate operating and information systems to integrate work across company boundaries. There is a need for good resource management in healthcare, which includes outsourcing services when justified adapting and applying supply chain management concepts to integrate and improve healthcare delivery.

3.3 What Is Resource Management?

Although a supply chain is a way for an organization to work with its vendors to coordinate efforts across companies and create value for customers, resource management is about organizing and using assets, people, and capabilities *whether they are within the organization or held by its suppliers.* Resources management involves information and financial exchanges among many firms so that they can work cohesively to create value for and with customers. It is part of a value creation process that links demand and supply and transforms inputs into services and goods that customers want. In healthcare, this means better quality care, access, and patient satisfaction for a fair price. This view considers resources broadly in both tangible form (e.g., labor, capital, materials, supplies, energy, equipment, and facilities) and intangible form (e.g., knowledge, skills, processes, partner collaborations, and customer demand for a service or good). It involves shaping customer demand and adjusting supply (sometimes referred to as capacity) to create the right balance, achieving both effectiveness and efficiency.[12]

3.4 Levers to Balance Demand and Supply

Patients generate demand, and healthcare providers obtain, apply, and manage resources that offer supply. To make the healthcare delivery system work efficiently and effectively, demand should include actual patients' needs, and supply should not be over- or understimulated by regulations or inappropriate incentives. Table 3.1 contains some key control levers generally used in industry to adjust demand and supply so that they are balanced. Demand-side levers include yield management, triaging work, delaying the start of work, and scope reductions.

1. Yield management is the use of financial incentives to shape demand to fit times when supply typically exceeds the need for the service or good. Movie theaters and restaurants provide useful examples of yield management. Most people are familiar with matinees at the movies or early bird specials at restaurants. These are programs designed to provide customers with discounts during nonpeak demand periods intended to shift some customers from peak times to periods when supply is high and typically goes unused.
2. Triaging work occurs when the needs of a specific customer are identified and matched with an appropriate level and type of resource. An emergency department provides an excellent example of triaging; when patients present

Table 3.1 Some Levers Used to Adjust Demand and Supply in Industry

Demand-Side Control Levers	Supply-Side Control Levers
Yield management	Staff: Hire, fire, and cross-training
Triaging work	Outsource
Delayed starts	Facilities and equipment
Scope reductions	Streamline processes

Source: Greenall, R. 2016. Effective resource demand management. http://www.pcubed.com/bulletins/effective-resource-demand-management (accessed February 3, 2016).

in the emergency department, they are quickly assessed to identify the type of care necessary (demand) and assigned to the proper provider (supply resource).

3. Delaying the start of work is a scheduling approach used to shift the demand to a time when the right supply of resources is available. This approach is often used in project management to shift resources, such as construction workers, from one job to another because the first job is not time-sensitive.

4. Scope reductions decrease the requirements of a customer order. For example, if a homeowner contracts with a painter to paint the entire interior of a home and then decides only to paint the bedrooms, this represents a scope reduction. All of these levers can increase or decrease to control or shape demand.

There are also supply-side levers used to adjust the capacity to meet demand. These include managing staff, outsourcing, facilities and equipment, and streamlining processes.

1. Staff can be adjusted to cope with changing demand. It is possible to hire additional or lay off existing staff as a way to ramp supply/capacity up or down to adjust to swings in demand. In addition, staff can be cross-trained to perform other jobs, thus increasing flexibility and capacity when a bottleneck exists. A bottleneck is a department or activity that limits an organization's ability to produce a service or good. For example, a bartender can be trained to wait tables in a restaurant, thereby increasing supply when the restaurant is busier than the bar.

2. Outsourcing can also be used to increase supply when needed. As touched on earlier with the discussion of markets, outsourcing allows firms to acquire specialized but rarely needed capabilities and increase the volume of supply when overflow demand occurs. Consider staffing agencies that supply well-trained employees in different functional areas, such as human resources recruitment, procurement, marketing, and accounting.

3. Facilities and equipment offer another opportunity to affect supply. This is more than simply building new facilities or closing existing ones in order to respond to a long-lasting increase or decrease in demand. It is about identifying bottlenecks in existing operations, which inhibit the delivery of a service or good, and finding ways to increase the capacity at the bottleneck activity. This can be done by finding new ways to use the equipment so that more work is accomplished or, if that is not possible, then to secure another piece of equipment. These ideas can be applied to a milling operation in a tool and die shop or radiology department in a hospital.

4. Streamlining processes improves productivity and reduces wasted effort and mistakes. As productivity increases and waste and mistakes are eliminated, available supply increases and costs decline. This is a concept that has been

well established in "lean manufacturing" when substantial productivity gains have been made by documenting, analyzing, and improving processes. Similar "lean" approaches are being applied to healthcare delivery.[13]

Ultimately, the performance of any system depends on the degree to which tangible and intangible resources are effectively managed. In other words, a system works well when *demand* for a service or good is reflective of a consumer's actual needs because the consumer is positioned to make rational purchasing decisions, and *supply* is managed so that the appropriate resources are used by professionals who have the right knowledge and skills to deliver that service or good. Under these conditions, customers receive exactly what they value, and resources are not produced in excess and wasted. So what does this have to do with healthcare?

3.5 A Patient-Centered Resource Management View of the Healthcare System

After considering the current state of affairs in the healthcare industry (Chapter 1) and the root causes of the underlying problems with the healthcare delivery system (Chapter 2), it seems clear that opportunities exist to enhance outcomes, improve cooperation and integration, and balance the demand and supply sides of healthcare. A significant problem is that resource management for healthcare is not organized to be patient-centered. This is particularly important because the healthcare value creation process should rely heavily on the patient to be an active and engaged cocreator of value. Value cocreation occurs when patients and providers share specialized knowledge for mutual benefit.[14]

In healthcare, patients must share information about their symptoms with providers, and in return, providers share information with patients about their diagnosis and treatment. All of this happens in real time without delay because patients and providers typically interact face to face. Thus, to produce value, which includes high-quality outcomes, fast access to care, strong patient satisfaction, and reasonable costs, the patient must be an active member of the value creation process. To do this, the value creation chain or network must be organized and resources managed in a patient-centered way. This is one important area where healthcare is different from manufacturing. In manufacturing, customer feedback is important, but the feedback is captured by the company and brought into the process for designing vehicles or appliances, which takes many months (annual model update) or years (new model introduction). Based on these inputs, the manufacturer creates a new design, and the cycle begins again as the manufacturer gathers feedback on the new design and engages in yet another redesign. Because patients and providers interact face to face, value creation in healthcare often takes place in a few minutes, hours, days, or weeks, and the cycle for manufacturing is typically months or years.

3.5.1 Effective Resource Management in Healthcare: A Stable Structure

Consider a house as a visual analogy for the healthcare delivery system. An effective, patient-centered resource management approach serves as the foundation creating balance between patients' demand for services and the healthcare system's ability to supply those services (see Figure 3.1). The left side of the house highlights the demand side of the healthcare systems, and the right depicts the supply side. *Financial incentives* align the decisions and behaviors of members with the desired outcomes of the system, and as a result, these financial incentives are foundational to balance demand and supply. In terms of the demand side, this idea rests in the thinking that consumers' decisions can be viewed rationally based on the value consumers perceive in a service. A patient-centered approach to resource management includes financial incentives for patients to engage in healthy behaviors to reduce the volume and severity of their claims. At the same time, providers would have financial incentive to support patients in their pursuit of better health and, when treatment is necessary, to provide it in an effective and efficient manner.

On the demand side, the resulting system would place substantial emphasis on wellness programing and resources for patients, and when they do develop a chronic condition, such as diabetes or high blood pressure, disease management resources, such as telephonic health coaches and online support, could help to manage the disease and improve quality of life. When care is necessary, it is delivered in a highly integrated way focusing on the unique needs of the patient. The intent is to create a substantial amount of health- and wellness-related activity (illustrated by the larger box in Figure 3.1) and reduce the amount of disease management–related activities and patient care (illustrated by the smaller box).

On the supply side, primary care physicians would play a critical role as resources for patients seeking health and wellness as well as diagnosing and treating basic health problems. Specialists—who treat specific aliments like oncologists,

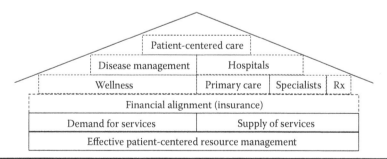

Figure 3.1   An illustration of effective resource management in healthcare: a stable structure.

or chronically diseased systems of the human body like cardiologists—would continue to provide their expertise as dictated by the needs of patients. The hope is that care by specialists may be reserved for highly acute patients, and care delivered by specialists may decline as patients become healthier. Pharmacies would continue to safeguard patients by monitoring prescriptions for accuracy and drug interactions; plus they would support patients' efforts to live a healthy life and could offer basic health services in the neighborhood. Pharmaceutical companies would continue to develop innovative drugs, but the hope is that a healthier population requires fewer rather than more prescriptions drugs.

Patients would be the focus of the healthcare value creation system and would be actively engaged in reducing demand for services through lifestyle choices (which include compliance with treatment protocols). When seeking services, patients would be active participants who make choices about when, where, and how to access care. The demand and supply sides of the healthcare delivery system would be integrated by providing wellness and disease management resources to patients on the demand side and effectively coordinating care among providers and patients on the supply side when treatment is required. As such, the boundaries encompassing wellness, disease management, the patient, primary care, specialty care, pharmacies, and hospitals would all be permeable (illustrated by dashed lines in Figure 3.1) with information flowing easily among the members of the system. Just like the illustrated house, demand and supply in healthcare would be balanced and stable.

3.5.2 Ineffective Resource Management in Healthcare: An Unstable Structure

Unfortunately, the present healthcare system is not balanced and stable (see Figure 3.2). The current approach is neither patient-centered nor effective. On the demand side, utilization of services may be higher than necessary given a health insurance system that insulates consumers from the cost of healthcare and lifestyle

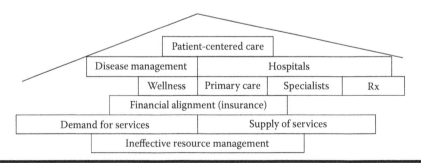

Figure 3.2 An illustration of ineffective resource management in healthcare: an unstable structure.

choices that lower their health and cause them to seek more care. Consider the discussion earlier about yield management (e.g., movie matinees and restaurant early birds). Patients have very little financial incentive (and even less information) to act as engaged participants in their health and well-being, particularly when accessing and consuming healthcare services. After patients pay deductibles, copayments, coinsurance, and their portion of insurance premiums (which is typically far less than the third-party payer shells out), they are completely insulated from the cost of healthcare services. An analogy would be consumers who pay the first $1 of the cost of a sundae, and the balance is paid by their employers or other third-party payers. The incentive would be to order extra sprinkles, chocolate chips, peanut butter topping, hot fudge, whipped cream, and nuts and to super-size the order given that consumers are held harmless for the costs beyond their payment of $1. In short, the financial incentive for patients in healthcare encourages consumption.

A logical insurance system would provide incentives for patients to engage in wellness activities, such as healthy eating and regular exercise. As discussed previously, although these factors certainly do not account for all of the claims generated by patients, these factors are key causes of disease and under the direct control of patients. This idea is explored in greater detail in Chapter 6, which emphasizes wellness and personal responsibility. The current insurance system largely insulates the consumer from the cost of care and only recently has begun to provide incentives for healthy living. Clearly, there are motivations against consumption, such as the inconvenience associated with disrupting a person's daily life to visit a provider, but the point about financial incentives remains an important driver of consumption.

Financial incentives on the supply side of healthcare are manifested through the "reimbursement system" or payment system for providers. The traditional payment system was centered on a fee-for-service model under which providers, such as primary care physicians, specialty physicians, and hospitals, received payment for each service provided. To some extent, this system emerged from Medicare's "cost plus" model that, as the title infers, was designed to enable hospitals to receive a reimbursement greater than their estimated cost to provide a service. With a cost plus model, the incentive is to provide more services, which is a corollary to the demand side on which the incentive is to consume more services. Admittedly, reimbursement models have changed and are continuing to change dramatically, such as value-based purchasing and accountable care organizations. These new reimbursement models are intended to incentivize providers to help patients maintain health and, when services are necessary, to deliver higher quality, better coordinated care. Although these new models are difficult to implement given the current lack of operational integration and supporting infrastructure among providers, these changes are positive steps toward better resource management.

Thus, under the traditional payment system, providers examined and ordered services for patients and were reimbursed for each service, and patients' objections were modest because they were insulated from the cost, largely born by insurers and, ultimately, third-party payers. The result is an unstable healthcare system in which both demand and supply exceed necessary levels. In terms of demand, incentives for wellness are primarily intrinsic and insufficient to encourage prophylactic measures, thus spurring potentially avoidable demand for services. At the same time, on the supply side, the reimbursement system incentivized utilization for both patients and providers, causing a surge of service provision.

Unfortunately, the negative effects of poor financial incentives do not stop at driving up claims utilization, which is often called the number of units of care generated. As discussed in Chapter 1, the total cost of healthcare is not driven solely by the number of units, but also by the price of each claim or unit of care. This is particularly important given the preceding discussion. The lack of focus on wellness and, to some extent, primary care means that when patients access care, they do so later in the disease progression process. As a result, patients present with more serious conditions and often need care from physician specialists. More claims (units) are generated for specialists who are more costly than primary care physicians, and this increases healthcare costs and leads to an imbalance between primary care (a smaller box in Figure 3.2) and specialist care (a larger box in Figure 3.2).

The lack of emphasis on wellness also influences preferences for pharmaceutical treatments. In many cases, patients would rather take a pill as opposed to engaging in wellness behaviors because it requires less effort and is very inexpensive under many insurance programs. Even though the cost to the consumer is modest, the portion of the cost of the drug paid by insurers, third-party payers, and employers of self-funded plans can be very expensive. As a result, pharmaceutical volume may be larger than needed, driving up healthcare costs (a larger box in Figure 3.2). Finally, using similar logic, when patients are admitted to acute care hospitals for services as inpatients, their conditions are severe, requiring expensive treatments (a larger box in Figure 3.2).

Summarizing, demand and supply have soared in healthcare because traditional control levers have not/could not be deployed fully and effectively. Many demand-side concepts have failed to be effective.

1. Yield management has no effect in the face of an insurance system that insulates the consumer from the cost of care.
2. Although triaging has been employed in microlevel environments (such as an emergency department), adapting the concept more broadly to link the right type of demand with the appropriate level of supply resources is just starting to gain some momentum. As an example, the role of nurse practitioners, a less costly resource than a physician provider, is expanding to improve access to care and reduce costs.
3. Delayed starts could be interpreted as postponing the need for specialty and highly acute care by improving the health status of patients.
4. Similarly, scope reductions can be thought of as limiting the need for acute care, again by focusing on wellness and improving the health status of patients.

On the supply side, healthcare leaders struggle to manage inefficient care delivery systems plagued by unused capacity, highly vertically integrated hospitals with comprehensive service offerings, ineffectively designed legacy facilities and processes, fragmented information flows, high material costs, and a heavy reliance on an insufficient pool of service providers.

3.5.3 A Patient-Centered, Resource Management Solution!

It seems clear that it is time to adopt a patient-centered, resource management solution to treat the ailments of the current healthcare system with an eye toward balancing supply and demand and stabilizing the system. Figure 3.3 lays out the solution. Ideas describing effective resource management are discussed in Chapters 8: Viewing Healthcare Trade-Offs Positively, 10: Accelerating the Use of Information Technology, 12: Reducing the Incidence of Malpractice and the Reforming Legal System, and 13: Rebuilding the Provider Network. Financial alignment is the foundation of balancing demand and supply. Reform depends on rethinking and redesigning health insurance and is discussed in Chapter 7. Wellness and disease management are mechanisms capable of influencing demand and are discussed in Chapter 6. Approaches to improving supply-side coordination among providers are discussed in Chapter 9: Improving Healthcare Strategy and Management. Patient-centeredness, the keystone of the future healthcare system, is discussed in Chapter 5. The book closes with Chapter 14, providing some final thoughts. Next, Chapter 4 contextualizes the nine elements of a comprehensive and integrated solution to the current state of affairs in the healthcare industry.

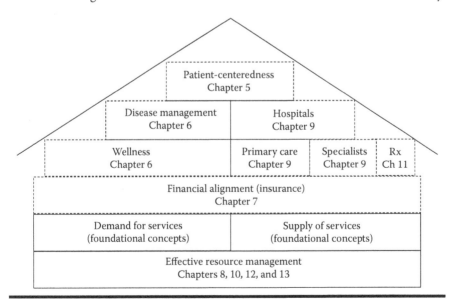

Figure 3.3   An illustration of effective resource management in healthcare: layout of the book.

References

1. Carroll, A. E. 2014. Why improving access to health care does not save money. *New York Times*, July 14, 2014, http://www.nytimes.com/2014/07/15/upshot/why -improving-access-to-health-care-does-not-save-money.html (accessed February 18, 2016).
2. Cogan, J., Hubbard, R., and Kessler, D. 2004. Healthy, wealthy, and wise. *Wall Street Journal*, A, 20.
3. Palmer, P. n.d. Why you need a hospital bill review. http://billadvocates.com/resources /need-hospital-bill-review/ (accessed February 18, 2016).
4. RWJF. 2012. Which approaches encourage patients to become more engaged in their own healthcare? Health Policy Snapshot, Health Care Quality, (January), 1–2. http:// www.rwjf.org/en/library/research/2012/01/which-approaches-encourage-patients -to-become-more-engaged-in-th.html (accessed on February 9, 2016).
5. Dobrzykowski, D., and Tarafdar, M. 2015. Understanding information exchange healthcare operations: Evidence from hospitals and patients. *Journal of Operations Management*, 36, 201–214.
6. AHRQ. 2010. National Healthcare Disparities Report. http://archive.ahrq.gov/research /findings/nhqrdr/nhdr10/Chap5.html (accessed February 1, 2016).
7. Institute of Medicine. Envisioning the National Health Care Quality Report. Washington, DC: National Academies Press; 2001.
8. Dobrzykowski, D. D., Callaway, S. K., and Vonderembse, M. A. 2015. Examining pathways from innovation orientation to patient satisfaction: A relational view of healthcare delivery. *Decision Sciences*, 46(5), 863–899.
9. International Alliance of Patients' Organizations (IAPO). 2006. Declaration on patient-centered healthcare. Retrieved December 13, 2011.
10. Rawson, C. 2012. Why Apple's products are 'designed in California' but 'assembled in China.' http://www.engadget.com/2012/01/22/why-apples-products-are -designed-in-california-but-assembled/ (accessed February 9, 2016).
11. Healey, J. R. 2013. Government sells last of its GM shares. http://www.usatoday .com/story/money/cars/2013/12/09/government-treasury-gm-general-motors-tarp -bailout-exit-sale/3925515/ (accessed February 9, 2016).
12. Greenall, R. 2016. Effective resource demand management. http://www.pcubed .com/bulletins/effective-resource-demand-management (accessed February 3, 2016).
13. Dobrzykowski, D., McFadden, K., and Vonderembse, M. 2016. Examining pathways to safety and financial performance in hospitals: A study of lean in professional service operations. *Journal of Operations Management*, 42–43, 39–51.
14. Callaway, S., and Dobrzykowski, D. 2009. Service-oriented entrepreneurship: Service-dominant logic in green design and healthcare. *Service Science: An INFORMS Journal*, 1(4), 225–240.

Chapter 4

Making Healthcare Work: A Comprehensive and Integrated Solution

To address the root causes of the underlying healthcare problems, there are a set of actions that, when taken together, form a comprehensive and integrated solution. The solution is comprehensive because it addresses a broad range of issues on the demand side and the supply side of healthcare. The solution must be integrated because there are many cross-currents among the underlying problems and root causes, which are discussed in Chapters 1 and 2 and summarized in Figure 2.2. As discussed in the prior chapter, the framework for the comprehensive and integrated solution is based on a healthcare delivery system that focuses on the needs of patients and allows them to be the key decision makers. The solution must effectively organize and manage healthcare resources, so patients get high-quality care, limited delays, good access, and fair and reasonable costs. The nine elements of the solution are interdependent, and the relationship between these elements and the root causes are illustrated in Figure 4.1, which is the organizing vehicle for this chapter.

The solution should not be viewed as a menu from which politicians pick the ones that are easy to do, and everyone agrees because no action meets these hurdles. As discussed in Chapters 1 and 2, these problems and their root causes are complex and challenging, and they did not come about overnight. The difficulty of the task helps to explain why so little has been done to fix the problems and why the Affordable Care Act (ACA) skirted most of these important issues. The solution

Solutions / Root Causes	Chapter 5: Implementing Patient-Centered Care	Chapter 6: Emphasizing Wellness and Personal Responsibility	Chapter 7: Rethinking and Redesigning Health Insurance	Chapter 8: Viewing Healthcare Trade-Offs Positively	Chapter 9: Improving Healthcare Strategy and Management	Chapter 10: Accelerating the Use of Information Technology	Chapter 11: Making Drug Costs Affordable and Fair	Chapter 12: Reducing the Incidence of Malpractice and Reforming the Legal System	Chapter 13: Rebuilding the Provider Network
1. Poor Lifestyle Choices	X	X							
2. Biased Trade-Offs	X		X	X					
3. Unused Facilities and Equipment		X	X	X	X	X			
4. Poorly Designed Policies and Processes	X				X	X			
5. Limited and Ineffective Information Technology	X					X			
6. High Costs of Drugs		X	X	X	X		X		
7. Excessive Legal Liability and Malpractice Insurance Costs	X	X	X	X	X	X		X	
8. Shortage of Healthcare Professionals	X	X	X	X	X	X		X	X

Figure 4.1 Comprehensive and integrated solution that addresses the root causes.

will take time to implement and even more time to feel its full effects, but the journey toward better health and healthcare must start now.

All participants in the healthcare delivery system, including patients, will be impacted and will need to adjust. There are elements in the solution that one group will like while another will not, but that is the nature of compromise: all sides gaining and giving ground. The ultimate test of the solution is asking will it resolve the problems with healthcare? To this end, the solution was built to addresses the root causes that created the underlying problems. The elements of the solution are presented here and discussed fully in the following chapters.

- Chapter 5: Implementing Patient-Centered Care
- Chapter 6: Emphasizing Wellness and Personal Responsibility
- Chapter 7: Rethinking and Redesigning Health Insurance
- Chapter 8: Viewing Healthcare Trade-Offs Positively
- Chapter 9: Improving Healthcare Strategy and Management
- Chapter 10: Accelerating the Use of Information Technology
- Chapter 11: Making Drug Costs Affordable and Fair
- Chapter 12: Reducing the Incidence of Malpractice and Reforming the Legal System
- Chapter 13: Rebuilding the Provider Network

As a summary, Figure 4.1 lists the root causes as the rows and the elements of the solution as the columns. The Xs in the body of the table identify where an element of the solution impacts a root cause. The chapters that follow describe these elements, including how they improve healthcare outcomes and what the driving forces for implementation are. There are discussions of difficult issues, such as personal responsibility and healthcare rationing. An effective solution must consider these issues even though they are difficult, and reasonable people may disagree on how to define them and how they help to shape the solution.

4.1 Implementing Patient-Centered Care

Before the widespread availability of insurance as a fringe benefit, physicians treated patients with help from hospitals and other healthcare professionals. Diagnoses and treatments were determined by patients and physicians without intervention from government, employees, or insurers. In most cases, patients paid physicians directly, so the transaction was simple and efficient. Physicians would often extend credit to patients or even provide charity care as appropriate. Today, healthcare usually involves third-party payers, so relationships between patients and physicians are different and more complex.

Now, governments, through federal and state laws; agencies, such as Medicare and Medicaid; and other third-party payers, require patients and physicians to follow their rules or guidelines. When decision making is placed in the hands of others, patients and physicians no longer have control. Choices are limited, and patients no longer feel responsible for monitoring and controlling costs or keeping healthy. Even when their intent is to help patients, these limitations degrade the relationship between patients and physicians. In addition, meeting these rules consumes resources as physicians take time to read the rules, design a system to address them, and execute the system to ensure compliance. In most cases, the quality of care suffers, and costs increase. This does not mean that all rules are bad. The important question is, What are the costs and the benefits of those rules and regulations?

To have better healthcare, which means care that costs less and leads to increased longevity and better quality of life, it is essential to restore the central role that patients once had and deserve to have again. Patient-centered care is more than being "nice" to patients. It requires patients to make decisions about their health and healthcare in consultation with professionals led by primary care physicians. It means that the patients, or their advocates when a patient is a minor or incapacitated, are the key decision makers, the focal point. The relationship between patients and their primary care physicians, a relationship built on trust and formed over time, is the place to turn for guidance.

Getting help with technical questions isn't abdicating responsibility; it is the smart thing to do. People ask experts to inspect their furnaces and help with appliance repairs. However, advice is information, possibly a recommendation, but it is not a decision. Considering advice as the decision is abdicating responsibility. If evidence is needed to illustrate the value of putting the patient back in charge, ask several friends who have sought second opinions about the advice they received. It is common to get different, even conflicting, opinions when more than one expert is asked. To make patient-centered care work, patients must be willing to learn about health and healthcare even though the topic is a vast and complex. Useful information is plentiful, and patients need to learn, ask questions, and take responsibility.

At the heart of patient-centered care is a personal health plan (PHP), which is created by patients and their primary care physicians. The plan, which would be updated periodically, has five components:

1. A medical history provides information about the health of a patient, which is extremely useful in constructing screening and testing plans as well as diagnosing and treating ailments.
2. A routine health screening plan is a set of indicators, such as blood pressure, heart rate, and body mass index, that monitor patient's health. The frequency of the screenings is determined by patients and physicians and is based on the patient's medical history and health status. Screenings should be inexpensive, easy to do, and common or very similar for all patients.
3. A preventive testing plan is a customized set of assessments that is based on factors such as age and gender, such as a pap test or PSA test, and known

medical conditions, such as an EKG for heart conditions or blood work for diabetes. Physicians and patients would determine the plan's contents and set the schedule.

4. A wellness plan would address diet and exercise and other lifestyle choices. It would be based on the patient's medical history and results from health screenings and preventive testing.

5. An end of life plan would make known the wishes of patients coping with death.

The PHP would change over time as the patient's health and healthcare needs change. Using a PHP is proactive healthcare that focuses on wellness, prevention, and early detection. This approach would allow primary care physicians to be compensated for having healthy patients who have low healthcare costs rather than paying physicians solely for treating the sick.

Having patients participate in healthcare is clearly the right approach. People do this when they seek repairs for appliances, cars, and other devices. Think about the outcome if consumers took their car to a repair shop, provided limited input, and did whatever repair the shop suggested? That is clearly not in their best interest. Even though mechanics have more technical knowledge than the average vehicle owner, the consumer has useful inputs to the process, has a better understanding of the outcome they want, and should make the final decision. Why should healthcare be different?

Figure 4.1 indicates that patient-centered care and the PHP are fundamental parts of the solution because they enhance wellness, improve lifestyle choices, and help people make better decisions about healthcare services and prescription drugs. The close relationship between patients and physicians increases their understanding and acceptance of new technology, such as electronic health records, as well as changes to processes and procedures that improve productivity and quality. The resulting improvements in health and healthcare reduce the likelihood of a malpractice lawsuit, which leads to higher job satisfaction and a willingness on the part of physicians to continue working in healthcare.

4.2 Emphasizing Wellness and Personal Responsibility

Wellness is consistent with the idea that health and healthcare should be patient-centered. When patients are more involved and more responsible for their health, they should no longer feel that health and healthcare are happening to them. Wellness is one of the most effective ways to improve quality of life, increase longevity, and control costs because when patients are well there are no healthcare quality issues, treatment delays, lawsuits, satisfaction problems, or costs. In fact, a focus on wellness should free resources to treat people who currently have only limited access to care.

When many people think of wellness, they think of testing that screens for diseases, an element of wellness, but wellness should be more than screening and testing. An effective wellness program provides education beginning as early as possible—preschool and kindergarten are not too early—and continuing for a lifetime. There should be education about nutrition, exercise, alcohol consumption, drug use, smoking, and other health risks. Wellness also means creating and developing information, websites, and public information announcements that emphasize the what, how, and why of wellness. It is also about creating incentives for patients to make healthy lifestyle choices. It should involve personal responsibility, which implies holding people accountable when they make choices that negatively impact their health. To summarize, wellness is

1. Having individuals take responsibility for their health
2. Educating people about the importance of good health and actions that deliver good health
3. Identifying and disseminating basic health information and goals that people understand
4. Providing feedback on people's health through basic screening
5. Using information from preventive tests to check for disease
6. Implementing incentives, such as lower insurance premiums, for those who make good decisions

Figure 4.1 indicates that efforts to improve wellness and personal responsibility should allow patients to make better lifestyle choices. As wellness is improved, fewer healthcare resources are required, so facilities, equipment, and healthcare professionals are available to work with those who currently are unserved or underserved. Wellness also leads to a reduction in drug usage and to fewer malpractice lawsuits because fewer procedures and treatments are required.

4.3 Rethinking and Redesigning Healthcare Insurance

For healthcare to be patient-centered, it is necessary to rethink and redesign insurance so that patients are in control and face decisions that consider the full costs and benefits of services. If patients receive the benefits of care and bear little or no costs, they are likely to opt for any care even when the benefit is small and the costs to the third-party payer are high. If the money came from patients' pockets, they may make different decisions. Following is a brief outline of how a redesigned health insurance system might work.

1. Preparing and executing the personal health plan: As a requirement for having health insurance paid for by an employer, Medicare, Medicaid, or other third-party payer, patients must create and follow a PHP. The preparation

and execution of the plan would be covered by insurance to encourage everyone to prepare and follow such a plan.

2. Routine healthcare: For routine office visits and prescriptions, it can be argued that patients should pay for these services. Part of the reason is that the costs to manage these transactions among the provider, the patient, and the insurer have become excessive, and the process is fraught with errors. It can cost as much or more to process the transaction and deal with errors and disagreements than it costs to provide the service. Also, if patients pay, they will make better decisions about whether the benefit of the service is worth the cost. There is clearly a delicate balance because the intent is not to deny people access to care they need, but to have them make good decisions about whether to see a physician every time they have a cold. One way to set up this system is with a tax-free health savings account in which the balances roll forward from year to year. Contributions could come from a variety of sources. Employers could contribute the equivalent of the insurance premium for this type of care, and/or they could match employee contributions. Medicare could provide an annual lump sum to cover routine services. The annual expenditures for routine healthcare would be capped, so expenditures over this limit would be paid through catastrophic coverage.

3. Catastrophic coverage: Insurance should help people cope with the substantial costs of serious health problems, such as major surgery and cancer treatment. It should not be designed to cover a $50 office visit or a $30 antibiotic prescription. Insurance is designed to share the risk of serious health problems with others in the insurance pool. Catastrophic coverage for healthcare is needed for the same reason people need fire insurance for their homes. They hope that they never use it, and they do not begrudge their neighbors if they have a fire and collect.

As shown in Figure 4.1, as insurance coverage is modified to put the patient in control, better choices are made about the use of healthcare and prescription drugs. This occurs when patients and physicians face a balanced view of costs and benefits. This is likely to lead to the consumption of fewer services, which means that facilities and equipment would be used less, and there may be fewer physician visits. Fewer tests and procedures should lead to less legal liability and lower malpractice insurance costs.

4.4 Viewing Healthcare Trade-Off Positively: A Paradigm Shift

In order to put patients in charge of their healthcare and help them make better decisions, people must come to grips with trade-offs. In healthcare, people have become accustomed to making decisions based only on the benefits. In addition to not bearing the costs for healthcare services, many people seem to believe that there are no negative consequences from testing and treatment. There are complications from all procedures: false positives leading to more testing and unneeded treatments, hospital-acquired infections, and many others. It is essential to learn how to evaluate trade-offs and make decisions that consider the benefits and costs of healthcare services.

With any trade-off comes the acceptance of risk. Anyone—patients, physicians, government bureaucrats, or insurance companies—will make errors in making healthcare decisions. Today, some people blame the profit-making, greedy insurance companies for charging excessive premiums and denying service to those in need in order to make more profit; never mind that some insurance companies are not for profit and millions are covered by Medicare and Medicaid, which are government sponsored. In turn, others insist that the government, under the ACA, is attempting to ration healthcare. It is vital to cut through this rhetoric and build a healthcare delivery system that provides the best care while keeping risks to a minimum. This is done by putting the best people, patients supported by their physicians, in a position to make these difficult trade-offs. This is another reason why the PHP is so important. It focuses on wellness and early detection, which enables patients to avoid ailments, thereby avoiding risky decisions and treatment costs.

No system can drive risk to zero, and with risk comes the possibility of injury, death, and lawsuits. If patients can file lawsuits naming a doctor or hospital as the guilty party any time a trade-off is made and the outcome is negative, then the healthcare system will be crippled. The right approach puts patients and physicians at the center of the decision-making process, so the patient is fully aware of the risks. Accepting risk means patients and physicians are willing to accept some chance that treatments will not be successful and may lead to serious complications and even death.

As shown in Figure 4.1, the ability to make trade-offs helps patients make better decisions about healthcare treatment and prescription drug use because the trade-offs are no longer biased. Having unbiased trade-offs is likely to lead to the consumption of fewer healthcare services, which could lead to a decline in the usage of facilities and equipment and physician visits. Fewer tests and procedures should lead to less legal liability and lower rates for malpractice insurance.

4.5 Improving Healthcare Strategy and Management

In recent years, hospitals, clinics, physician groups, equipment suppliers, and other healthcare organizations have consolidated through mergers and acquisitions, seeking better use of their capacity, reducing management costs, and achieving economies of scale in operations and purchasing. These moves have resulted in the elimination of smaller, older, and less efficient facilities in an attempt to match capacity with the demand. It is likely this trend will continue as healthcare transitions from small, localized providers to large healthcare organizations and partnerships that represent dozens or even hundreds of hospitals, clinics, and physician groups.

As this process progresses, what appears to be emerging is a tiered provider structure. Small rural hospitals are partnering with regional healthcare systems, and the regional systems are linking with top clinics, hospitals, and academic medical centers. This provides a pathway for treatment from the patient in rural Ohio, via Life Flight if needed, to a more complete set of services at a hospital in Toledo and, ultimately, to experts at the Cleveland Clinic. In addition to access to world-class care, the rural hospital is able to share managers and resources and participate in bulk purchases of goods and services that keep costs in check. This trend is likely to continue.

There are also a number of management practices that healthcare organizations should implement. In other industries, firms are putting resources—people, facilities, equipment, and systems—at the point of contact with the customer. These people are given better training and additional authority, which allows the firms to make better and faster decisions for the customer and reduces middle management costs. For hospitals, this would shift resources from management to direct patient care, and it would allow faster lab results and more accurate and responsive pharmacies, among other things. It also includes process improvement using techniques that have a proven track record, such as process mapping to find procedural problems, Lean thinking to reduce waste, and Six Sigma to improve quality.

It is also about managing the supply chain that provides the goods and services used by hospitals and clinics each day. How can hospitals work with drug companies to order pharmaceuticals? What is the relationship with suppliers who provide and service equipment in surgical centers? Should food services be outsourced? These are key decisions that can lead to significant annual cost savings.

Figure 4.1 indicates that improving healthcare strategy and management should enable hospitals and other healthcare entities to use facilities and equipment more efficiently, thereby increasing availability for others. Process improvements allow hospitals to diagnose and treat patients more effectively and efficiently, which increases productivity, lowers costs, and enhances outcomes. Better care reduces the likelihood of errors, so the legal liability is reduced. Making physicians and staff more productive helps to address the current physician shortage.

4.6 Accelerating the Use of Information Technology

To be effective, physicians need the "right" information, and they must be able to access, sort, and process it quickly and accurately. This system should have state-of-the-art communication technology; the latest in data storage, including sophisticated security to maintain privacy; and algorithms that can analyze patients' health data and provide possible diagnoses and treatment regimens.

The creation of regional and, eventually, national health information exchanges serves patients best because all relevant information is quickly accessible, and it can be easily shared. So when primary care physicians recommend that patients see specialists, patients' data are available to all parties, assuming, of course, that the patient grants permission. In addition, pharmacies, laboratories, testing facilities, and others can access and contribute to the patient's healthcare record.

The use of portable, smart devices allows physicians to access the latest diagnoses and treatment information, giving patients the best chance for success. Also, there are devices that allow healthcare managers to track and locate equipment as well as access maintenance and service information. There are systems that track patients, so staff knows if a patient is currently in X-ray or has been moved to another room. These technologies simplify management and reduce healthcare costs.

As shown in Figure 4.1, better information reduces delays, lowers costs, and drives better care, and better care reduces legal liabilities. The application of information technology also leads to a more efficient use of equipment because it can be tracked and put to use effectively and quickly. Because productivity is higher, physicians have the ability to serve more patients.

4.7 Making Drug Costs Affordable and Fair

Spending on drugs is driven by the amount consumed and the price paid, so efforts to reduce costs must examine both price and usage. When costs are borne in large measure by third-party payers, decisions about drug consumption are biased toward more use. Creating a realistic trade-off that requires decision makers to consider both benefits and costs should cause usage to decline. The PHP is a cornerstone for controlling usage because it identifies wellness goals, and wellness should lead to less consumption. Screenings and testing identify problems before they become serious, further reducing the need for medications. So consuming fewer drugs may actually be a sign of a healthier population.

In addition to usage, rising drug costs are driven by increases in the price charged, especially for new drugs. Price is driven, in part, by high research costs to develop innovative, breakthrough drugs. One study claims that the total cost to develop a new drug is one billion dollars or more and that it can take 10 or more years for a new drug to reach patients.[1] After making these substantial investments in research, drug companies must wait years before earning any revenue and even longer to see profits.

In addition to higher research costs, companies have always done extensive marketing to physicians. More recently, they have substantially increased direct marketing to patients, so patients are aware of treatment options and can ask their physicians about prescribing specific drugs. This has a twofold impact on what the United States spends on drugs as patients' requests stimulate drug usage, and more advertising raises costs and, ultimately, the price of drugs.

There is another factor affecting price and costs that should be considered. Often, drug companies charge one price in the United States and a lower price in other countries, such as Canada. The price in the United States covers the cost to produce the drug plus the full development and marketing costs, which are substantial. The price is much lower in Canada because development and marketing costs are not fully loaded into this price. In effect, the United States is subsidizing the price of drugs sold in Canada and other developed countries.

Reducing drug usage is addressed most effectively by improving wellness and resolving the biased trade-off faced by those with insurance that covers prescription drugs. As indicated in Figure 4.1, making drug pricing fair and affordable leads to lower drug costs. Reducing prices should focus on streamlining the drug development process and carefully assess the value of marketing, especially to patients. As drug usage declines, the probability of lawsuits drops.

4.8 Reducing the Incidence of Malpractice and Reforming the Legal System

If additional efforts are made to reduce the incidence of malpractice in healthcare, everyone, with the possible exception of lawyers, wins. Patients have fewer problems, physicians have lower malpractice insurance costs and are not taken away from their work to deal with these cases, and hospitals have lower costs and fewer distractions.

The intent in reforming the legal system is not to eliminate malpractice lawsuits. They serve a useful purpose as the method of last resort to resolve disputes. The intent of reform is to strike a reasonable balance between plaintiffs and defendants. Frivolous lawsuits, ones that have virtually no chance for success, should be eliminated. These suits increase healthcare costs, clog the courts, and delay the resolution of other lawsuits. Delays in legitimate malpractice cases often require plaintiffs to wait longer for a fair resolution of their case. The key is to balance the risk of winning and losing. When losing incurs little or no cost, a decision to pursue the lawsuit is likely even when there is virtually no chance for success. The attitude may be "What is the harm?" With luck, the defendant may settle out of court.

A solution should attempt to reduce the incidence of malpractice, so there are fewer errors; balance the decision to reduce frivolous lawsuits; and streamline the process, so valid lawsuits are settled more quickly. Figure 4.1 indicates that reforming the legal systems and impacting malpractice insurance will have a direct impact on controlling legal liability and insurance costs. In addition, if lawsuits are reduced, the shortage of physicians may be lessened because they need less time to respond to lawsuits, and fewer will leave the profession because of excessive litigation and malpractice insurance costs.

4.9 Rebuilding the Provider Network

There is a cross-current of effects that impact access to care. Some factors are driving up demand or reducing the capacity of healthcare professionals to provide care. New healthcare technology, diagnostic tools, and treatments are likely to increase demand, and the ACA gives millions of uninsured people access to insurance, which should increase demand. The United States' aging population is demanding more services from hospitals, primary care physicians, and specialists. At the same time, physicians are retiring and pursuing new career opportunities, reducing the supply. On the plus side, if wellness improves and patients face a more balanced trade-off when making healthcare decisions, there should be less demand. Occupations such as nurse practitioner and physician assistant are providing additional qualified healthcare professionals.

Analysis later in the book indicates that the net effect of these cross-currents is likely to be a shortage of physicians because about one-third of physicians are expected to retire in the next 10 years.[2] Following are some suggestions to cope with the pending shortage:

1. Expand admissions to medical schools: There are limits on the number of students admitted to medical schools. Admissions should be allowed to float in response to the anticipated need for physicians and the number of medical school applications from qualified students. This should help to keep capacity in line with demand.
2. Expand physician residencies: Sometimes it takes several weeks or months to see a specialist. This is caused in large part by limiting the number of slots for residents in certain specialties.
3. Alternate providers: Leverage physicians' time with physician assistants and nurse practitioners. Some specialists and primary care physicians are already doing this with great success.

Figure 4.1 indicates that it is critical to rebuild the healthcare professional network to address the shortage. The mix of physicians, physician assistants, and nurse practitioners can be adjusted to provide sufficient, high-quality care.

4.10 Key Issues in the Healthcare Solution

The nine elements described in this chapter combine to create a comprehensive and integrated solution that addresses the underlying healthcare problems related to cost, quality, delay, access, and patient satisfaction. Acceptance of the solution requires a different mindset than the one that commonly exists:

1. In which people tend to believe that everyone should be treated for everything regardless of cost
2. In which efficiency and productivity are considered dirty words because, after all, the purpose of medicine is to save lives, and saving money only gets in the way

The solution requires people to think about quality and cost not as contradictory variables where quality improvements must cost more, but as complementary variables where high-quality care can be delivered, and costs can be reduced. For example, getting healthcare right the first time enhances quality, lowers costs, and reduces delays. Increasing workforce productivity lowers costs, allows healthcare professionals to see more patients, and, when done properly, actually improves patient care. The application of tools, such as information technology, where healthcare is far behind other segments of the U.S. economy, facilitates the delivery of better care and helps to control costs.

It is about recognizing that there are trade-offs even in medicine: What are the costs and benefits of treatment? It is about recognizing that resources are finite: How much healthcare can the United States afford? If patients and their primary care physicians are unwilling to make trade-offs and if resources are limited, the implication is that some external entity must decide who gets care and who does not—in other words, rationing healthcare. Under these circumstances, insurers/employers or government, the third-party payers, do the rationing, and they often make bad decisions. It is time to put healthcare decisions and their associated cost–benefit trade-offs back in the hands of patients and physicians.

It is also about personal responsibility: How much should society spend to treat someone who continues to make poor lifestyle choices? There are many people who smoke, drink too much, eat too much, and exercise too little: Why should they pay the same amount for health insurance as others who take better care of themselves?

The chapters that follow describe these solutions in more detail and discuss how their implementation should improve performance in healthcare delivery. Those chapters provide insights about difficult and important questions. Should there be a limit on healthcare spending? Should healthcare spending have priority over education, better highways, medical research, etc.? How should the healthcare system cope with end-of-life issues?

4.11 A Call to Action

Making changes to the healthcare delivery system is difficult because it is a vast and loosely coupled group of organizations, including physician practices, hospitals, labs, pharmaceutical companies, device makers, and other entities that must work together. Over the years, there have been only limited efforts to examine the system carefully and create plans to improve its performance. The hope seemed to be that the system would self-correct, but it has not.

If the United States continues to wait, the healthcare delivery system will collapses under its own weight, and then the country will be forced to fix it. This is likely to happen in the next decade or so unless corrective action begins soon. As mentioned earlier, healthcare is about 17.2% of the U.S. GDP. This expenditure is likely to grow because of aging baby boomers; problems with obesity and its consequences, especially diabetes and heart disease; and extending access to healthcare to 45 million people through the ACA.[3] In addition, Medicaid funding is not adequate, and Medicare is expected to run out of money by 2024,[4] and it could be sooner. Estimates vary significantly, but one forecast has unfunded Medicare liabilities at $38.6 trillion.[5] This liability is calculated using a 75-year forward that subtracts future Medicare expenses from future Medicare revenue. The country should not wait for the healthcare system to collapse before addressing the issue.

How can changes be implemented? This is a critical national problem, and presidential leadership is essential to define the problem, articulate the pillars that form a solution, and bring representatives from various interest groups to the table for serious discussion. The president and congressional leaders must be part of the solution. The solution involves putting patients and primary care physicians back in charge of healthcare, using market forces and economic principles to address the root causes and underlying problems, creating incentives to encourage change, and applying information technology and management principles to improve care.

Clearly government agencies, such as the Center for Medicare and Medicaid Services; nonprofit organizations, such as the American Medical Association and the American Hospital Association; and private payers must be at the table if the country is to change policies and practices. It is likely that some legislation will be needed to implement the solution. The solution will not be easy, but the nation must engage and solve this problem starting now.

References

1. Drug Discovery World. 2004. Failure rates in drug discovery and development: Will we ever get any better? http://www.ddw-online.com/business/p148365-failure%20rates%20in%20drug%20discovery%20and%20development%3A%20will%20we%20ever%20get%20any%20better%3F%20%20fall%2004.html (accessed December 18, 2015).
2. Washington Policy Center. 2011. The looming doctor shortage. http://www.washington policy.org/publications/notes/looming-doctor-shortage (accessed September 10, 2015).

3. Young, J. 2013. Uninsured Americans 2012: More than 45 million lacked health insurance last year, CDC reports. Huffington Post (April 23). http://www.huffingtonpost.com/2013/03/21/uninsured-americans-2012_n_2918705.html (accessed November 29, 2015).
4. National Academy of Social Insurance. 2011. Medicare's fiscal future. http://www.nasi.org/learn/medicare/financial-problems (accessed December 18, 2015).
5. Goins, C. 2012. Medicare faces unfunded liability of $38.6T, or $328,404 for each U.S. household. cnsnews.com (April 23). http://www.usdebtclock.org/ (accessed October 13, 2015).

Chapter 5

Implementing Patient-Centered Care

The unfortunate truth is that patients have less to say about their healthcare than other parts of their lives, such as where to live or what cars to buy, in part, because choices are limited by reimbursement rules and regulations from third-party payers. Plus, healthcare has technical elements that often intimidate patients, who find it easier to give up control to highly educated professionals. Patients may not want to learn about their medical conditions or to be assertive by taking a leadership, or even an active, role in their care. The current system does not expect patients to do this, and in fact, it seems to discourage this behavior.

In addition, many people in the United States appear to accept the misplaced notion of the infallible physician. This overconfidence in the physician's ability to heal sets up unrealistic expectations that are not good for patients, who may make poor lifestyle choices and take a passive role in their health and healthcare because they believe physicians can fix their problems. With these high expectations, physicians are in a position where they can only disappoint patients, which increases the chance of legal action when expectations are not met regardless of the reason.

These feelings are reinforced by entrenched practices that act as signs and symbols of the patient's second-class status. Third-party payers usually determine what services they will pay for, who can provide the service, and the amount they will pay. Most of the time, patients have no idea how much these services cost. When patients have diagnostic tests, they do not get the results. In fact, if patients ask the laboratory or testing company for results, they are usually told to see the physician, who will explain the outcomes. Normally, patients don't get a copy of lab reports unless they ask for them and the physician agrees to provide them. After a hospital stay, patients don't receive a detailed bill. The bill is sent to the insurance company, government agency, or other third-party payer.

The one thing for which patients are responsible is fixing payment problems. When payments are delayed because the hospital or physician's office did not list the right information on the medical claim or the third-party payer is late in processing it, healthcare providers may demand full payment from patients, often without listing details about the services rendered. The patient has two choices: Pay the full amount even though they have insurance or make several phone calls to the insurer and provider to fix the problem. It is not uncommon to have patients threatened with collections because the healthcare provider, the payer, or both did not do their jobs correctly and/or in a timely manner.

It is time to put patients back in charge, making them, with the help of their primary care physicians, responsible for their health and healthcare. Patient-centered care (PCC) provides a mechanism to do just that. Before diving into PCC, it is important to note that many physicians have adopted PCC principles. For them, this is an opportunity to validate and reinforce this behavior, take the next steps in PCC, and be compensated based on how successful they are at having healthy patients.

5.1 Defining Patient-Centered Care

PCC, the centerpiece of effective and efficient healthcare, focuses on the needs of patients.

> PCC is based on two fundamental principles: The interests of patients are most important, and patients are the ultimate decision makers.

PCC requires patients to have a basic understanding of health and healthcare, be actively involved in their care, work closely with primary care physicians and their staffs, and create a personal health plan (PHP) that focuses on the following:

1. Keeping patients healthy
2. Finding problems before they become debilitating
3. Empowering patients as decision makers

The PCC must be respectful of patient's preferences, values, and beliefs. It is a partnership between patients and their primary care physicians. The physicians provide information about health status and wellness as well as diagnosis and treatment options, including their risks and benefits. Patients, assisted by their physicians, make decisions. The goal of the PCC is not to provide more and better care and treatment. The goal is to create circumstances in which patients need less but better treatment, thus reducing healthcare costs, improving longevity and quality of life, and freeing resources to treat others.

As shown in Figure 5.1, PCC begins with a strong and effective relationship between a patient and a primary care physician. When needed, a parent or legal guardian is present to provide information, help with decision making, follow through on recommendations, and deal with medical billing and payment. Think about what would happen if each time a patient saw a physician the patient saw a different one. At each visit, the physician would have to relearn the patient's medical history and health profile, which decreases their productivity and drives up healthcare costs. When a patient and a physician have a long-term relationship, the physician does not have to build knowledge and trust, and the physician can use his or her time more effectively and be more productive. There are fewer delays and missteps because the physician understands the patient's attitudes and behaviors, and the physician has a knowledge base and a health plan that the patient created. As a result, the patient responds better and is more likely to buy into wellness and work toward being healthy. When a patient has a health problem, he or she is more likely to get better and faster care. When insurance plans or government regulations disrupt the relationship between patient and physician, a patient is burdened with less effective healthcare.

Figure 5.1 also shows that patients and primary care physicians can draw upon a variety of physician specialists, medical professionals, and facilities to help execute the patients' health plan. Physicians, who specialize, such as cardiologists

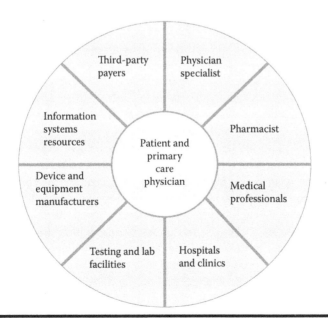

Figure 5.1   Patient-centered care.

and neurologists, and pharmacists can provide essential support when diagnoses and potential treatments are beyond the training and experience of primary care physicians. Medical professionals, such as physician assistants, nurse practitioners, nurses, and therapists, work with primary care physicians and physician specialists to provide hands-on, quality care. Hospitals and clinics have essential facilities, such as surgery rooms, cardiac care units, and physical therapy.

Figure 5.1 shows testing facilities, such as those specializing in magnetic resonance imaging (MRI) and laboratories that do blood work, tissue biopsies, and other analyses. These facilities may be housed within a hospital, clinic, or physician's office, or they may be independent. A bit further down the supply chain are device and equipment manufacturers who design and build healthcare products, such as joint implants, surgical apparatus, and testing equipment used by physicians to support patient care.

Physicians require fast and easy access to information about their patients, including medical history, test results, and drug allergies as well as access to the latest treatment options. Patients need to know about their health and healthcare. PCC is based on having organized and summarized information to support decision making, an essential part of electronic health records (EHRs). With this, patients and physicians can create a list of blood pressure or glucose results over the past five years and can quickly spot trends and determine if lifestyle changes or treatments are needed or have been successful.

5.2 Personal Health Plan

At the heart of PCC is the PHP, with which patients and their primary care physicians work in concert to create a blueprint for a healthy person. Although the structure of the PHP would be common for all patients, its content would be customized through patient and physician collaboration. Health, rather than healthcare, was chosen as the operative word because the focus of the PHP is achieving health. The traditional value of screening and testing is to identify problems that require diagnosis and treatment. With a PHP, screening and testing are used to adjust how patients live by providing information that guide lifestyle choices and determine health.

Shifting the relationship between patients and primary care physicians from one seeking solutions to problems through diagnosis and treatment to one seeking problem prevention through health and wellness may seem like a small change. In fact, this is an enormous change that can have a major impact on the process for delivering healthcare, the roles and responsibilities of patients and primary care physicians, and the method of evaluating and compensating primary care physicians and their staffs. These changes are vital and are discussed later. For now, being clear about the objectives and elements of the PHP is critical. The objective is simple and bears repeating, strive for the highest level of patient health. Ultimately, that is the primary objective for the relationship between patients and primary care

Personal health plan				
Medical history	Routine health screening plan	Preventive testing plan	Wellness plan	End-of-life plan

Figure 5.2 Personal health plan.

physicians. This means less healthcare: Patients need fewer surgeries, fewer pharmaceutical drugs, less therapy, and so on. This means better health, so patients have better quality of life and longevity.

As shown in Figure 5.2, the PHP has five elements on which patients and physicians collaborate. Medical history, the foundation of the PHP, lists all relevant information about the patient's health and healthcare. Second, a routine health screening plan outlines simple, fast, and inexpensive assessments, which are commonly used and important indicators of health. Third, a preventive testing plan is a set of tests given to patients that is based on the patient's medical history and the results of routine health screenings. It is dynamic because the tests and the frequency of testing change in response to the patient's condition. Fourth, the wellness plan is a set of lifestyle choices that patients make and pledge to follow with the support of their primary care physicians. The last part, the end-of-life plan, is essential because it requires people to think about and plan for this critical time in their lives. The following sections discuss each element of the PHP in more detail.

5.2.1 Medical History

The first element, medical history, is commonly used by physicians to provide a picture of the patient's past and current health. It includes the following:

1. Current symptoms: Each visit begins with a discussion of current symptoms, which are noted in the medical history. When life-threatening, time-sensitive problems are present, updating the medical history must take place after the emergency is addressed. With EHRs, physicians and patients can easily look back to determine how frequently and for how long these symptoms have occurred. It is also possible to see what treatments were used and how well they worked.
2. Immunizations: A list of vaccinations and other relevant information are included.
3. Medication: A list of medicines the patient is currently taking and allergies to medicines are part of the history.
4. Routine health screenings: Basic health assessment, such as blood pressure, pulse, and weight, are included.

5. Medical testing: Results from tests listed on patient's preventive testing plan and diagnostic testing ordered by physicians to address a specific ailment would be part of the record.
6. Personal medical history: A list of the patient's health conditions, such as anemia, gout, and kidney disease, are included.
7. Surgical history: Dates and types of surgeries are included.
8. Family history: Identify the health status of parents, siblings, and even grandparents. This would include causes of death when relevant.
9. Other health concerns: This includes a series of questions about lifestyle, including diet, exercise, drug and alcohol use, tobacco consumption, and other relevant information.
10. Personal information: This would include occupation, marital status, dependents, hobbies, and other factors that might impact health.[1]

The medical history is foundational for the PHP because it has a direct bearing on the type and frequency of the health screenings and preventive testing a patient needs as well as how the wellness plan would be constructed and implemented.

Before discussing the second element in the PHP, it should be noted that EHRs will make medical history a much more useful, accurate, and patient-friendly tool. Without EHRs, medical history is a paper-based, handwritten document created from a patient's memory, so it is likely to contain errors. Currently, each physician maintains a medical history for each patient. So when patients see multiple physicians, each medical history may be different. Periodically, physicians ask their patients to update their medical history by redoing it from scratch, so the same physician may have histories that are inconsistent. In addition, it is annoying to enter the same information over and over and over again. How many times should patients have to write about their appendectomy in 1955? With EHRs, the medical history is an integral part, and every physician has access to the same one. Once the data are in the medical history, it is only necessary to provide updates. Most updates should be done electronically and occur without special actions by physicians or patients.

5.2.2 Routine Health Screening Plan

A routine health screening plan contains quick and easy assessments of the patient's health status and is likely to include blood pressure, pulse rate, weight, and height as well as an overall health appraisal. There could be some screenings that are specific to the patients' health needs, such as a simple glucose test when diabetes is prevalent among family members. Screenings are important inputs for patients and their primary care physicians as patients adjust lifestyle choices to improve their health. Some of the assessments can be done at home and entered online into the patient's EHR. Others, including blood pressure, require equipment, so patients must come to their physician's office and have a technician do the screening and enter it into the EHR. This process can be simplified by having patients go to a local pharmacy where their blood pressure is measured and results sent electronically to their EHR. Using pharmacies as points of care is discussed in more detail in Chapter 13. Wearable fitness devices are able to make some of these assessments and upload the information electronically.

The frequency of the screenings is a variable and depends on various factors. For example, a young, healthy patient may need a blood pressure check once a year or once in six months, and someone who is older and who has a history of high blood pressure would be monitored more frequently. Patients and physicians would have access to this information, so a pattern of deterioration can be detected and acted upon before it becomes life threatening.

5.2.3 Preventive Testing Plan

The third element of the PHP is a preventive testing plan, which differs from the routine health screenings plan because the tests are more elaborate, usually require specialized equipment, and are more costly to perform. These tests as well as their frequency are specific to the needs of the patient. A young, healthy person may have little, if any, preventive testing, and patients who are older and have a history of health problems are likely to have several tests.

The need for preventive testing may be triggered by health screenings that indicate problems. For example, if a patient feels fatigued, a blood test may be administered to learn if the thyroid is functioning properly. If the thyroid level needs adjustment, medication is prescribed and future testing is done as part of the preventive testing plan to monitor the level and adjust medications accordingly.

As patients age, they become more susceptible to certain ailments, so tests such as colonoscopies become part of the preventive testing plan. Gender plays a role as mammograms and PSA tests are administered at specified intervals. The essence of preventive testing is having patients and physicians work together to catch and address problems early, preventing more serious problems and complications.

5.2.4 Wellness Plan

The fourth element of the PHP is a wellness plan, which evolves, in part, from the first three. The wellness plan is a set of actions that provides each patient with a customized pathway to a healthy life. Wellness is multidimensional as it includes physical, emotional, and mental health issues, and the wellness plan identifies a set of actions and goals that address lifestyle choices. Wellness includes programs that address addictions to cigarettes, alcohol, drugs, and even to food. It also includes actions that prevent illness, including vaccinations, flu shots, and the like. To the extent possible, patients are encouraged to address health problems by making better lifestyle choices, such as increasing exercise and changing their diet to eat healthier food, control weight, cope with diabetes, and lower cholesterol. Wellness planning is described in more detail in Chapter 6 on wellness and personal responsibility.

5.2.5 End-of-Life Plan

The fifth element of the PHP is the end-of-life plan, which is a way to cope with the difficult decisions faced at this stage of human life. Through serious accident, disease, or the gradual impact of aging, everyone approaches death. The important questions are the following: How should people be treated? What is their quality of life? What are the costs? According to an article in *Money* magazine, each year, "one out of every four Medicare dollars, more than $125 billion, is spent on services for the 5% of beneficiaries in their last year of life."[2]

When patients speak with their families and primary care physicians before facing their end-of-life struggle, they make thoughtful decisions, and they provide their loved ones with a plan that identifies the patient's wishes at this critical time. So patients have what they want, and their family does not face these difficult decisions wondering what to do. This discussion does not mean that everyone must make the same choices, have a healthcare power of attorney, and a "do not resuscitate" order. The patient's choice could be to prolong life as long as possible.

Following are brief descriptions of some important tools in end-of-life planning: living will, healthcare power of attorney, and "do not resuscitate" order.

1. Living will: This is a written instruction that identifies actions to be taken regarding the patient's health when he or she is unable to make those decisions because of illness or mental incapacity. The living will provides directives that healthcare providers are obliged to follow. It may also list certain actions that are not permitted, such as feeding tubes and other life-support activities. The living will can be either specific or general. Following is a typical statement found in a living will: If I am suffering from an incurable, irreversible illness and the physician determines that my condition is terminal, the physician is directed to withhold or discontinue life-sustaining measures that would serve only to artificially postpone my dying.[3]
2. Healthcare power of attorney: Like other powers of attorney, this document gives a third party the power to make healthcare decisions for the grantor. This tool is flexible, so it can provide decision makers with the power to terminate care and remove life support. It is sometimes called a medical power of attorney.[4] Some people prefer the healthcare power of attorney over a living will because vesting power in a person rather than a written document provides a way to deal with a wide variety of health issues. Of course, this places a greater burden on the third party and assumes that this person will act in the best interest of the grantor.

3. Do not resuscitate (DNR): This is also called a "No Code." A DNR is a specific legal order to withhold cardiopulmonary resuscitation (CPR) or advanced cardiac life support,[5] which is urgent treatment for heart attack or stroke. It does not preclude other treatments. DNR is most often used for patients who have advanced diseases, such as cancer, or have multiple medical problems. A DNR takes pressure off the person named as decision maker in a healthcare power of attorney.

What constitutes a good plan? Combining a healthcare power of attorney and a DNR can be an effective way to address end-of-life issues. Although these options may not provide a perfect solution, it is better than giving loved ones no guidance or, worse yet, ending up in court fighting over what to do. It should be clear that patients are not required to have any of these legal documents; they have the right to traditional care, including resuscitation, feeding tubes, and other life-support functions. Their plan may be as simple as "I want health-care professionals to follow normal patterns of treatment and prolong my life as much as possible." The goal of end-of-life planning is to give patients a full understanding of their options and have patients, supported by their primary care physicians and families, make an informed choice. A copy of the end-of-life plan should be included in the patient's EHR, so healthcare providers have access to these important documents. Patients or their legal guardians should also keep copies.

Another important question is when to start. Some people argue that it is never too soon because accidents and severe health problems can happen at any time. End-of-life planning could start at birth, but that may not be reasonable when the time and cost of planning is compared to the few instances when it is needed. The death rate for one- to four-year-olds is only 30 per 100,000, and it falls to 16.6 per 100,000 for five- to 14-year-olds. The rate jumps to 905.9 deaths per 100,000 for 55- to 64-year-olds.[6] Requiring an end-of-life plan as people become eligible for Medicare may be a reasonable option. Having an end-of-life plan for someone with a significant health problem, regardless of age, also makes sense.

5.3 Implementing Patient-Centered Care

As described earlier, implementing PCC drives change in the process, the roles and responsibilities of healthcare professionals, and the measurement and reward system that are part of healthcare. The result of these changes is a new set of attitudes, values, and beliefs for patients, primary care physicians, and their staffs. When done properly, there is an alignment of goals among the participants and coordinated actions toward the ultimate goal of patient health.

5.3.1 Process Change

With PCC, there are fundamental changes in the relationship between patients and their primary care physicians. PCC shifts the goal from diagnosing and treating problems to providing pathways to health. As patients and physicians work together to achieve better health for patients, the topics they discuss and the way they interact change. The PHP becomes a central topic for the patient–physician relationship and the vehicle for managing patients' health and healthcare. The interaction between patients and physicians shifts from physicians as directors or decision makers to expert support persons, and patients become active participants, even leaders, in the pursuit of health.

These changes drive changes in the skills that primary care physicians and their medical staffs need, so medical school curriculum, or at least what is taught in residency, would change. Recertification and continuing education would adjust to deliver these skills to current healthcare professionals. These ideas are discussed more fully in Chapter 13.

5.3.2 Changing Roles and Responsibilities

Primary care physicians and their staffs would have different roles with greater responsibilities and an expanded scope of work, including nutrition, exercise, smoking cessation, and other lifestyle choices. The patients' responsibility changes from passive to active as they make decisions that change their lifestyle, improve their health, and determine their future healthcare needs. Patients are responsible for learning and decision making and should be held accountable for poor lifestyle choices.

Primary care physicians must be good communicators, organize work effectively, and exhibit leadership to a staff that possesses a variety of valuable skills. They must work closely with patients, draw them into the process, and instill a set of attitudes and values, so wellness is seen as the best path to longevity and a good quality of life. Primary care physicians would still identify health problems and implement cures when needed.

With PCC, primary care physicians would search for cures within the context of wellness and lifestyle choices. They would understand the value of these choices, so when health problems arise, they can discuss lifestyle changes with their patients rather than moving first to drugs, surgery, or other medical procedures. To do this, primary care physicians and their staffs must have an expanded knowledge base, including information about nutrition, exercise, substance abuse, and more. These changes imply different methods of compensation for primary care physicians and their staff.

Because of this expanded knowledge base, primary care physicians may not, and probably should not, possess all the skills needed to build and carry out a PHP, so they may be supported by specialists in nutrition, exercise, and other areas. More will be discussed in Chapter 13 about how physician offices will be organized, including the use of physician assistants and nurse practitioners to share the work-load, keep costs in line, and add capabilities.

5.3.3 Changing Measurement and Compensation for Primary Care Physicians

Even if new processes are put in place and new job responsibilities are defined, actions and attitudes will not change unless the measurement and reward system reinforces this behavior. If primary care physicians are measured and rewarded according to what is valued, diagnoses and treatments, behavior will not change. It is critical to reward them for preparing the PHP and keeping patients healthy. It is also important to incentivize patients to adjust their behavior, which can be done initially by lowering insurance premiums for having a PHP and following it.

Primary care physicians would no longer be compensated solely for treating the flu, back pain, and other ailments. They would be paid to keep patients in good health. Currently, the Pioneer Accountable Care Organizations (ACOs) model is examining a payment system in which providers are paid for improving the health of their patients. This is being undertaken by the Center for Medicare and Medicaid Services (CMS) as part of the CMS Innovation Center initiative. The purpose is to test innovative payment and service delivery models that reduce cost as well as preserve and enhance the quality of care.[7]

In addition to being compensated for patient health, primary care physicians would be compensated for working with their patients to prepare and update the PHP. When patients require treatment, physicians would be compensated for this as well, but this must be done so physicians are not incentivized to withhold needed care because they are able to keep funds that are not spent on patients. Ultimately, the goals are to increase wellness and reduce treatment, allowing physicians to see more patients and make the same or more net income. Primary care physicians may have more patients in their practice because the patients are healthier and require less care.

Before moving on, it is important to make the following point. Patients who are not capable of making decisions would have parents or legal guardians to help them. This includes minors, adults who are mentally retarded or developmentally delayed, and the elderly with dementia.

5.4 Driving Forces for Change

Healthcare is different from other parts of the economy because patients receive the services but most of the bill is paid by third parties. If patients paid all or most of the costs for care, driving change would be easier because patients would benefit from being healthier. If patients made poor lifestyle choices and, as a result, had high healthcare costs, patients rather than third parties would pay the bills. Eventually, patients would see the value in PCC and PHPs and would want to participate. Patients would demand more efficient healthcare delivery systems and respond positively to healthcare providers who offer high-quality, low-cost care. As a result of this circumstance, change must be driven by the third parties who pay for the services—not by patients. So organizations such as Medicare, Medicaid, and employers along with their insurers must be brought to the table, and they must buy into PCC and PHPs. More is discussed in Chapter 7 on health insurance and the responsibilities of patients.

Patients must understand the value of these changes and be willing to participate actively, so patient education is critical to drive these changes. Education must focus on the following:

1. The value of good lifestyle choices and wellness to improve quality of life and longevity as well as the importance of preparing and executing a PHP to reduce healthcare costs
2. Understanding the patient's role in PCC and why that role is critical for improving the healthcare delivery system

Offering discounts on health insurance to patients when they actively engage in PCC and create and follow a PHP would provide strong reasons for their participation. Higher reimbursement levels for physicians and hospitals that use these tools would incentivize their participation. Along with education and financial incentives, it is essential for health insurance to pay most of the cost to prepare a PHP.

For the providers, there are interest groups that represent hospitals, physicians, and other medical professionals, including the American Medical Association (AMA) and the American Hospital Association (AHA). These are powerful entities that must be part of these important changes. Although there are fundamental differences that divide third-party payers from providers, the idea of putting patients in charge of their health and healthcare and having a plan that focuses on wellness are very attractive and would be difficult for these groups to oppose.

5.5 Impact of Patient-Centered Care on Healthcare Outcomes

Of all the proposed solutions, PCC and creating a PHP, which includes wellness (the topic of the next chapter), may have the greatest impact on healthcare outcomes by improving costs, quality, access, and patient satisfaction. Following is a description of the impacts of PCC as they relate to the relevant root causes. The root causes are discussed in Chapter 2.

1. Poor lifestyle choices: PCC and the PHP focus squarely on wellness and providing services designed to help patients maintain a healthy lifestyle (root cause #1 from Chapter 2). PCC and PHP create an environment in which lifestyle and health are connected because patients understand how their choices impact their health and they have the tools to create a new and better life.

2. Biased trade-offs: PCC also provides an environment in which patients and their primary care physicians make better choices. And better decision making has important interactions with two other parts of the solution set: rethinking and redesigning health insurance and viewing healthcare trade-offs positively. With patients and physicians as decision makers, the new approach to health insurance lays out and evaluates trade-offs effectively. This happens because patients and physicians see both the costs and the benefits of decisions, and as a result, they make unbiased choices about the need for diagnoses and treatments (root cause #2).

3. Poorly designed policies and processes: PCC creates a closer relationship among patients, primary care physicians, and their staffs. It allows patients to see and understand the policies and processes (root cause #4) that govern healthcare and enables them to understand the importance of effectiveness, efficiency, and productivity. When this insight is combined with creating unbiased trade-offs in healthcare decision making, physicians, hospitals, and other healthcare providers will examine more closely their policies and procedures to achieve better cost outcomes. This scrutiny is likely to initiate improvements in the other underlying problems, especially low quality, service delays, and poor patient satisfaction.

4. Limited and ineffective information technology: PCC reinforces the need to improve information technology (root cause #5) because it requires more and better information to make decisions, and it produces more and better information about the patient.

5. High drug costs: Fewer prescription drugs (root cause #6) are needed because PCC strives to improve health. When there are problems, PCC and the PHP seek solutions through lifestyle changes first. When these changes are successful, fewer drugs are required.

6. Excessive legal liability and malpractice insurance costs: PCC leads to better decision making because the relationship between patients and physicians is stronger and there is more and better information. Also, if PCC is successful, there should be fewer and more effective treatments and procedures. As a result, the likelihood of malpractice liability (root cause #7) should be reduced.

7. Shortage of healthcare professionals: PCC should lead to less rather than more treatment, easing the pressure on the shortage of healthcare professionals (root cause #8). It should also lead to restructuring healthcare delivery so that nurse practitioners and physician assistants as well as experts in nutrition and exercise can take on some responsibilities.

5.6 Summary of Recommendations

Following is a listing of the key recommendations contained in this chapter:

1. PCC is the centerpiece of the new approach to healthcare delivery. It is a partnership between patients and primary care physicians that requires patients to become actively involved and learn about their health and healthcare and to work closely with primary care physicians to make good decisions about lifestyle and treatments. PCC depends on creating an effective personal health plan (PHP).
2. Each patient would have a PHP, which focuses on creating a healthy patient. It has five important components:
   a. A medical history provides an overview of the patient's health and healthcare. It holds useful information about the patient's medical conditions and family history. It will be much improved and a far more useful tool once an EHR system is in place.
   b. A routine health screening plan is a basic set of simple and inexpensive health assessments, such as blood pressure and pulse rate, that provide indications of the patient's health.
   c. A preventive testing plan is a group of tests that are more complex and expensive. They would be different for each patient because they address health problems that may be identified from information in the patient's medical history or results from routine health screenings.
   d. A wellness plan is a set of activities that patients do to maintain and improve health. The plan is customized for patients and is based on the medical history, routine health screenings, and preventive testing. The plan would involve various aspects of life, including nutrition, exercise, smoking cessation, and substance abuse.
   e. An end-of-life plan addresses the difficult decisions that people face as they age. It outlines how they want to be treated when facing death, and it may include a living will, healthcare power of attorney, and a "do not resuscitate" order. Patients are free to choose any option including full medical treatment to save their lives.
3. Implementing PCC would require changes in the process, that is, how patients and primary care physicians interact, which drives changes in the roles and responsibilities of each party and the measurement and reward system for physicians.

References

1. Palo Alto Medical Foundation: A Sutter Health Affiliate. 2011. Adult health history for new patients. http://www.pamf.org/forms/143952_Adult_Med_Hx.pdf (accessed September 17, 2015).

2. Wang, P. 2012. Cutting the high cost of end-of-life care. *Time Inc.* (December 12). http://money.cnn.com/2012/12/11/pf/end-of-life-care-duplicate-2.moneymag/index .html (accessed October 19, 2015).
3. Randolph, M. 2015. What is a living will? AllLaw.com. http://www.alllaw.com/articles /wills_and_trusts/article7.asp (accessed October 19, 2015).
4. Lawyers.com. Elder law 2015. Health care power of attorney. http://elder-law.lawyers .com/health-care-power-of-attorney.html (accessed October 19, 2015).
5. Braddock, C. H., and Clark, J. D. 2015. Do not resuscitate (DNAR) orders. University of Washington School of Medicine: Ethics in Medicine. http://depts.washington.edu /bioethx/topics/dnr.html (accessed October 19, 2015).
6. Data360. 2015. U.S. death rate by age group. http://www.data360.org/dsg.aspx?Data _Set_Group_Id=587 (accessed October 19, 2015).
7. Center for Medicare and Medicaid Services. 2015. Pioneer ACO model fact sheet. https://innovation.cms.gov/initiatives/Pioneer-ACO-Model/PioneerACO-FactSheet .html (accessed October 27, 2015).

Chapter 6

Emphasizing Wellness and Personal Responsibility

It seems sensible to believe that everyone wants to have "wellness." After all, who does not want to be healthy and happy? Yet many people's actions suggest that they are not interested in being healthy, or they do not understand the consequences of their choices, or their cravings overwhelm their judgment, so they eat too much of the wrong food, smoke, take drugs, etc. So creating wellness must include the following:

1. Explaining the consequences of making poor lifestyle decisions
2. Providing knowledge so that people can make good lifestyle choices
3. Offering programs to help people cope with cravings and addictions
4. Giving incentives to encourage healthy choices

Patient-centered care (PCC) and wellness are integrated, interdependent, critical activities. The concepts and principles contained in these two activities are the best ways to enhance quality of life, increase longevity, and improve healthcare because these ideas work together to do the following:

1. Improve the quality of care as patients become the focal point and decision makers
2. Eliminate delays because there is less demand for healthcare resources

3. Expand access for those with limited or no access to care because resources become available
4. Reduce the costs of healthcare as people consume less
5. Increase patient satisfaction as care improves and costs moderate

Wellness is also about personal responsibility. When people consume more healthcare because they make poor lifestyle choices, shouldn't they pay more for it? There seems to be a direct and positive link between poor lifestyle choices and more health problems. Some argue that this is too harsh for people in poverty who are financially disadvantaged, often food-insecure, and in many cases, forced to make tough choices from among medical care, food, and affordable housing. Others argue that some people make the right decisions about wellness yet have serious medical problems. A key element in determining how much people pay for health insurance should not be how much healthcare they receive but if they make good lifestyle choices, which means they have a wellness plan and follow it.

6.1 Defining Wellness

Wellness is a state. Simply defined, it is having a good quality of life—a life that is enjoyable and does not require others to meet a person's basic needs.[1] Wellness is multidimensional, including physical, mental, and emotional health. It is the absence of illness or disease, and it allows people to participate in activities they like. A wellness plan is a customized pathway to a long, healthy, and productive life, and it is driven by personal initiative as people seek an optimal and holistic state of health.[2]

This does not mean that the goal of wellness is to achieve perfect physical, mental, and emotional health. No one is perfect. Everyone has limitations that must be addressed, which explains why wellness plans are not the same for everyone. Some people are born with or acquire conditions that limit their activities and reduce their quality of life. Children and young adults develop cancer even though they have led healthy lives. Some people are blind or have poor eyesight. Others have physical disabilities, so they cannot run or walk. Still others have limited mental capacity, so they require special education, or they suffer from emotional problems that require counseling and medication. The wellness plan must consider these conditions, work to overcome them to the extent possible, and design a program to achieve the best level of health given the circumstances.

Health and wellness are closely related to PCC because they are patient-centered. Patients, supported by primary care physicians and their staffs, are the architects of wellness plans. Experts in fields such as nutrition, exercise, and substance abuse can help to create plans that meet an individual's needs. Executing the wellness plan is the patient's responsibility, and mechanisms must be in place to track progress toward the plan's goals and provide feedback to patients.

Figure 6.1   Health and wellness are patient-centered and based on the personal health plan.

As shown in Figure 6.1, health and wellness depend upon creating and following a wellness plan. The wellness plan, in turn, is part of the personal health plan (PHP) and uses as input the first three elements of the PHP, which are listed here but are discussed in the prior chapter:

1. A medical history provides important background information about the patient's health, medical conditions, and substance abuse issues as well as family medical history.
2. A routine health screening plan provides basic health information about patients, which is used to identify actions that become part of the lifestyle choices component of the wellness plan. The information gathered by these screenings is also used to track progress toward the plan's goals.
3. A preventive testing plan is designed to catch health problems early and take appropriate action, thereby keeping people healthy.

A key ingredient of the wellness plan is a set of lifestyle choices that people make in order to maintain and improve their health. Another important aspect of the wellness plan is preventive treatment. These are discussed in the following section.

6.1.1 Lifestyle Choices

Lifestyle choices are a critical part of a wellness plan, and they include nutrition and diet, exercise, substance abuse, and mental and emotional health issues.

1. Nutrition and diet: Eating healthy—a so-called "balanced" diet—provides sufficient vitamins, minerals, and calories to support overall health and control weight, and it offers enough fiber to maintain digestive health. If done properly, many people will not require vitamins or other supplements. This call to eat healthily is not meant to advocate for a vegan, vegetarian, low-fat, low-carb, or other diet. Nutrition and diet are personal issues that people

commit to, and asking them to follow something they do not believe in leads to failure. What to eat depends on the needs and tastes of the individual. Some people have food allergies; others can tolerate more fat in their diet; and others may wish to avoid meat for religious or cultural reasons or simply to protect animals. Diet and nutritional needs change as people age and vary depending on many factors, including the amount of exercise a person gets. The key is for patients, primary care physicians, and their staffs to work together to find a diet that provides patients with appropriate levels of nutrients and calories at an affordable price so patients maintain their health.

2. Exercise: Everyone should maintain good cardio fitness, strength, flexibility, and balance. There are inexpensive exercises people can do at home. For example, a push-up requires no equipment or special clothing, and many people regard it as the best exercise to build overall strength, including core strength. Walking, jogging, or riding a bike can provide an effective cardiovascular workout. Once again, the exercise plan should be crafted to meet the needs and limitations of the individual. Some people have physical disabilities, such as missing limbs or paralysis, that must be accommodated. A person with lower back pain has different stretching and strengthening activities from someone with limited shoulder mobility. As people age, they may need to place more emphasis on maintaining strength, flexibility, and balance than a younger person. There is a strong link between nutrition and exercise, so these activities must be coordinated. For example, football players and assembly line workers usually need more calories than college professors or accountants. People who exercise more may require more carbs or may need more fat in their diet. Controlling weight with a good eating plan and a good exercise plan has a substantial and positive impact on a person's ability to avoid heart disease, diabetes, cancer, knee and hip replacements, back problems, and other ailments.

3. Substance abuse and mental and emotional health: It is essential to be out front on these issues by identifying problems early and resolving them before they become more serious.

   a. Substance abuse includes a number of harmful activities, such as smoking, drug use, alcohol consumption, and overeating. In many cases, these behaviors are triggered by mental or emotional problems that require treatment to address the underlying problems. Treatments, such as medication and counseling, must be part of a wellness plan because substance abuse often leads to serious health problems and early death.

   b. There are other mental and emotional problems, such as bipolar disorder and depression, that do not involve substance abuse. These problems should also be addressed as part of the wellness plan because people with these problems can become homeless and may harm themselves or others.

   c. Some people have intellectual disability and learning disorders. Intellectual disability, which is a less pejorative term for mental retardation, is defined as having an IQ below 70 to 75 and occurs in a small percentage of the population.[3] Many people claim that there are no known ways to increase IQ. People with learning disorders have inadequate development of specific academic, language, and speech skills. A common one is dyslexia, which is difficulty reading because it is challenging to identify speech sounds and learn how they relate to letters and words.[4] Learning disorders are not caused by low IQ or a lack of motivation. People with learning disorders are intelligent, but they see, hear, and understand things differently.[5] So it is essential to find mechanisms and teaching methods that allow them to learn and communicate to their full potential.

6.1.2 Preventive Treatment

Wellness is engaging in actions that help people avoid disease and stay healthy. Vaccinations, flu shots, and vitamin and mineral supplements may be part of a wellness plan. The most commonly known vaccines are given to children, and there are reports that some vaccinations have unintended, negative consequences. There are also questions about a conflict of interest in the approval process for mandatory vaccines, namely that the pharmaceutical industry has undue influence on the process. Many children are required to have 22 shots by the first grade.[6] On the other hand, the positive benefits of vaccinations are documented by the virtual eradication of common and serious diseases, such as polio and diphtheria, in developed countries where vaccinations are given routinely. A balance is needed between the risk of unintended complications of a particular vaccination and the risk of a serious disease outbreak when the vaccination is not given.

There are actually a number of vaccinations or treatments, such as the ones for shingles, typhoid, or malaria, that are given to adults. Several of these are recommended for people who travel outside the United States, especially to underdeveloped or developing countries.

Vitamin and mineral supplements are another tool for wellness. Currently, many people take vitamins and other supplements because of a poor diet or advertising claims that promote these products. With an effective wellness plan that has a diet rich in nutrients, the need for vitamins and supplements should be reduced and possibly eliminated. As with other aspects of wellness, patients, primary care physicians, and their staffs should work together to determine what actions to take.

6.2 Implementing Wellness through Education and Training

Wellness depends on individuals taking personal responsibility for their health. Wellness is not passing laws that force people to comply; it is providing information about why to, how to, and the health consequences when people are not healthy.

1. Why: The health benefits people achieve when they are well, the money they save as they avoid healthcare expenses, and incentives they receive from lower health insurance costs
2. How: The tools and techniques needed to achieve their health goals
3. Consequences: The risks people assume when they are overweight, smoke, or make other poor lifestyle choices

Information and education regarding these three elements are keys to creating a healthy population. In addition to traditional print media and videos, the Internet offers easy access to important information and smartphone apps can play an important role in monitoring health.

Achieving wellness depends on people following a continuous cycle of learning, understanding, making decisions, acquiring feedback, and taking action before starting the cycle anew. This leads to a critical transformation as the role of patients changes from passive to active with patients taking a leadership role in determining their health and directing their healthcare. At the same time, primary care physicians and their staff change from decision makers and action takers to experts who provide ideas, guidance, and support. These changes mean that patients and primary care physicians have wellness as a main focus. This implies changes in medical school curriculum, residency programs, and continuing education courses for healthcare professionals.

6.2.1 Educating and Training Healthcare Professionals

Educating professionals takes place in three settings:

1. Classroom education focuses on learning concepts. It should explain why wellness is such an important part of patients' health and healthcare, and it should discuss the basic principles behind wellness and the benefits of wellness to individual patients and the healthcare system more generally. If these educational requirements become part of the accreditation process for medical schools, nursing schools, and other schools that train healthcare professionals, it is very likely this message and supporting knowledge will be effectively integrated into the curriculum.
2. Practical, hands-on, action-oriented, learning guided by practicing experts helps healthcare professionals to learn how to practice medicine. Practice-based learning shows primary care physicians, nurses, and others how to help patients achieve wellness, create and follow wellness plans, and see the potential improvements in their health.

3. Continuing education keeps knowledge current. It provides opportunities for professionals to renew their understanding about wellness. It is especially important for the millions of well-trained and highly educated professionals who are currently working in healthcare because the whys, hows, and consequences of wellness must be delivered through this mechanism. An effective rollout will take time because the number of professionals to educate is very large. Initially, it may be necessary to create some intensive wellness programs to jump-start the process as wellness education is integrated into the continuing education cycle.

6.2.2 *Educating Patients*

Patient education is the key success factor. No matter how strongly physicians and other healthcare professionals feel about wellness, without patients' buy-in, the PCC, PHP, and wellness will fail. Patient education must do more than distribute knowledge. It must drive fundamental changes in the way people think about themselves, the importance of health, and the methods to achieve it. The plan must be more than a few public service announcements that trumpet the value of health and some websites that provide basic wellness information, although both are helpful. In fact, to some degree, this information is currently available. One thing is certain, it will take a long time to achieve the degree of wellness the United States needs because it takes time to change attitudes and values.

To understand how this might be accomplished for wellness, consider the environmental movement, which is thought to have begun in the 1960s after high-profile disasters, including the Donora, Pennsylvania smog in 1948, when a temperature inversion trapped air pollution in this town along the Monongahela River,[7] and the London smog in 1952 that killed thousands.[8] To make their points, environmentalists used a two-pronged approach to education. First, there was a public awareness campaign that focused on changing the minds of the adult population. It emphasized the problems with pollution and the benefits, including the health benefits, from having a cleaner environment. This was relentless, unfolded over decades, and was reinforced by environmental scandals such as the Love Canal, which is in Niagara Falls, New York.[9] Second, and probably more important, was using the kindergarten through 12th-grade education system to advocate first for the environment and then for recycling, reusing, and reducing consumption. This approach created a new generation for whom environmental responsibility is second nature. Virtually everyone who graduates from high school is a proponent of environmental responsibility.

Health advocates should adopt a similar approach to make wellness an integral part of day-to-day life. It should not be government passing laws that limit the size of soft drinks or regulate what people eat, thereby taking away freedom of choice and stirring controversy that creates opponents where there should be none. It should be people who make the choices, who decide when it is okay to splurge.

These people benefit from or bear the consequences of their decisions. Patients and not government must control wellness if it is to succeed. If some choose not to be responsible, there are consequences, but those consequences are not prescribed by government edict. They are the natural outcome of the patient's decision: poor health, low quality of life, shorter life span, and higher healthcare costs.

Selling wellness today should be easier than selling environmental responsibility in the 1960s and 1970s. There is a growing awareness that people in the United States are far less healthy than they should be. In addition, what is the downside to wellness? Patients win because they are healthy. Third-party payers win because costs decline, so insurance premiums should follow. If physician compensation is properly adjusted, as they work to achieve healthy patients, their income level should continue to attract well-qualified applicants. Even though demand for treatment is reduced because patients are healthier, it is not likely that demand for hospital beds, pharmaceuticals, medical devices, or other items in the healthcare supply chain will drop dramatically. There are about 45 million people in the United States who are currently uninsured, and baby boomers are likely to consume more healthcare as they age, so some of the slack will be absorbed. Even if there is a large drop in demand, which would be a pleasant problem to have, it will take time to materialize because the impact of wellness on healthcare consumption will not happen overnight. There will be sufficient time for healthcare providers to adjust.

There is a need to provide patients with knowledge and information about health and wellness in order to create advocates for good lifestyle choices. These efforts target the existing adult population just like the environmentalists did. Following are activities to drive awareness, create support, and provide patients with important information:

1. Public service announcements and advertising: It is essential to build awareness of wellness as a tool to improve quality of life, increase longevity, and reduce healthcare costs. As awareness increases, people need knowledge in order to act. Currently, there are some articles, editorials, and advertisements in magazines by the AARP and others that focus on wellness. In the future, the number and quality of these will expand.

2. Knowledge-based websites: Patients need access to information on a variety of subjects, such as how to eat well on a budget, designing inexpensive exercise programs, and ways to cease smoking. These sites should provide information about why wellness is important and describe a process for setting wellness goals, creating and executing a plan to reach those goals, and measuring outcomes to give feedback so that people can assess progress and make adjustments when their efforts are not working. In addition, patients need general health information as well as the ability to investigate diseases and treatment options, so they can be informed decision makers. Websites such as WebMD or the Mayo Clinic represent a good start in providing information that patients need to live a healthier life and work cooperatively with

their physicians. These websites and others would hold information that helps patients to prepare a wellness plan and, for that matter, to prepare a PHP.

3. Cost and benefit analysis: Different people are motivated to be healthy by different factors. In some cases, people recognize it is the right thing to do for themselves and their family. Others feel better because they are in shape and don't suffer the side effects of smoking or excessive drinking. Still others are motived because being healthy has economic benefits. Showing the costs of an unhealthy life, including medical payments, lost time from work and leisure, and purchasing cigarettes and alcohol may provide additional motivation. Pursuing health does not have to cost a lot. Eating better can cost the same as eating poorly, and it can cost less.

If these efforts are successful, parents and other adults are in a position to set good examples for children.

Following the approach used by environmentalists, phase two involves launching educational programs in primary and secondary schools to improve children's health and make them life-long advocates for wellness. Some of the ideas are throwbacks to the past, but that does not make them bad.

1. Health education: In many schools, health education has been eliminated or deemphasized. This can be reversed by doing three things: First, bring back a learning module on health that focuses on why and how people maintain wellness. This would include information about nutrition, exercise, and substance abuse as well as the importance of vaccination and disease prevention. This curriculum would grow with the students from kindergarten through 12th grade. Second, make adjustments in the science curriculum to discuss the costs and consequences of diseases caused by poor health, specifically diabetes and heart problems. This would be applicable in elementary and junior high as well as general science and biology courses in high school. Third, find ways to make wellness a competition among students. Unlike sports, this is a competition in which everyone can win because everyone can improve their health. Extracurricular activities, class projects, and clubs that emphasize health and healthcare provide focus and give students reasons to participate. It is possible that enthusiastic students may drive change at home.

2. Educate by example: If students are expected to learn and be motivated to be healthier, then their environment should support and reinforce that outcome. There have been discussions and some actions about enhancing the nutrition of lunch for students. The results are mixed, in part because students do not understand why they should do it, and they are excluded from the process. The health education program could be tied to the student lunch menu with discussion of the nutritional value of foods. It could go as far as giving students some decision-making authority in determining the menu using their understanding of nutrition. A key is to avoid extremes, so students eat neither

pizza nor bean curd five days a week. In addition, food and drinks available in vending machines should contain healthy options. Let students and parents have a say in whether high-sugar snacks should be banned from schools during class time or at all times. Another element of educating by example is for faculty, administrators, and staff to participate in wellness programs. In any case, they should be doing this for their own benefit. It will help them improve their health and lower their healthcare costs, and it should help the school district control its insurance costs.

3. Exercise: Physical education was, for many years, a part of grade school and high school curricula. Also, schools had intramural sports activities as well as varsity and junior varsity teams. Now, most schools support only varsity and junior varsity sports, which tends to serve a very small percentage of the students. Bringing back physical education would be a good start. In addition, more programs, either school-based or community-based, are needed to provide students with opportunities to get exercise and/or participate in sports that lead to a high level of fitness. Building an exercise routine early in life is a key to maintaining one as an adult.

6.3 Coping with Addictions

Addiction to cigarettes, alcohol, drugs, and even food is a significant problem for both adults and children, so it is important to have programs that deal with these issues, such as Alcoholics Anonymous, rehabilitation centers, hypnosis, and smoking cessation. There is an abundance of counselors, psychologists, and psychiatrists who can support these programs as well as cope with mental and emotional health issues. Investing healthcare dollars in identifying and resolving these problems is important, and it should begin as early as possible to avoid the substantial costs to treat the complications that often result. Patients working with their primary care physician may be able to identify these problems early and find ways to address them.

6.4 Embracing Personal Responsibility

The legal system and the capitalistic, free-market economy depend on personal responsibility. It is a cornerstone of society. When a person commits a crime, they are responsible for their actions except for the rare cases of mental incompetence. Managers and workers do what is expected because their compensation is linked to their job performance. They are responsible for doing their jobs well.

Why should it be different for health and healthcare? If people know about the value of wellness and the methods to attain it and if they do not pursue it, should they be accountable and face the economic consequences of their poor choices?

A growing number of people in the United States make bad decisions about lifestyle, and as a result, the negative consequences of these choices are on the rise.

Theoretically, this is not different from car owners who know little about vehicles or who have the know-how but are too busy to address routine maintenance needs and fix small problems. Because warning signs are ignored, they pay higher repair bills, and their cars do not last as long. For example, if owners do not have their vehicles' wheel alignment checked, they can have uneven tire wear that results in premature tire replacement and possibly more serious problems. They pay for the alignment, and they pay for new tires before they need to. If owners ignore an engine warning light or do not understand the significance of unusual noises, they may have a breakdown on the highway and more expensive repairs. If the owner learns to do some basic repairs and maintenance, such as replacing light bulbs and wiper blades, they can save money and time. People are motivated to learn about cars because it costs them more if they do not. Paying more for poor health choices, up to now, has not impacted persons with health insurance significantly because third-party payers covered all or most of the costs.

Some people may argue that paying more for healthcare, or car repairs for that matter, is not fair to people who do not have knowledge about their health or their cars. But the knowledge is available to everyone. It shows initiative, good judgment, and common sense for people to learn so that their quality of life is better and the costs of these services are lower. It is the responsible thing to do. In general, people with more knowledge about goods and services are better off than people with less knowledge. Among many differences, people with more knowledge earn more, have better health insurance, and live in safer neighborhoods. The solution is to improve the educational system, thereby enabling people to qualify for better jobs and earn more so that they have better healthcare, housing, etc.

6.4.1 Is Personal Responsibility the Answer?

Some would argue that having people pay more for health insurance and healthcare because they are sicker is not fair because being sick is outside of their control, and that may be true to some degree. However, personal responsibility means holding people accountable for choices that lead to an increased likelihood of being sick. Smokers should not pay more for insurance and healthcare because they are sick; they should pay more because they made a poor choice. That may seem like a fine distinction, but it is an important one. The decision to smoke has consequences, as do other poor choices, so health insurance should cost more for smokers than nonsmokers because smoking increases the likelihood or risk of health problems, and health insurance is about dealing with risk. Smokers also may have a higher deductible and larger copayment than the nonsmoker. More is discussed about this issue in Chapter 7 on rethinking and redesigning health insurance.

Others would argue that there are people who cannot help themselves. It is their genetics, environment, or another factor that forces them to smoke, overeat, or take drugs. There is likely an element of truth in this statement as well because it appears to be easier for some to quit smoking, control eating, or abstain from alcohol or drugs than for others. However, there are many individual differences that impact peoples' lives in various ways. Some have reading disabilities making them work harder to succeed in school; others are not athletic, making a career in professional sports very unlikely, and still others have a below-average capacity to learn, which limits their opportunities for advanced education.

People with reading disabilities are often very intelligent and with the proper training and support can reach their full potential. Primary and secondary schools are mandated by government to identify students with this problem and provide interventions to address it. There are drills and exercises for people to improve their strength, endurance, coordination, and balance, which determine their athletic ability. Fortunately, there are plenty of life pursuits in which athletic ability is not a requirement. IQ is not the sole or even the primary determinant of success. Hard work, time management, planning, and techniques to make learning easier lead to success even when IQ is less than people would like. There are aptitude tests that identify jobs that fit peoples' skill sets. The bottom line is that people with these and other conditions have options, and pursuing those options may help them to overcome deficiencies that are inherent in their being. They may require help to overcome these problems, but it is their responsibility or the responsibility of their parents or legal guardians to find ways to do so. There are many programs offered by the government, religious organizations, and communities to provide assistance.

It is important to clarify that some things are within a person's control, and others are not, and people should accept the consequences for things that are within their control. The problem is getting people to agree on what is in their control and what is not. Clearly babies or young children bear no responsibility for their health circumstances, but just as clearly well-educated, affluent adults should be responsible for decisions, such as smoking or drinking excessively. There is a very large gray area between these extremes, and this book is not able to define with precision a "bright line" that marks things for which people should and should not be responsible. For some guidance, consider the legal system in the United States, in which adults, regardless of their life circumstances, find it difficult to escape responsibility for their actions. Adopting the same approach for healthcare may be appropriate.

6.4.2 Addressing Obesity

Obesity is becoming the most important determinant of health in the United States. Obesity is not being a little overweight. The simplest and most commonly used measure of obesity is the body mass index (BMI). Normal weight is a BMI from 18 up to 25, and 25 up to 30 is considered overweight. Obesity is a BMI of 30 or more.[10] Although BMI is easy to calculate, it is not the most accurate predictor of obesity, especially for people who exercise and are muscular. Better but more expensive tests, such as skin fold caliper tests and hydrostatic weighing, measure body fat percentage more accurately. BMI is a place to start with other tests used to provide more precise measurement when needed.

People in the United States have seen decades of movies and advertisements using men and women with "perfect" bodies, accomplished in nearly every case through retouching and Photoshop. More recently, there has been pushback and significant efforts to "accept the way we look." This can be a double-edged sword. On one hand, it is important that people do not do things to themselves to meet some "ideal" body image, especially when those actions can be harmful. This has led to eating disorders and other medical problems. On the other hand, it is important that the notion of accepting the way we look is not used as an excuse to avoid healthy choices.

Also, there are groups who claim that society discriminates against people based on size.[11] Is it fair to charge people who are obese more for health insurance? Is that discrimination? Discrimination is legal in many cases. If a person has a big appetite and wants a second hamburger, the restaurant has the right to charge for two sandwiches. The person who only can eat only a half sandwich has the right to take the other half home. If a person wants a triple-X sweatshirt, the manufacturer has the right to charge more because it consumes more material and requires more sewing time. Teachers discriminate when they assign different grades to students. Basketball teams discriminate in picking their players because the average height of the team is much greater than the height of the general population. On the other hand, discrimination based on race, religion, ethnicity, gender, and some others factors is unlawful.

There is substantial evidence that obesity increases health risks and therefore increases healthcare costs.[12] Much like smoking, the linkages are well known. The point is not that people cannot be obese if that is their choice. The point is that if they do choose obesity, there are consequences for that decision, and those consequences lead to higher healthcare costs and poor health. If eating is an addiction, there are supportive services that can help people see food differently. For those seeking help to address an eating disorder, health insurance should cover the expenses.

6.5 Driving Forces for Change

The forces that push wellness to succeed are similar to those that drive PCC because patients are critical in determining its success or failure. If patients had been focusing on quality of life and longevity, wellness would already have taken hold, and health would be increasing. It is essential for third-party payers, specifically employers and the government, to endorse wellness and make it a pillar of their health insurance programs. These third-party payers and the insurance companies they work with are essential for motivating physicians and hospitals to participate and for providing the incentives to nudge patients toward wellness. They are also important in creating websites and other information access points so that people can learn about wellness.

To educate kindergarten through 12th-grade students, it is critical to involve the U.S. Department of Education and the state boards of education to change curriculum standards so that health and wellness are important elements of their education. To change medical education so physicians understand and are capable of helping patients achieve wellness, medical schools and the American Medical Association (AMA) must be on board. The payment system for primary care physicians must be changed to reward them for creating well patients. This is easier with buy-in from the AMA and the American Hospital Association (AHA), and it may require efforts from government, including laws that require some level of participation.

6.6 Impact of Wellness and Personal Responsibility on Healthcare Outcomes

Wellness is closely related to PCC, and the PHP and if practiced faithfully will have a substantial, positive impact on health and the costs of healthcare. Following is a summary of the impacts of wellness on the relevant root causes, which are discussed in Chapter 2:

1. Poor lifestyle choices: Patients who are fully engaged in wellness and accept responsibility for their actions will make better choices, leading to better health (root cause #1 from Chapter 2).
2. Unused facilities and equipment: If wellness is achieved, patients will use fewer healthcare services, spend less time in hospitals, and have fewer medical tests (root cause #3).
3. High drug costs: As patients become well, they require fewer prescription drugs (root cause #6).
4. Excessive legal liability and malpractice insurance costs: Better health, fewer tests, and fewer procedures mean there is less opportunity for errors. As a result, there should be less legal liability and lower malpractice insurance costs (root cause #7).
5. Shortage of healthcare professionals: Fewer tests, physician visits, and hospital stays mean less demand for physician services, including diagnoses and treatments (root cause #8). This frees resources to treat patients who are currently underserved.

6.7 Summary of Recommendations

Following is a listing of the key recommendations contained in this chapter:

1. Patients must have a wellness plan. The plan is customized and multidimensional, including physical, mental, and emotional health. Wellness is patient-centered and includes a wellness plan, which is based on the following:
   a. A medical history that provides important background information about the patient
   b. A routine health screening plan that provides basic health information to guide decision making and track progress toward the goals in the plan
   c. A preventive testing plan that is designed to catch health problems early
   d. Lifestyle choices that address nutrition and diet, exercise, substance abuse, and mental and emotional health
   e. Preventive treatment that deals with vaccination, vitamins, and supplements
2. Successfully implementing wellness depends on an individual taking personal responsibility for their health. Implementation depends on education and access to information. This means the following:
   a. Educating and training healthcare professionals with classroom education in medical school, hands-on training in residency, and continuing education during practice
   b. Educating adult patients through public service announcements, knowledge-based websites, and cost–benefit analysis of healthy choices
   c. Educating students in primary and secondary schools so they are able to make good decisions about health
3. Offering programs that address substance abuse.
4. Holding people personally responsible for decisions that impact their health.

References

1. Merriam-Webster Dictionary. 2015. Definition of wellness. http://www.merriam-webster.com/dictionary/wellness (October 27, 2015).
2. National Wellness Institute. 2015. The six dimensions of wellness. http://www.nationalwellness.org/?page=Six_Dimensions (accessed October 27, 2015).
3. MedicineNet.com. 2015. Definition of mental retardation. http://www.medicinenet.com/script/main/art.asp?articlekey=20174 (accessed October 27, 2015).
4. Mayo Clinic. 2015. Dyslexia definition. http://www.mayoclinic.org/diseases-conditions/dyslexia/basics/definition/con-20021904 (accessed October 27, 2015).
5. HelpGuide.org. 2015. Learning disabilities and disorders. http://www.helpguide.org/articles/learning-disabilities/learning-disabilities-and-disorders.htm (accessed October 27, 2015).

6. Association of American Physicians and Surgeons. 2015. Fact sheet on mandatory vaccines. http://www.aapsonline.org/testimony/mandvac.htm (accessed November 4, 2015).

7. Murray, A. 2009. Smog deaths in 1948 lead to clean air laws. NPR, (April 22). http://www.npr.org/templates/story/story.php?storyId=103359330 (accessed October 28, 2015).

8. Boyd, C. 2012. London's great smog of 1952. PRI's The World, (December 5). http://www.pri.org/stories/2012-12-05/londons-great-smog-1952 (accessed October 28, 2015).

9. SUNY Geneseo, History Department. 2015. Love canal—A brief history. http://www.geneseo.edu/history/love_canal_history (accessed October 28, 2015).

10. WebMD. 2015. Weight loss and body mass index (BMI). http://www.webmd.com/men/weight-loss-bmi (accessed October 28, 2015).

11. National Organization for Woman. 2015. Love your body. http://now.org/now-foundation/love-your-body/ (accessed October 28, 2015).

12. WebMD. 2015. Obesity—Health risks of obesity. http://www.webmd.com/diet/obesity/obesity-health-risks-of-obesity (accessed October 28, 2015).

Chapter 7

Rethinking and Redesigning Health Insurance

As patient-centered care (PCC) from Chapter 5 and wellness from Chapter 6 are closely related topics, so are the topics of this chapter, reconfiguring health insurance, and the next chapter, healthcare trade-offs. Addressing the latter set of topics requires considering important questions, such as how much healthcare can the country afford, and how should healthcare resources be allocated? If resources are unlimited, everyone could have any healthcare procedure they desire and, for that matter, anything else they want from luxury cars to the finest cuisine. There would be no difficult healthcare decisions and no trade-offs. Unfortunately and in spite of what some people would like to believe, the United States does not have unlimited resources for healthcare or any other aspect of people's lives. So, the United States must find ways to use resources more effectively and allocate them in a well-reasoned manner. The country must come to grips with the fact that resource allocation is a polite way to say that healthcare must be rationed; in other words, someone must evaluate trade-offs and make difficult decisions about who gets care and who does not. Patients, not government or insurance companies, are in the best position to examine costs and benefits and make trade-offs and, through this process, to ration healthcare.

The current system is plagued with biased trade-offs with which patients receive the benefits of care but incur little if any cost, which leads to overconsumption of services. There are reports identifying surgeries that are often done unnecessarily, such as cardiac angioplasty and knee replacements,[1] as well as tendencies to be too quick to prescribe drugs, especially new ones that are usually more expensive.[2] To be better consumers, people must find ways to be healthier so that they consume less, not more, healthcare. They should avoid healthcare services that have little or no value or that may have negative impacts on their health. Medications have side effects and problematic interactions, and medical procedures have complications that put patients' lives and health at risk. People should ask, are the potential benefits of a treatment worth the complications?

This chapter describes a different vision for health insurance, explains why this vision leads to better utilization of healthcare resources, and discusses the impact of the vision on healthcare outcomes. It also considers activities that enhance competition among healthcare providers and health insurers. This begins with open and transparent prices for services, so people understand the full cost of healthcare, which should encourage people to shop for the best value. Facilitating competition among insurers, specifically allowing competitors to cross state lines, is a way to keep insurance premiums competitive. The chapter also examines critical facets of the Affordable Care Act (ACA), including eliminating maximum payment limits for policies, jettisoning the preexisting condition doctrine, allowing adult-aged children to be on their parents' insurance until they are 26, and extending insurance coverage to the uninsured.

Chapter 8 explicitly examines how decisions may be different when patients compare the full cost and potentially negative consequences of healthcare tests and treatments with their benefits. When patients see only the benefits, they are likely to make poor choices. What decisions would consumers make if they could buy a new car or have a professionally landscaped yard and someone else paid 80% or more of the cost?

7.1 Understanding the Financial Side of Health Insurance

To create a different vision for health insurance, it is essential to understand the purpose and the financing of insurance. These concepts apply to all types of insurance, not just health insurance. The primary purpose of insurance is to protect people from catastrophic losses that could drive them into bankruptcy, homelessness, or worse. Insurance should not be used to pay for small expenses, such as minor storm damage to a house, paint scratches on a car, or an office visit for a sore throat. Any good financial planner would suggest that an emergency fund is a better way to cope with this type of unexpected expenses.

The value of insurance to protect people from devastating loss is shown with the following example: Suppose a family's home, which it owns free and clear, is destroyed by fire. The family's annual income is $80,000, and the house is valued at $200,000. How does the family rebuild? Without insurance, the family has two options. First, it can save enough money for a down payment and buy a new house on credit. If the family can save $12,000 of its $80,000 annual income for this purpose, which is a significant task, then 16 months are needed to accumulate a 20% down payment. Then, the family has a mortgage to pay for up to 30 years. Second, to pay cash for a similar house, the family would have to save $12,000 a year for 16.67 years. In the meantime, where do they live? With insurance, the family has the money to buy a home almost immediately. Insurance is protection against catastrophic loss; it allows consumers to reduce risk. For completeness, it should be noted that no bank or other institution provides a home mortgage unless the house is fully insured, and the lender is listed on the policy as a beneficiary. Lenders demand protection.

So families buy house insurance and hope they never use it. They benefit through peace of mind because they are covered for catastrophic loss. They make this choice even though they pay premiums of hundreds or thousands of dollars a year, which is neither recoverable (unless, of course, the house burns down) nor tax deductible. Financially speaking, insurance policies from the collective perspective of all purchasers are money-losing propositions. Here is why: People who want insurance pay into a pool that is controlled by an organization, usually an insurance company. In a typical insurance pool, the largest part of these insurance premiums is paid to the few people who have a house fire, car accident, death in the family, or major surgery. These unfortunate few receive much more than they paid in, and most people will receive no payout. That is the risk-sharing nature of insurance. The reason insurance is a money-losing proposition, on a collective basis, is the total amount all people pay into the insurance pool is more than the total payouts to all the claimants. Why? (The only exception is a government that is willing to put money from other sources, such as general tax receipts, into the risk pool to subsidize the health insurance payouts from Medicare and Medicaid—more on that later.)

As shown in Figure 7.1, the premiums paid into the pool have different uses. The largest share is a payout for claims. People have house fires, car accidents, deaths in the family, or serious medical problems. Premiums also cover administrative costs, marketing and sales expenses, and operating expenses, such as processing and approving applications, evaluating and paying claims, and providing customer service. Managers guide the organization and its personnel, and teams of actuaries and lawyers design and write the policies. These important functions also have costs, which are paid from customers' premiums. Capital is required to build administrative offices, fill them with furniture and equipment, and acquire computer hardware and software. Ultimately, the company must repay this capital to the bankers and bond holders. In addition to returning capital, in the form of principal repayments, bankers and bond holders want an interest payment for using their money.

If the insurer is a for-profit company, investors provide capital and hold stock, and they want their investment back plus a fair return on it. For stockholders, the return of capital comes when investors sell their stock, hopefully at a higher price,

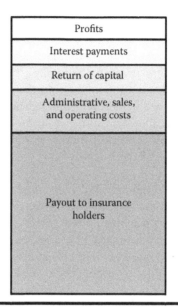

Figure 7.1 Payout and cost structure for a typical insurance pool. (The diagram is not to scale but shows the order of magnitude of these factors.)

because they get their original investment back plus more. This stock appreciation happens when the company makes a profit that investors feel is reasonable for the level of risk in the stock. The insurance companies may also pay stockholders an annual dividend from their profits, which is another part of their return. Profits are also a source of capital when companies reinvest them to grow the business, improve efficiency, and provide better service to its customers.

As illustrated by Figure 7.1, insurance is a money-losing proposition for policy holders because people who pay into an insurance pool receive, on the average, less in payouts than they paid in premiums. So the only logical reason to have insurance is to reduce risk, specifically to deal with the possibility, however remote, of catastrophic loss.

7.1.1 Insurance Companies' Profits Are Too High

Some have argued that insurance companies make too much money. They claim that if these companies would cut back or eliminate their profits, the premiums customers pay would drop dramatically. The prior discussion seems to indicate that the reduction in premiums would be small as payouts to policyholders, the biggest expense by far, would not change because they are defined by legal contracts.

To provide specifics, Table 7.1 contains the income statements for Aetna's healthcare insurance business for 2012, 2013, and 2014 in billions of U.S. dollars. Aetna is one of the largest and best-known insurers in the United States. Revenue

Table 7.1   Aetna Healthcare Income Statements 2014, 2013, and 2012 (in Billions of Dollars)

	2014	*2013*	*2012*
Total revenue	$55.11	$44.40	$33.01
Healthcare costs	$40.75	$32.90	$23.73
Selling expenses	$1.54	$1.24	$1.02
General and administrative expenses	$8.80	$7.06	$5.48
Total operating expenses	$51.09	$41.20	$30.23
Amortization expenses	$0.24	$0.21	$0.14
Income before taxes	$3.78	$2.99	$2.64
Taxes	$1.59	$1.08	$0.95
Income after taxes	$2.19	$1.91	$1.69
Percentage of profit to revenue	4.0	4.3	5.1

Source: Aetna Inc. 2014. Aetna annual report. https://materials.proxyvote.com /Approved/00817Y/20150313/AR_239789/#/24/ (accessed August 26, 2015).

in 2014 was $55.11 billion, and outflows for healthcare costs were $40.75 billion, meaning Aetna paid out approximately 74% of its revenue in claims. Aetna's profit from healthcare operations was only about 4% of total revenue, and that has been declining since 2012. So if policyholders could snap their collective fingers and force Aetna to return its profits to them, the impact on insurance premiums would be quite small. It is possible, even likely, that Aetna deserves to make a profit because it may provide better service and be more efficient than not-for-profit insurers.

There are many not-for-profit health insurers covering millions of people across the United States.[3] They must make payouts for claims and cover the costs for application reviews, claims administration, and other costs. They would incur sales expenses unless the company enjoys a monopoly, which is typically not the case. Not-for-profit insurers must organize effectively and compete for sales, and they have managers, actuaries, and lawyers. Not-for-profit insurers must acquire money to build facilities and have computer equipment, and these funds must be repaid with interest to bond holders and bankers. With not-for-profit insurers, there are no profits to reinvest in the business, so they need capital to support their operations and make improvements in the business. Plugging this capital gap usually comes in the form of additional loans from bankers and bond holders, which must be repaid with interest.

If the capital needs for a not-for-profit insurer are one billion dollars, then 100% of this amount must be borrowed from banks, bond holders, and other sources. A for-profit insurer, with similar capital needs, could choose to sell stock to raise part of its capital—for discussion purposes assume 50%. Mixing bonds and stocks to raise capital is a common way to finance for-profit companies. A not-for-profit insurer must pay interest on one billion dollars and be capable of repaying this amount. A for-profit insurer must do the same for 50% of the billion dollar capital requirement. The other 50% comes from stockholders who get their return in two ways:

1. Stockholders often receive a dividend, which is typically paid quarterly and is paid at the discretion of the board of directors, so it is not guaranteed. For tax and other purposes, interest payments on loans and dividends on stocks are different, but they serve a similar purpose because dividends provide part of the return for stockholders.
2. Stockholders receive the other part of their return in the capital appreciation of the stock they own. Profits are a signal to investors regarding whether a for-profit insurer is doing well or poorly. When it is doing well, other investors bid up the stock price, giving current investors opportunities to sell their stock at a higher price, thus earning the second element of their return.

The sum of dividends paid and stock appreciation on each dollar invested is, in theory, more than interest paid on each dollar borrowed. The justification for this premium for stockholders is that stockholders take more risk. Dividend and stock appreciation are not guaranteed; plus the company could go bankrupt, meaning stockholders would lose their entire investment. Bond holders have guaranteed returns, and if bankruptcy occurs, they are paid before stockholders.

For-profit companies, such as Aetna, have an important advantage over not-for-profit insurers because the profit motive drives the following:

1. Innovations, which improve product offerings and processing capabilities
2. Efficiency improvements, which reduce costs
3. Enhancements in service quality, which improve customer satisfaction

As a result, for-profit insurers can compete on price and services with not-for-profit insurers. The following logic supports this claim. If not-for-profit insurers perform as well as or better than their for-profit rivals and if not-for-profits charge less because they do not have to generate profits, then not-for-profit insurers would drive their for-profit competitors into bankruptcy. Who wants to pay more for the same or lesser service? For-profit insurers seem to be able to provide a good value with value being defined as what customers pay for the services received.

7.1.2 Buying Insurance: How Much Is Too Much?

The question involving the "right" amount of health insurance is hidden from view for most people because they have employer-based insurance or are enrolled in Medicare and/or Medicaid. As consumers, they typically have few choices; they must accept the insurance or opt out and receive no benefits. Most employer-based policies do not allow employees to take cash in lieu of insurance. Even if this option is available, employees are unlikely to find insurance with the same coverage for the same premium because most company plans have a group rate with a large and diverse risk pool. Also, cash payments to employees would be taxed, so after paying federal, state, and local income taxes, there is less money to buy insurance. Medicare recipients pay only a small monthly premium, about $100. They cannot buy an equivalent policy in the open market for that amount. Medicaid patients have no options.

Over the years, the tendency has been for insurance to cover more and more facets of healthcare until all expense were covered. Basic hospitalization insurance expanded to include physician visits, drug coverage, routine health screening, and preventive testing. For employers, this was a way to make tax-free payments to their employees. Essentially, this made healthcare free because third parties paid 100% of the premiums and covered 100% of the expenses. This wiped away all financial uncertainty with respect to healthcare because literally everything was covered, and as discussed in detail in the next chapter, this led to poor decision making about healthcare.

The notion of risk elimination is an attractive one, and the United States has become a nation seeking certainty, to the point of making poor choices about purchasing insurance. This tendency is seen in many aspects of life in the United States. When people buy cars, smartphones, or appliances, companies are eager to sell them maintenance plans or warrantee extensions that cover repair costs and other expenses. These are nothing more than insurance against future expenses. People trade a known, upfront cost to buy the insurance to save unknown future costs for repairs that are unlikely to occur. This insurance is available on very inexpensive items, such as $40 hedge trimmers or $30 calculators.

As an example, an extended warrantee for a gas stove that sells for $1500 costs the consumer $209 for a two-year period. If 100 customers purchased this insurance, it would generate $20,900 in revenue. Even if 5% of the ranges sold had to be replaced completely in the first two years, which is an extremely high number, that would cost the company only $7500 ($1500 times five stoves). Actually, this cost is much less because the retail price, $1500, is far more than the cost to manufacture and deliver a new stove. Also, there is already a one-year warrantee on the stove, which may not cover its replacement but does cover repairs. The gross profit for the insurance after the payout is much more than 50%.

People should be in a position to be self-insured for low-cost item, even a $1500 appliance. Their monthly budget should have enough slack or their emergency fund should have enough money to cover these costs. Emergency funds can be built if consumers take the money they would have spent on insuring things such as stoves, refrigerators, and calculators and use it to replace or repair these items. They will be surprised at how much money they can save in five years.

A negative outcome of a culture that strives to eliminate risk for all expenses, large and small, is a state of mind in which people feel comfortable living paycheck to paycheck. They no longer feel the need to build an emergency fund to deal with unexpected car repairs, dishwasher replacements, or medical expenses. This helps to explain why the United States has low savings rates. With limited risk and uncertainty, what is the benefit of deferring gratification and saving for the future? This mind-set spills over into retirement. Previous generations had social security, pensions, and job-based savings plans to rely on. Young workers typically have social security, which many believe will not be there for them, and a 401k plan that is most likely substantially underfunded.

If risk reduction is good, what is wrong with eliminating risk through insurance? A big part of the answer is to recall that insurance is a money-losing proposition. When people buy insurance, on the average, they will receive less back than they paid in. People should only be willing to pay insurance premiums to avoid major expenses that could send them to financial disaster. From a systems perspective, it does not make financial sense to have insurance to cover a $50 office visit. From the perspective of an individual, it makes sense only when someone else is paying the insurance premium.

7.1.3 Dealing with Routine Healthcare Costs

Not all healthcare expenses should be covered by insurance because insurance carries with it other costs that must be paid. For example, the physicians' office has additional compliance procedures and paperwork that it must file with the insurer so physicians are paid, and there are government regulations for physicians to comply with. The costs of these activities are buried in the physician's fee. Because of these administrative and compliance costs and the extra costs associated with creating an insurance pool, which were discussed earlier, insurance is not a cost-effective way to pay for small medical expenses. If these routine healthcare expenses are paid directly by patients and not paid by insurance, these visits would cost less because the costs of creating an insurance pool, and the administrative and transaction costs incurred by patients, insurers, and healthcare providers would be gone.

Further, with three main participants—patients, insurers, and healthcare providers—the opportunities for errors increase with patients in the middle. If healthcare providers do not file the paperwork correctly or insurers make errors and claims are not paid, patients must step in and fix the problem. Ultimately, healthcare providers hold patients responsible for payment, so this means multiple phone calls to resolve problems even when patients did nothing wrong.

When insurance transitions from providing protection against catastrophic loss to covering office visits, a process with very high administrative expenses and transaction costs is created. If patients have an emergency fund and accept some financial risk, they can save money and spend less on healthcare.

7.1.4 A Health Insurance Monopoly: Why or Why Not?

The only significant cost advantage of a monopoly is to reduce sales expenses because there are no competitors. Everyone buys from the monopoly, and sales become an order-taking and paperwork-processing task, which should cost less. There are payouts; there are claims to review and pay; there are managers, actuaries, and lawyers doing their jobs; and there are facilities and equipment to finance.

However, a monopoly has downsides—the most obvious being that a monopoly can set a very high price, and consumers have little choice but to pay it. Customers are in no position to push back because most people want healthcare insurance, and there are no competitors to drive efficiencies and improve services, which keeps prices low and pushes quality higher. There is less reason to control fraud because fraud is accepted as part of doing business and passed on to consumers. So monopolies, even "benevolent" government monopolies, will not provide the highest quality and most cost-effective health insurance. In fact, insurance coverage offered by a monopoly may cost more than insurance offered by for-profit and not-for-profit insurers operating in the competitive marketplace.

The best insurance is provided by open and competitive markets, which should include for-profit and not-for-profit insurers and could even include government entities as long as they do not subsidize insurance premiums. Competition drives innovation, controls costs, and improves quality. Healthcare and health insurance need competition and choice.

7.1.5 But Medicare Is a Monopoly and Has Nearly Universal Support

The government provides Medicare to about 41.5 million people who are 65 and older and about 9.5 million people with disabilities.[4] Some may argue that Medicare is not a monopoly because people could procure other insurance, and even if eligible for Medicare, they are not required to participate. However, Medicare is a virtual monopoly because nearly all U.S. citizens and permanent residents are eligible for it, and nearly all who are eligible enroll. The reality is that people select Medicare because they were required to make payments into Medicare when they worked, and Medicare is subsidized by the government—more on that later.

Altruists believe that government can be an effective, benevolent monopolist, one that provides a good product at a fair price. They believe government is not motivated by profit, is concerned about its citizens, and would not overcharge the consumer. They reason that Medicare must be the best option. Seniors who qualify for Medicare, and that is nearly all of them, choose Medicare because they paid for it their entire working life. If they decide not to enroll in Medicare, there is no cost-effective insurance pool with which seniors can share risk with people of various ages and health conditions unless they continue to work at a company that offers employment-based health insurance. By its actions, the government monopoly has limited the health insurance market for those 65 and older, and it has created a large market for supplemental policies because Medicare covers only part of the costs.

In addition to having few options, another important reason why seniors like Medicare is that its costs, looking forward, are small. Seniors were required by law to pay for Medicare while they worked, and they cannot get their money back. At 65, the costs of Medicare are $0 per month for Part A, which is hospitalization; $104.90 per month for Part B, which is medical insurance; and a variable, but modest, amount for Part D, which is drug coverage.[5] Recipients with a modified adjusted gross income above certain amounts pay an income-related monthly fee that increases Part B and Part D costs. Even with the adjustment, Medicare is a very good deal for senior healthcare because future premium payments and other out-of-pocket costs are far less than the likely payouts seniors will receive during their lifetime.[6] So, at 65, nearly everyone who is eligible, signs up for Medicare because it is a bargain. They are further encouraged to sign up because there is a penalty for signing up late. The government with its power to tax and make rules has made Medicare very attractive.

If seniors who paid into Medicare could withdraw their payments at retirement and if there were viable insurance options, would their decision be different? The answer is probably not; they will most likely opt for Medicare. Why? Medicare is run differently from for-profit and not-for-profit insurers because the government loses money on Medicare even when the Medicare payroll deductions are considered. The federal government uses general tax revenues to subsidize Medicare. Medicare is a money-losing system for the government and taxpayers. According to the Urban Institute, a couple earning $89,200 per year and turning 65 in 2010 would have paid $122,000 into Medicare and can be expected to take out $387,000 in benefits.[6]

In addition, Medicare is loaded with fraud. Fly-by-night pharmacies bill Medicare for drugs prescribed to patients who are deceased, are fictitious, or are alive but did not order or receive the medications. There are physicians who bill for treatments that are not needed and in some cases were never given. Medicare is not very effective at finding, prosecuting, and eliminating fraud. In 2010, the General Accounting Office estimated that improper payments totaled $48 billion or almost 10% of the Medicare expenditure.[7] CBS News estimates total Medicare fraud at $60 billion annually.[8]

In addition to fraud, Medicare services may be overused. Even when a service adds little value, recipients often opt for treatment because they pay little, if any, of the costs. For seniors residing in assisted living or nursing care facilities, this may be especially true because these organizations can generate additional revenue by providing rehabilitative and other supportive services. This is perfectly legal, but in many cases, the services add little value. Guardians often opt for these services because they want to do all they can to help their loved one, and there usually are no out-of-pocket costs.

7.2 Implementing a Different Vision for Health Insurance

A new vision for insurance requires knowledgeable consumers, a focus on increasing wellness, and more attention to preventive care. Consumers must know the costs of services, understand how they might benefit from those services, and make difficult decisions. They must work with their primary care physicians to create a personal health plan (PHP) that moves them toward wellness and design a health-care regimen that emphasizes prevention over care. These fundamental changes will cause people to think differently about healthcare. The ideas proposed here could apply to employer-based insurance and Medicare.

7.2.1 Becoming a Knowledgeable Consumer

In a revamped healthcare system, patients and their primary care physicians are the key decision makers, evaluating options and examining trade-offs. To do this effectively, they must know the full costs as well as the benefits of their decisions. Currently, patients and physicians are most often unaware of the costs of testing and treatment, and even if they are aware, most patients pay only a small part of these costs. If patients and physicians know the costs and if patients have "skin in the game," they should make better decisions about whether or not to have care. These competitive forces, including patients paying a meaningful portion of the costs, should put pressure on providers to find ways to be more productive and effective. A key in this new vision is to find balance between patients paying for services yet having insurance to address catastrophic healthcare problems that can cause financial ruin.

So what motivates patients and primary care physicians to consider costs and make better decisions? They must have knowledge and control. Knowledge is a prerequisite to PCC care and the PHP, which gives patients and physicians greater authority and flexibility in determining how to care for patients. Currently, third-party payers, including government, and regulators often restrict options. Patients can only see this physician and use that hospital, must follow certain patterns of treatment, and cannot take a medication because it is not covered by insurance. At the same time, patients and physicians need tools to achieve wellness, do simple screening, and engage in preventive testing that improve wellness and avoid serious health problems. In addition, patients need health insurance to avoid paying for catastrophic healthcare problems.

For discussion purposes, healthcare expenditures are divided into three parts:

1. Preparing and executing the PHP, which may be the most important element because it requires patients and physicians to focus on creating healthy patients who need less care
2. Routine care, which addresses minor health problems
3. Catastrophic coverage, which involves health issues that are life threatening and/or are very expensive, which is where insurance makes sense

7.2.2 Preparing and Executing the Personal Health Plan

As described in Chapter 5, the PHP has five elements: the medical history, routine health screening plan, preventive testing plan, wellness plan, and end-of-life plan. Each facet of the PHP is important because it has the potential to improve the quality of life and reduce costs. Creating and following a PHP would become a requirement for having health insurance that is paid for by a third party. This condition would be set by third-party payers, not by government mandate. Third-party payers have the right to make this stipulation; after all, they are paying all or a big part of the insurance premium. Setting similar conditions is not new. Some employers will not hire people who smoke. Others require employees who smoke to pay a larger share of the insurance premium than nonsmokers.[9] Even the ACA has penalties for smokers.[10] In return for having and following a PHP, the cost to develop the plan, except for the end-of-life plan, would be covered by insurance.

Medical history is an important part of healthcare, and it would be more important under the PHP. It becomes the basis for determining health screenings and testing requirements as well as the content of the wellness plan. As discussed in Chapter 5, the current process for collecting these data is haphazard and fraught with errors. When electronic health records are fully implemented, the accuracy of the data will increase, and the cost of collecting, organizing, searching, and accessing the data in the medical history should decline. Currently, collecting data for the medical history is an integral part of healthcare and is covered by insurance. That would continue.

Routine health screening collects a standard set of data that is used to monitor a patient's health. These screenings would be inexpensive, simple, easy-to-do actions, such as measuring blood pressure and pulse. The interval for data collection would depend on the patient's health: Younger, healthier people would have a longer interval than older, less healthy ones. It is likely that the cost of doing the screenings and recording the data would not increase healthcare costs substantially because many of these screenings are currently done. For example, height and weight used to calculate body mass index (BMI) are collected routinely when patients see their primary care physicians. Plus, automating and routinizing data collection should keep costs low. Ways to do this inexpensively are discussed in Chapter 13. Routine health screenings would be covered by insurance.

An individualized preventive testing plan would be constructed by patients and their primary care physicians based on the patient's medical history, routine health screening, and medical conditions. Preventive tests are different from screenings because the tests are usually more complex, time-consuming, expensive, and tailored to the patient. A healthy young patient may have no preventive tests, and a diabetic male in his 60s may have several different tests performed each year.

It is difficult to gauge whether the cost for preventive testing will increase or decrease as the PHP is implemented. On one hand, preventive testing may increase because more people will have insurance that pays for it, and patients are required to prepare and follow a PHP in order to have their insurance paid for by a third party. On the other hand, a certain amount of preventive testing is being done, and some of it is duplicative, so a well-designed plan may reduce testing. Also, if the PHP works as it should, the population will be healthier and require less preventive testing. Even if there is a cost increase, it should be offset by early diagnoses and treatments that lead to fewer serious, long-term health problems. All preventive testing identified on the PHP would be covered by insurance.

Although a wellness plan might not be new for everyone, for many people, it is a big and important step in the right direction. Patients would work with their primary care physicians and the physicians' staffs to create individual plans that meet patients' needs. They would set targets for important metrics, such as blood pressure, sugar levels, cholesterol, and BMI. The initial actions would be lifestyle changes, such as diet, exercise, and smoking cessation. Patients would ultimately be responsible for executing the plan and meeting their targets. Insurance would cover the costs to develop a wellness plan, but the costs of its execution would be shared by patients and the insurers. It does not seem reasonable for insurers to pay for gym memberships to get in shape or a chef to make healthy food. There are simple, inexpensive ways to get in shape: Doing push-ups, which requires no equipment, is one of the best total body muscle-building exercises, and there are many inexpensive and easy-to-use cardio routines. There are dozens of websites that tout exercise programs and hundreds of books, pamphlets, and websites on healthy eating. On the other hand, it may be appropriate for insurance to pay for therapy to combat drug addiction or counseling to address smoking, drug dependency, or eating disorders, such as anorexia or bulimia. Insurance would cover vaccinations but would not cover vitamins and supplements. Although this book can provide insights as to what is covered by insurance, the details require additional analysis, thought, and discussion.

An end-of-life plan identifies how people want to be treated as they approach death. A critical question is does it make sense for everyone to have a plan? The answer seems to be not for the young and healthy, who have a very low probability of death. There is no reason to prohibit this group from making such a plan, but it may be reasonable to require an end-of-life plan as a prerequisite for receiving Medicare. Applicants would be free to customize their plan and to choose one that extends their life as long as medically possible. The cost of preparing the plan would not be eligible for Medicare or health insurance coverage, but Medicare should provide a standard set of documents, such as do not resuscitate or healthcare powers of attorney, that individuals could customize to fit their situation.

Some people may suggest that Medicare cover these expenses. The answer, in large part, is to imagine how a Medicare applicant might be deluged by requests from "legal experts," not necessarily lawyers, to help him or her find the "best/most complicated" end-of-life plan with outsized fees for their preparation. Seniors who have difficulty preparing such a plan could have help from experts at Medicare, knowledgeable family members, or court-appointed guardians.

7.2.3 Routine Healthcare

The difference between routine healthcare and catastrophic coverage is judged by severity and costs with routine healthcare being low in both. Catastrophic coverage takes over when annual healthcare expenditure reaches a certain level, commonly referred to as the annual plan deductible. The deductible amount for each policy is determined by the third-party payer and the person being insured. The deductible amount would not be mandated by government laws or regulations.

Routine healthcare includes office visits and standard treatment, such as prescription drugs for things such as low thyroid levels or high blood pressure. These treatments are not covered by insurance but handled in a different manner. In lieu of coverage, third-party payers may place a specific amount, say $200 per month, into a health savings account controlled by the insured, who would use this money to pay for routine services. The third-party payer may require the insured to contribute monthly to this account with pretax dollars. Even though these expenses are paid by patients, they would be paid at rates negotiated by the third-party payer and not the "full" price listed by the provider. If patients find a provider who offers the service at a lower price than the negotiated rate, they can use that provider.

The annual deductible is higher than the third-party payers' contributions to the health savings account—for discussion purposes, assume the annual deductible is $4500. Annual expenditures above this amount are considered catastrophic and covered by insurance. All routine expenditures paid by the insured count toward the deductible, and once the annual deductible is reached, routine expenditures are covered in full. In effect, the insured is responsible for the difference between the annual deductible, $4500 in this example, and the amount contributed to the health savings account by the third-party provider, $2400. The insured could chose to contribute pretax money to the health savings account to cover all or part of this difference, which, in this example, would be $2100. Under these circumstances, the insured faces a balanced healthcare decision that includes the full cost and the benefit for treatment. When facing this decision, the insured is likely to inquire about the cost of treatment and may shop around for the best healthcare value.

Money remaining in the health savings account at the end of the year would automatically roll over to the next year. Another set of deposits is made, and the process continues. Patients could accumulate money in the health savings account that they could use to pay all or part of the annual deductible in future years. Continuing the example, in a future year, if a patient incurred $50,000 of health-care costs, the first $2400 is paid by the employer's contribution to the health savings plan, and the amount over $4500 is paid by the catastrophic insurance. The patient is responsible for $2100 ($4500 minus $2400). If the patient had accumulated $1200 in his or her health savings account by carefully managing health-care expenses in prior years, the patient's out-of-pocket costs would be only $900 ($2100 minus $1200). The numbers used here are for illustrative purposes and are not intended to be the "right" values for health savings contributions or deductible limits. In effect, the health savings account becomes an emergency fund to deal with unexpected healthcare costs.

What is important is that patients, supported by their primary care physicians, become responsible for knowing the cost of healthcare services, including medications and for making good decisions about what services to consume. Patients, in reality, become consumers and decision makers rather than objects of the healthcare delivery system. Compensation for primary care physicians changes significantly, so they do not benefit from withholding tests and treatments or pushing tests and treatments that are unnecessary. Their primary compensation is based on having healthy patients.

In addition to these benefits, health insurance reform can be used to reduce regulatory burdens, which introduce delays and drive up costs. If the transaction for routine healthcare is simplified with direct payment from patients to their primary care physician, administrative costs could be reduced, and the processes for dealing with claims, at least for routine care, could be simplified.

7.2.4 Catastrophic Coverage

Insurance is designed to deal with catastrophic loses. People pay into insurance pools to share risk and have access to funds, so they can avoid serious financial problems. Insurance should never be designed to cover a $50 office visit. Buying health insurance is sensible for catastrophic expenses even though the insurer takes some of the money to manage the company, design the policies, and administer the pool.

Catastrophic coverage has two relevant numbers. When does it kick in? What is the maximum amount for which the insurance company is liable? The question about when catastrophic coverage kicks in is setting the deductible because after patients reach their annual deductible their healthcare is fully paid. Patients with high wages and/or significant investment income can afford to take greater risk, so they may opt for a higher deductible, therefore paying more out of pocket, but their catastrophic insurance policy would cost less. If they are rich enough, they may prefer not to have insurance and pay all their medical expenses. On the other hand, people with lower incomes may want a smaller deductible so that their out-of-pocket costs are less but their catastrophic coverage costs more. The deductible amount is not set by government; it is determined by what is best for individuals and third-party payers.

With very minor exceptions, the ACA prohibits lifetime limits on health insurance. These limits mean that once a patient's total payouts reach a certain amount, the insurance company is no longer responsible for paying its share of the costs. Placing a cap on insurance coverage is a somewhat common practice. Car, house, and life insurance all have limited payouts that are clearly defined in the contract. In fact, when someone buys life insurance, they pay for a certain dollar amount of coverage. So was eliminating the maximum payout in health insurance the right thing to do?

Prior to the ACA, 45% of health insurance policies had no lifetime maximum, 22% had caps of $1 million to $2 million, and 32% had caps of $2 million or more.[11] So about 55% of the population had lifetime limits on healthcare insurance payouts that were $1 million or more, and the rest had none. Of the group with a limit, a very small percentage might become extremely sick and run out of health insurance coverage. Policies without limits cost more but not substantially more. Raising the lifetime limit from $1 million to $5 million would increase costs by 0.6% to 0.8% or about $3 per month for an individual and $8 per month for a family. The corresponding change from $5 million to $10 million would be about 0.1% or less than $1 per month for an individual or family policy.[11] On one hand, the purpose of insurance is to protect people from catastrophic losses, and a multimillion-dollar healthcare problem certainly qualifies as catastrophic. Given the uncertainty and the fact that healthcare is so expensive, having an uncapped health insurance policy is a safe and reasonable decision. Although this government mandate may be reasonable, it does take away the opportunity for people to choose. If they make a bad choice, they are the ones who suffer the consequences.

7.2.5 Important Guidelines for the New Approach

The intent of the new approach is not a guise to allow third-party payers to offer lesser coverage. The guidelines are to have the following:

1. Third-party payers spend about the same amount for the new insurance coverage as they did before.
2. The insured spend about the same amount for out-of-pocket costs.

If this new approach to health insurance is put in place and other aspects of the solutions are fully implemented, third-party payers and patients should eventually see their healthcare costs and insurance premiums decline because (a) patients are healthier and make better decisions about how they use healthcare and (b) providers improve their strategies and practices to enhance quality and lower costs.

7.2.6 Applicability to Medicare and Medicaid

As discussed earlier, the ideas presented here can be applied to Medicare or similar payment systems, but there may be value in delaying full implementation to allow Medicare recipients to adjust to the changes. Empowering Medicare and Medicaid recipients to be knowledgeable consumers, requiring them to have a PHP (especially the ideas of prevention, wellness, and end-of-life planning), and paying for their PHPs are things that could begin quickly. For Medicare, the new payment scheme could be implemented once there is some experience with applying the changes to employer-based insurance. Medicare implementation may also require a phased approach, in which the current recipient could keep the existing payment system or opt for the new one, and future recipients must participate in the new system. For Medicaid, the payment scheme is not an issue because the government pays for everything.

7.2.7 A Mindset Change

This new approach to healthcare and health insurance should help people make better decisions about medical treatments, improve their quality of life, and change patients' attitudes and values about what is important for good health. Patients should think differently because wellness is a central theme, and decision making is restored to patients and primary care physicians working as a team. Wellness and what patients need to do to become well are core issues. Patients believe that they have control over their health, which helps them understand that sickness and disease are not things that happen to them.

In addition, their perspective on healthcare costs change because patients are now responsible for managing their healthcare savings account and paying for their routine healthcare—at least the amount up to the annual deductible. They are incentivized to know the cost of healthcare, consider alternatives that may cost less, shop around for healthcare providers who focus on both outcomes and costs, and in general become better consumers of healthcare. This new mind-set should carry over to other facets of healthcare, including preventive care and catastrophic care, which are covered by insurance. Patients could be encouraged and even incentivized by insurers and third-party payers to work with them to report fraud and control the costs of tests and treatments covered by catastrophic insurance.

7.3 Key Elements of the Affordable Care Act

There are four elements of the ACA that many people believe deserve further consideration:

1. Eliminating the maximum lifetime limit on health insurance
2. Forbidding the use of preexisting conditions as a reason to deny health insurance

3. Allowing children to remain on their parents' health insurance policy until they are 26
4. Extending health insurance coverage to everyone

The first element, eliminating lifetime maximums, was discussed earlier, and this idea is consistent with the notion that health insurance should protect people from catastrophic healthcare costs. The others are discussed here.

7.3.1 Preexisting Conditions

Some people have used preexisting conditions and the practice of using them to deny coverage to vilify insurance companies as profit-oriented, heartless organizations. Although many, but not all, insurers are profit-oriented, the people who run insurance companies are not heartless. As described earlier, insurers and third-party payers are, by default, the gatekeepers that ration healthcare.

There is a good reason why the idea of a preexisting condition is commonly used by both for-profit and not-for-profit health insurers because without it people can "game" the system in the following way: People decide not to have health insurance and save several thousand dollars each year by not paying insurance premiums. If denying coverage for preexisting conditions is illegal, people could wait until they have a serious health problem and buy insurance, which the insurer would be required to provide. As a result, the insurer is liable for healthcare expenses caused by this preexisting condition.

Once cured, the patient could cancel the policy and go without insurance until the next significant health episode. Patients who jump in and out of the pool did not pay into it for the past several years and will not pay into it once treatment is complete, and they can repeat this tactic over and over. The missing payments to the insurance pool would have helped to cover some of the treatment costs. Patients who engage in this tactic get the full benefit of health insurance yet pay into the pool only while having treatment. As a result, the premiums for everyone else in the pool must increase.

What if the persons who decide not to have health insurance never have a significant illness and thus never join the insurance pool? They never buy healthcare, but they do not take money from the insurance pool. Isn't that okay? The answer is no because risk avoidance is the idea behind insurance. People buy insurance to cope with the risk of a future illness—just like people who insure their homes to cope with the very unlikely event that it burns down. The very few who are "never sick a day in their life" and those who are seldom sick subsidize those with serious health problems. All insurance programs, including the ACA, are built on this premise.

To understand the value of the preexisting condition doctrine, consider this: What happens if government applies the ban on preexisting conditions to car, house, and life insurance? The short answer is these markets would be in chaos. People could buy house insurance after a fire, car insurance after an accident, and life insurance after a death, and then argue that their claim cannot be denied because these are preexisting conditions. People would quickly learn this trick, and insurance pools would break down, causing the cost of car, home, and life insurance to skyrocket.

How does the ACA deal with preexisting conditions? The answer is simple. The ACA requires everyone to have insurance, and if they do not have insurance, they must pay a penalty. In spite of the Supreme Court ruling that this penalty is a tax, the penalty is in reality a health insurance premium. So under the ACA, if everyone has insurance, there are no preexisting conditions.

How does Medicare and Medicaid deal with this? For Medicaid, the answer is simple, the people with Medicaid do not have insurance coverage. Their healthcare is paid by the government. For Medicare, the bulk of the premiums were paid while the person worked. They have already paid into the Medicare insurance pool in a substantial way. Medicare does not allow people to jump in and out of the system, so the notion of preexisting conditions is a nonissue. Based on earlier discussions, one could argue that people should pay more for Medicare, but that is a topic for another time.

Although most people are in favor of eliminating the possibility that coverage can be denied because of preexisting conditions, it is clear that some guidelines must become part of the system to eliminate the potential for "game playing." There are sound reasons why people may have gaps in their insurance coverage. For example, students who graduate from college in May might not find employment until August. When starting a new job, health insurance coverage may not kick in for 90 days. These are situations in which invoking the preexisting condition doctrine is unreasonable. Currently, this problem is handled by the Consolidated Omnibus Budget Reconciliation Act of 1985, more commonly known as COBRA, which is temporary insurance that can bridge gaps in coverage.[12]

7.3.2 Children Covered by Parents' Policy until 26

Another popular measure in the ACA allows parents to keep children on their health insurance until they are 26. At first glance, this appears to be a good idea because these young adults will have health insurance if they cannot find a job that comes with coverage or cannot find a job that pays well enough to allow them to buy insurance.

An underlying question is by what age do children become adults? Legally, adulthood begins at 18. Persons of this age can vote, can chose to serve in the military, can enter into contracts, do not have to follow their parents' directives, and are not subject to child labor laws. A century or more ago, many people would marry at or before this age. They would often seek employment to help their families make ends meet. Today, many 18-year-olds enter college and have four or five years of preparation before starting their career. Others pursue technical degrees, community college diplomas, and trade school certificates to prepare for good jobs. As a result, it makes sense to allow additional time, say to the age of 22, 23, or possibly 24, for young adults to remain on their parents' health insurance. What is the rationale for selecting age 26? If 26 is good, isn't 28 or 30 even better? Extending the age to 26 puts society on a slippery slope. There is no compelling logic for 26, so once it is in place, what can be said against pushing it higher? Raising the age to 26 seems not only unnecessary, but potentially harmful because it provides an excuse for those who might be reluctant to work or might be intimidated by the prospect of working. It sends a message that people are not expected to fend for themselves until they are 26.

7.3.3 Extending Health Insurance to Everyone

A key goal of the ACA is to extend health insurance to all people in the United States. A substantial majority of the people in the United States have insurance through employment or Medicare, and both groups have earned this through working and paying taxes. There is a much smaller group that purchases insurance through the private market with money they earn. Military veterans have earned government-provided healthcare through the Veterans Administration although the care it provides has come under substantial criticism.

On the other hand, Medicaid provides insurance for many who do not have the means to pay. In addition, the government provides medical assistance through a variety of programs to the mentally challenged, prison inmates who are not permitted to work, and people with physical disabilities who cannot work. One of the goals of the ACA is to provide coverage for what is sometimes referred to as the working poor, those who do not have insurance through employment, make too little to afford health insurance in the private market, and make too much to qualify for Medicaid. Providing healthcare coverage to this group is a goal that the nation should pursue, but the question is how.

Although the goal of providing insurance to everyone is laudable, there are better ways than subsidies. The solution comes in two parts:

1. A stronger economy and robust job growth build wealth for the nation, provide employer-based insurance coverage that is better than Medicaid, increase tax revenue because people are earning a living wage and paying taxes, and reduce the federal budget deficit because Medicaid and other support programs have less demand.
2. Current healthcare programs should be reconciled. This would involve carefully reviewing existing programs for the purposes of consolidating duplicate programs, eliminating programs that are not working, and expanding programs that are needed and effective.

The goal should be to provide access to health insurance for those who want it. There still may be a need for subsidized insurance, but the need would be smaller. Also, buying health insurance should not be required by law. People should have a choice in this important matter.

7.4 Expanding Competition

For the two largest third-party providers of health insurance, employers at about 55% and the government at about 31%, lack of competition is not a serious concern. Many competitors exist for employer-based insurance, especially for large organizations or small organizations that are part of a purchasing group. And when they do not like the offerings, they can choose to be self-insured. Government provides the funding for its programs but teams up with insurers such as Aetna to administer them. About 10% of the people buy insurance in the private market,[13] and for them, competition is critical.

For the private insurance market and for small firms in the employer-based market, it makes sense to find ways to increase competition among insurance providers. One way is to allow competitors to sell health insurance across state lines. Competition would force insurers to examine their cost structure and increase efficiency. State health departments could create websites that list the options for purchasing insurance in the private market. These sites would offer basic information about health insurance policies offered by various companies, much like the apples-to-apples websites that many state public utility commissions operate so that residents can find the best deals for natural gas and electricity.[14]

Another important factor in stimulating competition for any good or service is letting customers know how much it costs. When someone buys an appliance, gets a haircut, or engages in a contract with a realtor to sell a home, the price is posted or identified as part of a contract. This is not the case for healthcare, and there are three key issues:

1. Patients do not seek information about the price of a service because in most cases a third-party payer is covering all or most of the cost. Not only is this information unknown to most patients, most physicians are unaware of the cost. In fact, prices vary substantially from one provider to the next. The *Wall Street Journal* identified stunning differences between prices for services in the same state. The average charge for joint replacement surgery ranged from $5300 in Ada, California, to $223,000 in Monterey Park, California. In Jackson, Mississippi, the charge for treating a case of heart failure is $9000 in one hospital and $51,000 in another.[15]
2. The prices negotiated between insurance companies and a single healthcare provider can be very different even for the same service. For example, an MRI for a knee, hip, or ankle without contrast at a particular healthcare system in Michigan varies from a low of $335 to a high of $1990. The provider's list price for the service is $2844. If a patient walks in off the street and wants to pay cash, the price is $695.[15] How can patients and physicians shop for services with a confusing process and so many different prices?
3. On top of that, a provider has two prices for a service. The following is an illustration taken from an actual explanation of benefits. The "amount billed"

by the service provider for an X-ray of the left wrist is $581. The "amount allowed" by the insurer is $53.60, which is less than 10% of the amount billed. The very large price difference, $527.40, is neither paid by the insurer nor the patient. It is waived by the provider. This is illustrative of the pricing game in healthcare in which providers ask for very high prices, and insurers attempt to negotiate very low actual payments. There are three other amount categories on the explanation of benefits: "your deductible," "your coinsurance," and "excluded expenses." The patient is responsible for these costs. The pricing game is complex and difficult to understand, and it must be simplified.

As the new approach to insurance is implemented, it is essential that patients get the best price for routine healthcare, which is not covered by insurance.

1. The patient must have bargaining power. In the current system, when a patient has health insurance, all healthcare payments are under this umbrella, so even if the insurer pays nothing because there is a deductible, the patients pays only the "amount allowed" and not the "list price" or the "amount billed." As illustrated earlier, the "allowed amount" is much lower than the other amounts. The new approach to health insurance must allow patients to pay the "amount allowed" for routine services that are not covered by insurance.
2. How do patients know the actual price charged for a service? For diagnostic tests and routine procedures, providing actual pricing data can be done via a provider website. Eventually, entrepreneurs will develop websites that list prices for healthcare services, so patients and physicians can easily access data and compare prices for tests, flu shots, and other services.

Skeptics may argue that healthcare is more complex than other services such as renting a hotel room or buying an airplane ticket, so it is more challenging to set an accurate price. A heart catheterization can have complications, such as a stroke or heart failure leading to additional expenses, or it may not succeed, and the patient may require bypass surgery. It is also possible that even if "successful" the problem is not fully resolved and additional care is required. Although this is a challenge, healthcare providers can address these problems in discussion with patients prior to surgery. This is not radically different than what happens in other circumstances. A contractor bids on replacing a glass enclosure, which covers two sides of a homeowner's shower. The other two sides have ceramic tile over wallboard that appears to be in good shape. As the contractor carefully removes the frame for the glass panels, which is attached to the ceramic tile walls, the tile comes off the wall because the wallboard supporting the tile is waterlogged. The tile and wallboard must be removed and replaced. This is not the contractor's fault. A good contract anticipates this and other complications, and the contractor prepares the homeowner ahead of time. The homeowner and the contractor work out a solution.

7.5 Driving Forces for Change

Making a radical change to something as important as health insurance requires significant effort and a well-devised plan. After the controversy surrounding the ACA, including implementation issues with the website, it is understandable why people may be reluctant to endorse major changes to healthcare and in particular to health insurance. Most people with employer-based plans are comfortable with their current insurance because most expenses are covered. They are unlikely to be enthusiastic about changing to a new system that requires more decision making and trade-offs. It is unclear who will advocate this change.

Not only will patients be asked to put forth more effort, they will be asked to accept more risk when it comes to healthcare for a promise that at some future time their health will be better and their healthcare costs will be reduced. Physicians, especially primary care physicians, will be asked to switch from emphasizing treatment to focusing on wellness, with which they have little training. In addition, their method of compensation will change to include payments based on patient wellness. Healthcare providers, including hospitals, are likely to be leery because they have faced cuts in reimbursements over many years. On top of that, they are being asked to provide accurate pricing data and find ways to lower costs and improve quality. They are fearful that providing more data on pricing will give consumer groups, insurers, and third-party payers more ammunition to seek further reimbursement reductions. Insurance companies are fearful that changing the way insurance works and increasing competition will bring new challenges. In addition, more claims and more healthcare costs lead to more revenue and profit.

The leaders who must drive this change are the third-party payers, which include employers who provide insurance through the workplace, unions who insure their members, and the government in the case of Medicare and Medicaid. It becomes a partnership among these three entities because they pay most of the costs of healthcare. They have the power to change the system. Over the past three decades or so, third-party payers have tried to deal with rising healthcare costs by shifting the cost burden to the following:

1. Healthcare providers by reducing reimbursements
2. Patients by increasing premium payments, deductibles, and coinsurance

Although these efforts have achieved some savings, they have not gotten at the heart of the issue. For the most part, these efforts have only shifted the cost burden rather than actually lowering costs and improving quality.

Lowering healthcare costs can make U.S. companies more competitive in global markets. Remember, healthcare spending in the United States is about 17.2% of the gross domestic product, which is more than twice the amount spent by the United States' trading partners. This extra spending is a millstone for U.S. companies because it reduces their ability to compete. As healthcare costs increase for employers, those costs are passed along in the form of price hikes to consumers, which make U.S. products less competitive. The intent of redesigning healthcare and health insurance is to do the following:

1. Push wellness to make people healthier and need less care
2. Change health insurance in ways that make people better decision makers
3. Focus on eliminating waste in the system

Shifting healthcare costs to the government, as happened for seniors when Medicare was introduced, is not the answer because this increases the federal debt, which leads to a different set of problems.

7.6 Impact of Rethinking and Redesigning Health Insurance on Healthcare Outcomes

Making changes to health insurance coverage has several important impacts on outcomes. Following is a summary of the impacts on the relevant root causes, which are discussed in Chapter 2:

1. Biased trade-offs and high drug costs: Rethinking and redesigning health insurance should allow patients to make better decisions about using health-care services (root cause #2) and prescription drugs (root cause #6). Patients will face balanced trade-offs that present the full costs and the benefits of seeking healthcare. This should make healthcare consumers think more thoroughly and carefully about heading to an emergency room for a routine illness that could be handled just as well in the physician's office, taking medication because it might do some good, or engaging in risky behavior that could require healthcare if something goes wrong. Knowing and paying the full cost of routine healthcare should motivate people to lead healthier lives. It changes the mindset of the patient and makes them better consumers of healthcare.
2. Unused facilities and equipment: As this new approach to health insurance leads to less consumption, there will be less demand for healthcare facilities and equipment (root cause #3).
3. Excessive legal liability and malpractice insurance costs: As patients make better decisions about consuming healthcare and using drugs, there will be fewer opportunities for mistakes, including misdiagnoses, ineffective or dangerous treatments, serious complications from treatments, and drug interactions. It is difficult to watch television for more than 30 minutes without seeing an advertisement to join a class action lawsuit for one medical malady or another. With better decision making and the consumption of less

healthcare, there will be fewer opportunities for errors, less legal liability, and lower malpractice insurance costs (root cause #7).
4. Shortage of healthcare professionals: Better decision making should lead to the consumption of fewer resources, which should cause lower demand for physician services (root cause #8).

7.7 Summary of Recommendations

Following is a listing of the key recommendations contained in this chapter:

1. Create a new approach to health insurance that would put patients in control. This vision requires knowledgeable consumers and would have the following characteristics:
   a. Patients must prepare and execute a PHP, which focuses on improving their health and reducing their need for healthcare. Nearly all of this would be covered by insurance. This would apply to all insurance, including Medicare and Medicaid.
   b. Patients would be responsible for paying for all routine services up to what many would consider to be a high annual deductible. Third-party payers would contribute to a tax-free health savings account to defray part of these costs, and these funds would be under the control of patients. This would not apply to Medicaid because the government pays for everything. Implementation for Medicare would likely come after some experience with the employer-based insurance market.
   c. Catastrophic insurance would pay in full all of the healthcare expenses above the annual deductible. This would be the case in all insurance, including Medicare.
2. There are certain elements of the ACA that would become part of the new approach to health insurance.
   a. Health insurance would come without maximum lifetime limits as legislated in the ACA.
   b. Preexisting conditions would not be a reason to deny coverage provided there is a justifiable reason that a patient does not have insurance. Rules must be in place to prevent people from jumping into health insurance when they are sick and out when they are well.
   c. Extending insurance coverage to adult-aged children would be cut back to 24-year-olds from 26-year-olds.
   d. Efforts would be made to extend health insurance coverage to the uninsured first by improving economic growth and jobs, second by savings that result from reconciling existing programs, and third by offering subsidies for the working poor.

3. Competition would be expanded by the following:
   a. Allowing competitors to cross state lines to sell insurance. This would be facilitated by a website that holds costs and coverage information about all insurance providers.
   b. Providing information about prices for healthcare services so patients and primary care physicians can shop for the best deal. This would provide access to information on the Internet for easy comparisons.

References

1. Eisler, P. 2013. Six common surgeries often done unnecessarily. *USA Today*, (June 19). http://www.usatoday.com/story/news/health/2013/06/19/surgeries-unnecessary -patients-medical/2439075/ (accessed August 27, 2015).
2. Joelving, F. 2011. Hold those drugs, doctor. Reuters, (June 13). http://www.reuters .com/article/2011/06/13/us-hold-those-drugs-doctor-idUSTRE75C5K720110613 (accessed September 25, 2015).
3. Health Insurance Providers. 2012. Do non-profit health insurance companies exist? http://www.healthinsuranceproviders.com/do-non-profit-health-insurance-compa nies-exist/ (accessed September 29. 2015).
4. Center for Medicare and Medicaid Services. 2012. Medicare enrollment—Aged beneficiaries and Medicare enrollment—Disabled beneficiaries. https://www .cms.gov/Research-Statistics-Data-and-Systems/Statistics-Trends-and-Reports /MedicareEnrpts/index.html (accessed September 25, 2015).
5. Center for Medicare and Medicaid Services. 2015. Medicare 2015 costs at a glance. http://www.medicare.gov/your-medicare-costs/costs-at-a-glance/costs-at-glance .html (accessed September 25, 2015. Since this was accessed, the costs paid by Medicare recipients has increased modestly.).
6. Jacobson, L. 2013. Medicare and social security: What you paid compared with what you get. *Tampa Bay Times*, (February 1). http://www.politifact.com/truth-o-meter /article/2013/feb/01/medicare-and-social-security-what-you-paid-what-yo/ (accessed September 25, 2015).
7. Merrill, M. 2012. Medicare and Medicaid fraud is costing taxpayers billions. *Forbes*, (May 31). http://www.forbes.com/sites/merrillmatthews/2012/05/31/medicare-and -medicaid-fraud-is-costing-taxpayers-billions/ (accessed September 25, 2015).
8. CBS News. 2009. Medicare fraud: A $60 billion crime. (October 23, 2015). http:// www.cbsnews.com/news/medicare-fraud-a-60-billion-crime-23-10-2009/ (accessed November 10, 2015).
9. Olanoff, L. 2015. St. Luke's policy on hiring only non-smokers a success, network says. *LehighValleyLive.com*, (August 30). http://www.lehighvalleylive.com/news/index.ssf /2015/08/st_lukes_controversial_ban_on.html (accessed September 25, 2015); Zupek, R. 2007. Smokers drag down a workplace, study says. *CNN.com*, (August 1). http://www .cnn.com/2007/LIVING/worklife/08/14/cb.smokers/ (accessed September 25, 2015).
10. Alonso-Zaldivar, R. 2013. Penalty could keep smokers out of health overhaul. *Yahoo News*, (January 24). http://news.yahoo.com/penalty-could-keep-smokers-health -overhaul-205840155.html (accessed September 1, 2015).

11. Terry, K. 2010. No lifetime limit on health coverage is a good deal for Americans. *cbsnews.com*, (September 23). http://www.cbsnews.com/news/no-lifetime-limit-on -health-coverage-is-a-good-deal-for-americans/ (accessed September 25, 2015).
12. U.S. House of Representatives. 1985. H.R.—Consolidated Omnibus Budget Reconciliation Act of 1985. https://www.congress.gov/bill/99th-congress/house -bill/3128 (accessed September 25, 2015); Wikipedia. 2015. Consolidated Omnibus Budget Reconciliation Act of 1985. http://en.wikipedia.org/wiki/Consolidated _Omnibus_Budget_Reconciliation_Act_of_1985 (accessed September 2015).
13. Wikipedia. 2015. Health insurance in the United States. https://en.wikipedia.org /wiki/Health_insurance_in_the_United_States (accessed September 30, 2015).
14. Ohio.gov. 2015. Energy choice Ohio. http://energychoice.ohio.gov/ (accessed September 30, 2015).
15. Beck, M. 2014. How to bring the price of health care into the open. *Wall Street Journal*, (February 24): R1–R6.

Chapter 8

Viewing Healthcare Trade-Offs Positively

When speaking about healthcare, it may seem like an oxymoron to put the words *trade-off* and *positively* together. A trade-off is giving up one thing to gain another. For example, people buy full-size pickup trucks to haul stuff and pull trailers for work, but the gas mileage is much lower than small economy cars. Plus, pickup trucks can cost twice as much. Similarly, investors who wish to save money buy and sell stocks online, but these investors do not get the advice and council of a full-service stock broker. However, when it comes to their health, few people believe they should compromise—that is, make trade-offs and be satisfied with something less than the "best" care. In addition, a trade-off is a mechanism for allocating scare resources, and many people believe and act as though healthcare is a limitless resource.

The notion that healthcare is an unlimited resource collides with the reality that resources in the United States, or any nation, are finite. Even if there is a way to spend the United States' entire gross domestic product (GDP) on healthcare, the available resources are still finite. With all resources devoted to healthcare, every job would be in healthcare directly, such as nurses and physicians, or indirectly, such as biotech researchers and surgical equipment designers. All facilities and equipment would be converted to healthcare use. This leaves no one and no equipment to purify water, grow food, make clothing, construct houses, build transportation infrastructure, or provide other essential goods and services. No country can do this, so healthcare spending must be substantially less than the GDP. This begs the following questions:

1. How much can the United States afford to spend on healthcare—that is, what percentage of the GDP is the right amount?
2. How should these finite healthcare resources be allocated?

From a free market perspective, the first question is the wrong question. The United States does not set GDP targets for how much to spend on mobile phones, food, or tax accounting services. Demand and supply for these items are set by markets in which people make decisions or trade-offs that determine how they allocate their limited resources. Decisions to purchase items depend on their costs and benefits. This book examines and attempts to change the phenomena that underlie healthcare decision making. Key objectives of this book are to clarify why trade-offs are necessary and help people make good choices by considering both sides of the demand–supply balancing act. The solution accomplishes this by doing the following:

1. Reducing demand for healthcare services as people pay more attention to and put more effort into being healthy (Chapters 5 and 6)
2. Improving decision making, so resources are used wisely, which provides capacity to treat those with limited or no access to healthcare (the essence of Chapter 7 and this chapter)
3. Matching supply with demand while making the healthcare delivery system more efficient, more productive, and less wasteful plus enhancing the quality of care (Chapters 9 through 13)

These three factors are critical for addressing the more important question: How are finite healthcare resources allocated or rationed? It is consumers operating in the marketplace that ultimately determine how much the United States spends on healthcare as they do with mobile phones, food, tax accountants, and other goods and services.

8.1 Evaluating Trade-Offs: Allocating Healthcare Resources

The pejorative term that is often used when discussing how to allocate healthcare resources is *rationing*. Whether the phrase "allocating a scare resource" or "rationing a scare resource" is used, the meaning is the same: Not every part of the U.S. economy has all the resources it needs, and not every patient receives all the care they might like. When it comes to healthcare, which can be a life-or-death situation, deciding who gets treatment is not a popular job. Yet the ability to allocate resources is required whenever resources are finite, which is all of the time. As discussed later, allocating resources is easier when the economy grows because there are more resources.

Prior to World War II, most people paid for their healthcare the same way they bought groceries or clothing. There was no Medicare for senior citizens or Medicaid for the poor. Few people had employer-paid health insurance or purchased individual insurance policies on their own. Most people, young or old, rich or poor, retired or working, made decisions about their healthcare based on its costs and benefits and paid the bill. The trade-offs they made determined how resources were allocated and the amount of healthcare consumed. Patients decided when it was appropriate to see a physician and when it was not.

Because patients made the choices and paid the bills, there was competition among providers and pressure to keep costs under control. When third-party payers, such as employers and the government, began to provide health insurance the following happened:

1. Patients used more healthcare services because they received the benefits and paid little if any of the costs. As a result, the trade-off between the costs and benefits of healthcare became biased toward consumption.
2. The pressure on healthcare providers to keep costs low slipped away. There was little reason to reduce cost, increase productivity, and keep prices low because the price of services did not seem to matter to patients, who were paying little if any of the expense. For many years, the third-party payers covered the ever-increasing costs of healthcare.
3. Insurers and third-party payers replaced patients as gatekeepers, so they were thrust into a position to ration healthcare. As healthcare costs escalated, the new gatekeeper decided who would be treated for what and how much would be paid for the treatment.

8.1.1 Understanding Healthcare Rationing: The Current System

The United States is a wealthy and innovative country that should have enough resources to provide a high level of healthcare services to all of its citizens, assuming the system is effectively designed and properly managed. It is a much different story in underdeveloped countries where resources are insufficient to provide even basic care. Their economies often cannot provide clean water, basic nutrition, or rudimentary housing. Children suffer and die from malnutrition, and they die from diseases that have been eradicated in developed countries. There is a very strong correlation between the level of economic success that countries achieve and their ability to provide good healthcare.

However, even developed countries must ration care. There are circumstances in which healthcare professionals are required to make judgments about who gets life-saving treatments and who does not. In cases involving disasters, when those needing care overwhelm available medical resources, there must be a way to ration care at least until additional resources become available. When there are earthquakes, terrorist attacks, or military battles, the number of casualties can be great, so a process called *triage* is used in which someone or a small group of people sets priorities. Triage divides the injured into three groups: those who are likely to live regardless of what care they receive, those who are likely to die regardless of what care they receive, and those for whom immediate care would increase their likelihood of survival.[1] Triage diverts scarce resources from those who do not need immediate care and from those for whom care may not matter to those who will benefit. These are difficult decisions, and fortunately, they do not happen often.

It would be naive to believe that rationing occurs only in emergencies. Rationing happens in more subtle ways than triage and comes in various forms. For people without health insurance, rationing happens because healthcare is expensive, and they cannot afford to pay. Rationing may occur even when people have insurance because they have high deductibles and copayments. Their portion of the cost may not be affordable, or they can afford it but decide there are better ways to spend their money.

Because insurance companies have become the de facto gatekeepers for healthcare, they have created procedures and practices that limit patients' access to care. One common method is to create treatment pathways that require patients to have less expensive drugs, physical therapy, or other treatments before progressing to more expensive options. Some drugs and procedures are listed as experimental and are simply not covered. Requiring preapproval is yet another way to restrict access. These may or may not be reasonable ways to control cost, but they tend to work. As a result of these and other actions, many people have negative opinions about insurance companies. Rationing healthcare is a job that someone must do, and insurers are in this position by default.

In fact, insurers act on behalf of third parties, who pay the lion's share of healthcare costs in the United States through premiums paid to insurers. Third-party payers pressure insurance companies to find ways to control costs and limit usage because healthcare costs and the associated premiums have grown at such an alarming rate. Many insurers are not-for-profit companies and therefore do not enrich themselves or their shareholders by limiting access to care. This includes the government that pays Medicare and Medicaid claims. For not-for-profit insurers, it is not possible to argue that the primary reason for rationing is to increase profits because these insurers have no profits. Also, some companies, that many people consider to be "insurers," do not offer insurance. They act as administrators for large firms that choose to be self-insured, meaning the company, not an insurer, pays the patients' claims. These companies only pay a fee to the insurer for processing claims. They do not pay premiums to insurers.

Ultimately, healthcare rationing is driven by third-party payers, not by insurance companies. Third-party payers include for-profit companies, such as IBM and GE; not-for-profit entities, such as universities and foundations; public employee retirement systems; and federal, state, and local governments that offer insurance to their employees. In addition, there is Medicare and Medicaid, which are offered by the government. The percentage breakdown for healthcare spending by source of funds for the United States in 2012[2] is given in Figure 8.1. Medicare and Medicaid account for 35% of spending. Private insurance accounts for 33%, and it includes people with employer-based insurance from both for-profit and not-for-profit insurers as well as those who buy insurance on the open market. It seems unfair to blame limited access, low reimbursements, and denial of claim entirely or even substantially on for-profit insurers.

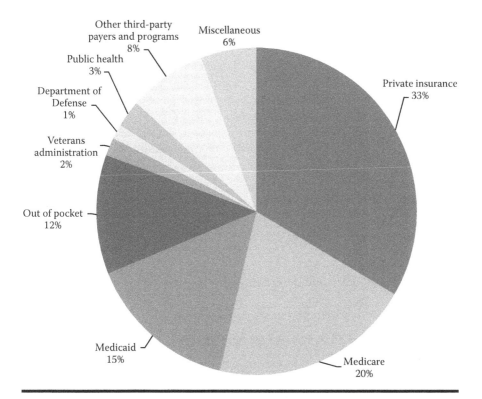

Figure 8.1 **U.S. healthcare spending by funding source for 2012 (spending total was $2.8 trillion). Note: Out-of-pocket costs to consumers is 12%, but they do not include premiums paid by individuals for private insurance. (From Center for Medicare and Medicaid Services, 2014, National health expenditures by type of service and source of funds, CY 1960–2013, https://www .cms.gov/Research-Statistics-Data-and-Systems/Statistics-Trends-and-Reports /NationalHealthExpendData/NationalHealthAccountsHistorical.html (accessed October 11, 2015.)**

In fact, the federal government uses tactics that are similar to those used by for-profit insurers to ration healthcare. Medicare has deductibles and requires coinsurance payments. Medicaid's reimbursement rates are so low that some physicians attempt to avoid Medicaid patients. This is a significant deterrent and is an effective, and probably an unfair, way to ration care. Medicare and Medicaid also have limits and restrictions on care, such as preapprovals and pathways to care, that ration healthcare.

The need for rationing becomes more acute when healthcare costs grow faster than the U.S. economy. As this happens, it is necessary to do one or more of the following:

1. Take resources from other parts of the economy to fund the increase
2. Employ additional mechanisms to further ration care
3. Borrow money to pay the increase as only the federal government can do

To reduce the need for rationing, the United States should have a robust economy that grows faster than healthcare costs and change the demand–supply relationship as described earlier: better health, higher productivity, and better decisions. This should drive down healthcare costs and free resources so that the United States can spend more on innovations that power economic development and job growth.

Before discussing how to change the system to more effectively ration care, the key points about healthcare rationing are summarized:

1. Rationing is necessary because the United States does not have unlimited resources.
2. Rationing has always been, is now, and will forever be a part of healthcare. As payment responsibilities have shifted over time, different groups have been responsible for rationing.
3. Rationing is currently implemented by or on behalf of third-party payers, including the government.

8.1.2 Rationing Care: A New Approach

The new approach encourages and supports efforts by individuals to have better health and make better decisions about their care and by healthcare providers to offer better care at a lower cost. With this change, decisions are made by customers or patients, not by government mandates, which means patients supported by their primary care physicians will again become responsible for their health and healthcare. The intent is not to return to the pre–World War II era when employer-based insurance was rare and many people could not afford basic healthcare. That approach effectively rationed care and kept healthcare costs low, but it did not deliver high-quality care to a large portion of the population.

In addition, employer-based insurance has worked well, and most people with these plans are very satisfied. Employer-based plans have several important benefits. Usually, employment groups naturally make good risk pools because they are typically large and diverse by age and health conditions. Smaller firms can band together through industry groups or associations to form effective risk pools. Insurance benefits are tax free, which effectively lowers their cost. The new approach would continue to rely on employer-based insurance as a primary instrument for delivering healthcare but would place patients, supported by their primary care physician, in charge of decision making.

There are three other substantial segments of the U.S. population that have insurance. The first two are Medicare, which serves those 65 and over and some people with disabilities, and Medicaid, which serves the poor. The third is insurance purchased by individuals in the open market, which serves people who are working but do not have employer-based coverage. The individual insurance market and Medicare, like the employer-based market, uses the same approach and methods to address rationing. Medicaid has different characteristics and presents somewhat different problems.

The new approach, which is based on three programmatic changes, should increase the health of the U.S. population, improve access to coverage, enhance the quality of healthcare, and spend healthcare dollars more effectively. These actions will make healthcare more responsive to patients' needs and reduce the need to ration healthcare.

1. Patient-centered care puts patients in control of their health and healthcare, and changes to health insurance require patients to control a pool of money that pays for routine healthcare. This refocuses healthcare on the patients' needs and puts pressure on providers to deliver better care at a lower cost. With patients controlling spending, websites and other information sources would spring up to provide pricing data for healthcare services. This information would allow patients to make better choices and stimulate competition among providers.

2. Wellness and prevention are center stage, so patients are healthier with less demand for care. Plus, inexpensive health screenings and preventive testing detect and solve problems early. Websites exist that provide information about wellness, health screenings, and preventive testing, and these will increase in content and quality as patients seek more and better information. These efforts will lead to less demand for care and will free resources to treat others who need care and currently are not receiving it.

3. Improvements in the healthcare delivery system will enhance patient safety and satisfaction, increase system-wide productivity and efficiency, and eliminate waste in the system. So existing resources would be used more effectively, leading to increased access to care and less rationing.

With this new approach, patients would make decisions about and be responsible to pay for their routine healthcare. Even though insurance pays for the personal health plan (PHP) and catastrophic care, patients would take interest in the costs of these aspects of healthcare because they understand the importance and value of controlling costs, are encouraged by third-party payers to participate, and are motivated by a desire to make healthcare better.

Patients would have access to price data for services offered by various providers, information about patient satisfaction from those providers, and itemized bills that patients or their advocates would review to check for accuracy and potential fraud. Using this information, patients would decide where to go for care. Patients could be incentivized with lower premiums, deductibles, coinsurance, and copayments for providing input to insurers about their quality of care and the accuracy of their bills. The intent is to change the mind-set of patients from passive "victims" to active participants, in fact leaders, who chart their path to better health. This will have a far greater impact on improving health, enhancing the quality of care, and controlling cost than pages and pages of government regulations.

This approach should work well for employer-based insurance, the individual market, and Medicare but will need adjustments to work for Medicaid, where the government pays 100% of the cost, making it more difficult to incentivize patients to be active participants in healthcare decision making. This should not stop efforts to make Medicaid more patient-centered, have Medicaid patients prepare PHPs, and involve them in making better choices.

To consider how to incentivize the right behavior, answer this question from the patients' perspective: What is the most serious problem with Medicaid? The answer seems to be finding providers who will accept Medicaid patients because of low reimbursements. Even if Medicaid patients find providers, it is difficult to build a long-term, effective relationship. One option is to incentivize providers with higher reimbursement levels when patients have and follow a PHP. As a result, patients and physicians could have an ongoing and effective relationship, and patients would have access to physicians who consider them a priority because their reimbursement is comparable to other patients. Medicaid patients who are unable to manage their healthcare could be supported by family members or court-appointed guardians. Dollars to support better Medicaid funding would come from a healthier population, both Medicaid and non-Medicaid patients who need less care, early detection that catches problems before they are catastrophic and expensive, and a more efficient healthcare delivery system.

8.2 Difficult, Unanswerable Questions

This discussion circles back to the question: How much can the United States afford to spend on healthcare? This question was dismissed earlier because spending should be determined by market forces, not by government directives. But there is a practical significance to this question because for many years spending on healthcare grew faster than the GDP. This impacts the economy because consumers spend more on healthcare so that they have less to spend on other goods and services. Also, U.S. firms that offer employer-based health insurance pass along its high cost to their customers, which damages their global competitiveness by increasing prices for their goods and services both in the United States and abroad. Recall, the United States spends more than 2.5 times the per capita average for the other 33 countries in the OEDC.[3] Hence, the percentage of the GDP spent on healthcare is important and can become a useful measuring stick to broadly assess the overall performance of healthcare services in the United States, but it should not be used as a policy tool to set spending limits.

In spite of these concerns, some suggest that the United States should not worry about spending on Medicare, Medicaid, and other government programs because the federal government can continue to borrow money to fund them. But there is a limit to how much countries and individuals may be willing to loan the United States to fund future spending. The United States has been borrowing for decades and amassed a debt that exceeded $18.4 trillion in October 2015.[4] This does not include unfunded liabilities, which are expected future benefits from programs, such as Medicare and Medicaid, that are not funded by expected future revenue collected to pay these benefits. The amount for Medicare alone is estimated to be $38.6 trillion, or more than twice the current national debt.[5] It should be noted that estimates for U.S. government unfunded liabilities vary widely.[6] In 2015, spending on Medicare, Medicaid, the Children's Health Insurance Program, and subsidies offered by the Affordable Care Act totaled about $1 trillion, topping Social Security spending at $882 billion for the first time.[7]

Because healthcare spending has limits and must be rationed, people may not get all of the care they want or need. This is certainly a quality-of-life issue, and it can be a matter of life and death. Hidden underneath this need to ration healthcare resources is a question that people and politicians would like to avoid: What is the value of a human life? Any decision to ration healthcare or any other resource that impacts lives implies an economic value of a human life that is less than infinite.

The following sections explore these two questions in greater depth. Please don't be disappointed when no specific amount is set for how much to spend on healthcare or the value of a human life. The ultimate answer is to find ways to be healthier, have a better quality of life and longevity, and use fewer healthcare resources so that care can be extended to those who do not have it.

8.2.1 How Much Healthcare Can We Afford?

As a measuring stick, is 10%, 15%, or more a reasonable percentage of the GDP to spend on healthcare? In truth, the "correct" percentage of the GDP should be a variable that depends on a variety of parameters, including the health of the population and its average age. Looking at the percentage of their GDP other developed countries spend on healthcare is a way to benchmark spending, but like all benchmarks, this one has its flaws. The biggest problem is there are no guarantees other countries have it "right." There is an implicit assumption in claiming that the United States should spend as much on healthcare as other developed countries, which is that the United States should get the same or better outcomes. The United States should strive to have the healthiest population and offer the best care in the world, meaning the highest longevity and best quality of life, and the United States should do so at the lowest cost. It is the dual mandate of high-quality outcomes and low cost that should drive the healthcare delivery system. If the United States achieves this dual mandate, it will get the best value from its system because it gets more and better care for each dollar spent. When most U.S. consumers buy flat-screen TVs, house-painting services, or real estate, they want value, which means both high quality and low cost—why not for healthcare?

In addition to population health and demographics, the amount the United States can and should spend on healthcare is related to the size and strength of the economy. Robust economic growth provides more wealth and resources, which allow a nation to consume more goods and services, including healthcare. However, in at least one way, healthcare is different because consumers are better off if they need less. The ultimate goals are to have better health and consume less care, which is a fundamental premise of this book. If the United States has a growing economy and properly redesigned its healthcare system, the amount the United States "can" afford to spend on healthcare may approximate what it "should" be required to spend to "meet everyone's needs." A growing economy provides more resources (increasing what it "can" spend). Healthier consumers and a productive and efficient healthcare delivery system reduce costs (decreasing what it "should" spend). The other important choice of words is to "meet everyone's needs," which may be doable, rather than to "meet everyone's wants," which may not.

Some people claim that it is not possible to simultaneously reduce healthcare spending and improve outcomes. As an aside, that was the perspective of U.S. car companies in the late 1960s and into the 1970s and 1980s when the Japanese built better cars, sold them at a lower price, and made money. Aligning one's thinking with auto industry executives from this era does not provide strong support for a claim that high-quality healthcare and low costs are incompatible. Back on point, this book provides a roadmap to achieve these apparently conflicting but actually compatible and reinforcing outcomes. This is accomplished by improving hospital management and organization, applying information technology, focusing on reducing the costs of drugs, reducing the incidence of malpractice, reforming the legal system, and changing the provider network. These topics are discussed in the following chapters. For now, here are calculations that show it is feasible to reduce spending without disrupting and devastating the healthcare delivery system.

In 2012, the United States spent about 17.2% of the GDP on healthcare.[8] If the United States extends the current system with all of its faults to the approximately 45 million uninsured, spending would increase to about 20.16% of the GDP. This estimate was determined by dividing the number of people in the United States with insurance (314 million [the U.S. population] minus 45 million [the uninsured]) into the number of uninsured. The result is a 16.7% increase in healthcare use. This would increase healthcare spending by 2.87% of the GDP (0.167 [the increase needed to cover the uninsured] times 0.172 [the portion of the GDP spent on healthcare] = 0.0287). Total healthcare spending as a percentage of the GDP would be about 20.07% (17.2% + 2.87%). The spending increase on healthcare would be about $465 billion (0.0287 times $16.2 trillion in GDP in 2012[9]), which is substantial. Who must give up what to spend an additional $465 billion on healthcare?

So it would take a bit more than 20% of the GDP to cover everyone, assuming the current lifestyle and health status and using the current inefficient delivery system. This is a ballpark estimate, a very big ballpark, with many assumptions that could be challenged. The point is not to suggest that this is the right number for healthcare spending, but to set an approximate upper bound on the amount needed to cover everyone using the current system.

The United States is already an outlier with respect to healthcare expenditures. Most other developed countries spend between 8% and 12% of their GDP on healthcare. As mentioned in Chapter 1, the United States spends on a per capita basis about 2.5 times as much as the other 33 OEDC countries.[3] Increasing this to 20.07% would put the United States at about three times the OEDC per capita spending. These data points indicate that the United States is spending substantially more on healthcare than other OEDC countries and, as noted earlier, is achieving results that are average or below average. This very high spending for average or less-than-average outcomes suggests that the United States should be able to spend less and achieve better results.

No one knows with certainty the right amount to spend on healthcare, and no one is suggesting that a number be placed into law that would set a spending limit, but a discussion is warranted. To begin, assume that spending 15% of the GDP on healthcare is the "right" amount. This is less than the United States spends on healthcare, but it is much higher than the average spent by OEDC countries both as a percentage of the GDP and per capita. This target implies that through better health, improved efficiency, better decision making, and stronger economic growth, the United States may be able to have the healthiest population and the best care. It will take time to get there because there will be a lag between implementing the solutions and realizing the results.

A decline in the percentage of the GDP spent on healthcare from 17.2% to 15% can be implemented over time without reducing actual dollars spent. These calculations are based on 2012 data. If the U.S. economy can grow at a compounded rate of 3% per year, which is certainly achievable, and the dollars spent on healthcare do not increase because people are healthier and spend these dollars wisely, it would take about 4.7 years to reduce healthcare spending to 15% of the GDP. The 3% assumption is reasonable because the annual compounded growth rate for the U.S. GDP from 2000 ($10.3 trillion), when the economy was very strong, to 2012 ($16.2 trillion) is 3.85%. If the United States finds ways to provide better care and spend less money, or if the economy grows faster than 3% per year, this timeline could be reduced further. The basis for this calculation and others to follow is the following:

1. Divide 2012 healthcare spending, which is about $2.8 trillion, by 0.15 to determine what the GDP should be in a future year, so healthcare spending is 15% of the GDP. When this is done, the GDP must be about $18.7 trillion.
2. Divide $18.7 trillion by the GDP in 2012, which is $16.2 trillion, and the ratio is 1.154. This means that the GDP would have to increase by about 15.4%.
3. Using logarithms, determine the number of years needed to reach a 15.4% increase in the GPD if it grows at a 3% compounded annual rate. The result is about 4.7 years.

If the assumptions change slightly and the economy grows at 3% per year but healthcare costs increase 1% per year, it would take about 7.0 rather than 4.7 years to achieve the target.

Table 8.1 shows these two scenarios in a simpler arithmetic way. As shown in column 2, if the U.S. GDP begins at $16.2 trillion and grows by 3% each year, in eight years it will be approximately $20.5 trillion. Column 3 holds healthcare constant. Column 4 shows that U.S. healthcare spending as a percentage of the GDP drops below 15% during year 5. Columns 5 and 6 are the same calculations, but the assumption is that healthcare costs grow by 1% per year. With these assumptions, healthcare spending as a percentage of the GDP reaches 15% at the end of year 7.

To get from 20.07% of the GDP, which is the amount needed to cover the 45 million uninsured, to 15% of the GDP will take about 10 years if the economy grows at 3% per year and healthcare spending remains constant. These calculations are not shown in Table 8.1. These timelines are optimistic because there will be a lag between implementation and better outcome, but starting now is much better than waiting.

This exercise illustrates that hitting a healthcare spending target of 15% of GDP is achievable. With the approach laid out in this book, it may be possible to spend less than 15% and actually achieve better health outcomes. An important accelerant to spending 15% of the GDP or less is finding ways to grow the U.S. economy faster than the assumed rate of 3%. A stronger economy creates more high-quality jobs with healthcare benefits and allows the United States to reduce the percentage of the GDP spent on healthcare.

Table 8.1   Calculation for Healthcare Spending as a Percentage of GDP

Year	U.S. GDP[a]	U.S. Healthcare Spending[b]	Healthcare Spending as a Percentage of GDP[c]	U.S. Healthcare Spending[d]	Healthcare Spending as a Percentage of GDP[e]
(1)	*(2)*	*(3)*	*(4)*	*(5)*	*(6)*
Current Year	$16.2	$2.7860	17.2%	2.7860	17.2%
Year 1	$16.7	$2.7860	16.7%	2.8139	16.9%
Year 2	$17.2	$2.7860	16.2%	2.8420	16.5%
Year 3	$17.7	$2.7860	15.7%	2.8704	16.2%
Year 4	$18.2	$2.7860	15.3%	2.8991	15.9%
Year 5	$18.8	$2.7860	14.8%	2.9281	15.6%
Year 6	$19.3	$2.7860	14.4%	2.9574	15.3%
Year 7	$19.9	$2.7860	14.0%	2.9870	15.0%
Year 8	$20.5	$2.7860	13.6%	3.0168	14.7%

[a] U.S. GDP (column 2) grows at a compound rate of 3% per year.
[b] U.S. healthcare spending is constant (column 3).
[c] Column 4 is healthcare spending as a percentage of the GDP (column 3 divided by column 2).
[d] U.S. healthcare spending grows as a compound rate of 1% per year (column 5).
[e] Column 6 is healthcare spending as a percentage of the GDP (column 5 divided by column 2).

8.2.2 What Is the Value of Human Life?

When a society has finite resources to spend, trade-offs must be examined and decisions must be made to determine how its resources are used. By implication, this places a finite value on human life. On the other hand, there are religious, ethical, and moral arguments for doing everything possible to save lives without regard to the costs or consequences. Because healthcare is only part of the U.S. economy, resources must be allocated to other activities, such as building safer highways and cars, growing more and healthier food, supporting education, and investing to spur business activities and economic growth. The first two examples seem clear; better highways and cars save lives and support the economy, and better food leads to healthier people and less starvation. This logic does not specify the precise amount to allocate to each activity, but it does provide a rationale for investing in them.

Funding education is vital for many reasons, including but not limited to supporting future innovations in healthcare and training the next generation of healthcare workers.

Investing in business activities is justified because growing the economy leads to greater prosperity as measured by the GDP, which provides more resources for all activities, including healthcare. This becomes clearer when examined at a microlevel. When a farmer buys equipment, the farmer plows more ground, plants more crops, and harvests more produce and grain. Fewer farmers are needed, so there are "former farmers" who can now be trained to do other things, such as building a stronger and more efficient manufacturing economy or becoming a healthcare professional. This transformation has been happening for hundreds of years as the United States went from an agrarian economy with more than 90% of the workforce engaged in agriculture to an industrial economy. Next, manufacturers invested in technology and automation, allowing their workers to produce more. Fewer people were needed to design and build things, freeing people to propel the knowledge economy. Operating in a capitalistic environment, these people developed and improved healthcare, information technology, and many other facets of human life. These impacts have been staggering in scope and scale and have enriched people's lives.

8.2.2.1 Some Factors to Consider in Valuing Human Life

It is beyond the capability of mortals to determine the value of a human life. There are, however, ways of thinking about life that may provide some understanding and put this difficult question in perspective. These points of view offer insights as to why allocating resources is necessary and how it impacts life, health, and quite possibly death.

In 2012, the U.S. GDP per capita was about $51,500.[9] On an aggregate basis, one could make the claim that $51,500 is the average annual economic value of each person in the United States. On an individual basis, judges, lawyers, and jurors frequently estimate the value of human life when they determine a settlement for a wrongful death lawsuit. Using experts, they project the earning power of the person for the balance of his or her expected lifetime. That amount becomes part of the settlement. So if a 38-year-old CPA is killed in a car accident, the settlement would reflect the lifetime earning power of this individual.

Many people recoil from the notion that a dollar amount is placed on human life because life is sacred. They believe that placing a value on it is crude, inappropriate, and wrong. They further argue that a human life is priceless and should be preserved no matter the cost. They often personalize their claim by pointing to a specific person with a problem and argue that society is cruel and unreasonable if it does not do all it can to help, regardless of the costs or circumstances.

These conflicting points of view—that there is a limited amount of money to spend, and all human life is priceless—are inconsistent but must be reconciled. These facts and beliefs come from two very different perspectives.

1. The first one is a depersonalized, fact-based, macro view of what society can afford to spend; it is grounded in reality and requires careful thought about how the nation spends money on healthcare and other things.
2. The second is a highly personal, emotional, ethical, and sometimes religious view of what a person should do to help loved ones.

This dilemma sets up a useful tug-of-war between constraints and aspirations.

The first perspective leads to an annual per capita amount to spend on healthcare, and the second requires spending more in cases in which the need is great. This, in fact, can be achieved. It is possible to spend more on some people because not everyone consumes their "full share" of healthcare dollars each year. This is the essence of insurance as it allows risk pooling so that healthcare dollars from people who do not need them now can be used to help those whose needs are critical and immediate. Unfortunately, even this does not allow society to spend an unlimited amount on healthcare or eliminate the need for rationing. Most likely, difficult decisions about a person's healthcare and the healthcare of their loved ones are still required.

The individual nature of healthcare was dramatized in the movie *John Q* in which John Quincy Archibald's (Denzel Washington) son is diagnosed with a life-threatening heart condition and is denied surgery because it is not covered by insurance. John takes hostages, demands care, and eventually gets it for his son. This speaks to the need to have compassion and flexibility about healthcare delivery while wrestling with the difficult task of controlling healthcare spending. If the U.S. population wants to do all it can to save lives, then it is essential to become healthier as a nation, so less care is needed to make the healthcare system more efficient and less wasteful and grow the economy so that there are more resources for healthcare and other basic needs. That is the best way to help John's son.

It is critical to reconcile the United States' aggregate ability to pay for healthcare as determined by the size of the economy, competing priorities for things, such as national defense and education, and heart-wrenching appeals to do all society can for a person with a serious health problem. To put this in perspective, examine how people make decisions for themselves, their children, and others that imply that people make trade-offs that involve human life—even their lives and the lives of their loved ones.

If society values human life infinitely, why do people text and drive? Why is texting while driving not a criminal offense in every state? Distracted driving—including eating, talking on the phone, tuning the radio, or drinking water—may contribute to accidents, injuries, and even death.

To go a step farther, should the United States ban driving altogether? In 2012, there were 33,561 people killed in traffic accidents in the United States. This is down from the peak of 54,589 deaths in 1972.[10] Still 33,561 is a lot of deaths. Why is driving legal? The answers are that driving is popular and is an essential part of the economy. Short of banning driving, the maximum speed limit could be set at 25 miles per hour because crashes at that speed are far less likely to be fatal. Why not take this simple step? The answer seems to be that life without convenience and access is unacceptable—plus the U.S. economy would suffer because moving goods would take longer and cost more. In other words, society through government actions makes the implicit trade-off that things such as convenience, jobs, and economic prosperity are desirable outcomes that society should seek even if people are more likely to be seriously injured or killed.

There were two paths to reducing highway deaths: make both highways and vehicles safer. In the decade of the 1950s, when the greatest generation was driving down the highway with their baby-boomer children riding in the car, nearly 360,000 people were killed on U.S. roadways.

Today, highways are much safer. Prior to the late 1950s, most roads were two-lane state or federal highways. The major push to have a grade-separated, four-lanes-or-more, limited-access, interstate highway system, which virtually eliminated head-on collisions on these roads, was passed under President Eisenhower in 1956. This law was known as the National Interstate and Defense Highways Act because of the president's vision to create a network that could efficiently transport troops and equipment across the country during times of war. Although that is certainly true, it also provides roadways that are safer than two-lane highways; plus the network supports the efficient movement of goods, thereby stimulating economic growth and prosperity. This shows that there are opportunities, other than healthcare, with which government can invest to improve the quality of life and save lives.

In the 1950s, vehicles were also far less safe. Dad was driving, mom sat in the front seat holding the baby, and three children occupied the backseat. There were no seat belts, no airbags, no antilock braking systems, and there were certainly no car seats for the children. The only protection in a panic stop was for dad to brace himself using the steering wheel and hold out his right arm to keep others in the front seat from hitting the windshield or the dashboard. The children in the backseat were on their own. Seat belts, actually a lap belt, such as those used on airlines, emerged slowly, initially meeting resistance from consumers. Nash was the first U.S.–produced vehicle to offer a lap-style seat belt option in 1949.[11] By the early 1960s, seat belts were in limited use in the United States. During that decade, many automotive repair centers offered lap-style seat belts that could be easily and inexpensively installed. Why didn't consumers rush to these stores and buy them? There certainly was evidence that they worked, and common sense indicated they would reduce injury and save lives. In 1968, the federal government required all passenger vehicles, except buses, to have seat belts, but a large percentage of the population refused to use them. In 1984, New York was the first state to require drivers and passengers to wear seat belts.[12] The story for air bags is not that different. It took many years for air bags to be embraced by consumers. The difficult question to answer is why?

Travel today is much safer. In 1950, the number of deaths per 100 million vehicle miles traveled (VMT) was 7.24. In 2012, the number was slightly more than one. Since the 1950s, the U.S. taxpayer through the government and the U.S. consumer through the automobile companies have invested heavily in making safer roads and safer vehicles. If the federal government had decided to stop spending on highways to increase spending on healthcare, and if consumers were unwilling to pay for safer vehicles, the impact on the economy would be negative, and highway deaths would be much higher. If the death rate per 100 million VMT was the same today as it was 1950, then the number of deaths on U.S. highway in 2012 would have been nearly 215,000 rather than 33,561.

People make trade-offs when they travel. A family of four from the Midwest decides to take a Florida vacation. Flights and a rental car for a week cost $1500 or more, and that does not include meals, lodging, and venue tickets. The cost of gasoline to drive the family car on the 2400-mile round trip is about $300. The parents decide to drive and do so in one day each way so that they have maximum time in Florida. The chance of being killed in a driving accident, especially driving 20 hours straight each way, is much higher than the likelihood of being killed in an airplane crash. Why take the risk? If parents value their lives and the lives of their children infinitely, they would pay to fly or not take the trip.

People drive too fast, run red lights, smoke tobacco, and have a second doughnut with their morning coffee. Children often start playing football in fifth grade and some continue through high school, college, and the professional ranks even though they risk debilitating injuries, including paralysis and concussions, even death. When individuals ride motorcycles or jaywalk, they are increasing their risk of injury or death. Even a walk around the block or riding a bike carries a risk of serious injury or death. If people value life infinitely, why would they take these risks? The point is that people take risks every day that endanger their lives and the lives of their families to save money, save time, and/or increase convenience. There are cases in which people take big risks for enjoyment. Otherwise, how can anyone explain bungee jumping or even riding a monstrous roller-coaster? Underlying these decisions is the acceptance of injury, ill health, or even death. This is the essence of a trade-off.

8.2.2.2 Are All Lives of Equal Value?

A related question that is also difficult to answer is, should everyone have the same level of healthcare? The retort by most people would be of course everyone should be treated the same. But, in fact, this is not the case. The U.S. president receives far better healthcare that costs much more than the average person. The same is true for senators, congressional representatives, governors, business executives, and university presidents. Some part of the difference is their earning power, which gives them access to better care; another part is their status and the symbolic nature of their position, and yet another part is their importance in providing leadership for government, commerce, and higher education.

There are circumstances in which some people are considered more valuable than others and receive better treatment and/or deserve more protection. During World War II, General Eisenhower ordered millions of men to hit the beaches at Normandy on D-Day. Thousands of those men died. Eisenhower was not criticized because he did not lead the charge from a landing craft at Omaha Beach or jump from a C-47 with the paratroopers. He was honored as a hero and elected president twice. His safety and protection were more important to the cause than the typical foot soldier or paratrooper.

Wealthy people can afford more and better healthcare than the average person. People seem willing to accept the fact that wealthy people have nicer clothes, eat at fancier restaurants, drive sleeker cars, and own better houses than the average person, but the notion that the wealthy can have better healthcare often carries with it a negative response. Critics argue that this is not fair, saying everyone should be treated equally. This strong response may be the result of a clear and direct link between better healthcare and better quality of life or longevity.

There are also interesting questions to explore, such as should a young child with a correctable heart defect receive the same level of care as a senior citizen with terminal cancer? The young child has a long and potentially bright future, and the senior will most likely have a poor quality of life in his or her remaining weeks or months. It is not for a government board or insurance company panel to make these decisions. The reasonable and humane answer for seniors is to help them or their guardian understand their situation and make the best decision for them. This movement is underway as seniors consider living wills, healthcare powers of attorney, and do not resuscitate notices to cope with end-of-life issues. The final decision about treatment is theirs.

8.3 Putting Things in Perspective

As promised, the discussion does not give specific answers to the following questions:

1. How much healthcare can the United States afford?
2. What is the value of a human life?

The first question must be answered by consumers as they examine their available resources and decide how to allocate those resources to best meet all of their needs. They must make trade-offs among their many needs. Should they forgo a vacation to buy a new car? Should they cut back on restaurant meals to save money for new clothes? This applies to healthcare as well because patients must consider their resources and decide the kinds and amount of care they should have. Should they spend less on entertainment to buy health insurance? Are there better, less costly alternatives to expensive drugs, surgeries, and other treatments? Would lifestyle changes reduce the likelihood of needing heart surgery? These decisions about resource allocation or rationing cannot be made effectively by the government or insurance companies. The questions and the decisions are most likely different for different people, so they must be made by patients supported by their primary care physicians. For patients who are incapable of deciding, a parent or court-appointed guardian must be there to help. For patients with limited resources, Medicaid and other programs are available.

This chapter raises the point that resource allocation decisions outside of healthcare also impact quality of life and longevity, such as having nutritious food, a good education, and safe transportation. The chapter goes into some detail on transportation to illustrate the negative consequences of driving and the progress that has been made as the United States allocates resources to enhance innovations.

The second question was discussed to illustrate that every decision has risks, and risk has two parts: the consequences or outcomes and the probability that a certain consequence will happen. Consequences can be positive or negative. So when someone decides to drive a car or ride a bike, they understand that the probability of a good outcome, getting to their destination safely and enjoying the trip, is very high, and the chance of having a serious, life-threatening outcome is very small. People are rational, so they continue to drive cars and ride bikes because the chance of a life-threatening injury is small. They may take actions to avoid a negative outcome by driving defensively or riding the bike on marked trails rather than on roadways to reduce the probability of a negative outcome. They may also wear protective gear such as safety belts and helmets to mitigate the severity of their injuries if an accident does occur.

When patients control their healthcare, they along with their primary care physicians can assess the risk of a decision. The decision may have negative consequences, but the probability of these consequences may be very small. If they are rational, they should be willing to accept a small risk of a negative outcome. For example, patients considering whether to have physical therapy after surgery may opt to do the therapy at home rather than work with a physical therapist. Patients believe they are capable of doing the therapy at home, estimate the likelihood of a negative outcome to be very small, and save money by doing therapy at home. This is a perfectly rational trade-off that saves money while accepting a very small chance of a negative outcome. It is important to understand that therapy with a trained physical therapist may have negative consequences as well.

8.4 Driving Forces for Change

The essence for changing how healthcare trade-offs are made or, using less pleasant terminology, "how healthcare is rationed," is putting consumers back in their role as decision makers. This is difficult. Who wants to move from a situation in which consumers have as much care as they want when they want it and have to pay little or nothing for it to a system in which they have to make difficult decisions that require analyzing trade-offs and assessing risks? The answer, of course, is almost no one.

The driving force for this change comes from continued pushback by third-party payers who work through their insurance companies to hold the line on costs. In some cases, private sector employers opted to greatly increase their employee's portion of the insurance premium or to eliminate coverage altogether, which shifts responsibility for payment from employers to the employee but does not address the underlying problems. This process will continue to unfold over time and is likely to result in solutions that miss the heart of the problem.

Although there is a certain amount of reluctance to suggest that the government should have a role in redesigning healthcare, the reality is that government is already heavily involved in healthcare via Medicare, Medicaid, the Affordable Care Act, and other regulations as well as providing coverage for its employees. Several of the proposed remedies, including implementing patient-centered care, making drug costs affordable and fair, and reforming the legal system require government support. Ultimately, a coalition of third-party payers, insurers, hospitals, physicians, drug companies, and government representatives must provide leadership to put the consumer back in a position of responsibility. Without this critical and fundamental change, serious and effective redesign of the healthcare delivery system cannot be successful.

8.5 Impact of Making Effective Healthcare Trade-Offs on Healthcare Outcomes

Changing the process for making health trade-offs is central to improving the healthcare system in the United States. Following is a summary of the impacts of this issue on the relevant root causes, which are discussed in Chapter 2. These are closely related to the impact of rethinking and redesigning health insurance on the relevant root causes, discussed in the prior chapter.

1. Biased trade-off and high drug costs: When the consumer is put back into the position of decision maker, who must examine the costs and benefits of each action, it is much more likely that patients will make better, unbiased decisions about using healthcare services (root cause #2) and prescription drugs (root cause #6).
2. Unused facilities and equipment: More careful analysis of the trade-offs is likely to reduce healthcare usage, so there will be less demand for healthcare facilities and equipment (root cause #3).
3. Excessive legal liability and malpractice insurance costs: When patients make better trade-offs, they should consume less healthcare, which leads to fewer opportunities for errors and less legal liability and lower malpractice insurance costs (root cause #7).
4. Shortage of healthcare professionals: Better analysis of trade-offs should lead to consuming fewer resources, which should cause lower demand for physician services (root cause #8).

8.6 Summary of Recommendations

Following is a listing of the key recommendations contained in this chapter:

1. The new approach to rationing healthcare would lead to better decision making.
   a. Patient-centered care makes patients, supported by their primary care physicians, key decision makers. Patients would have access to information about diagnostic and treatment options, including their costs. They would understand and consider the risks of having healthcare and be willing to accept a small chance of a negative outcome.
   b. Wellness and prevention become critical elements, so the need to ration care is reduced because demand for healthcare is less.
   c. Improve the effectiveness of the healthcare delivery system to enhance patient safety and satisfaction and increase productivity, thereby freeing resources so access can be extended to those who do not have care.
2. Patients would be incentivized with lower premiums, deductibles, coinsurance, and copayments for providing feedback about care and working effectively with primary care physicians and insurers.
3. Medicaid patients and their primary care physicians would be incentivized with higher physician reimbursement when there is a long-term relationship between patients and physicians and patients prepare and follow PHPs.
4. Growing the U.S. economy creates high-quality jobs with healthcare benefits and allows the United States to reduce the percentage of the GDP spent on healthcare.
5. To provide lifesaving care for everyone who needs it, the United States must become healthier, so illnesses caused by lifestyle choices are reduced substantially, its healthcare system is made more efficient and less wasteful, and its economy grows to provide more resources.

References

1. MedicineNet.com. 2015. Definition of triage. http://www.medicinenet.com/script/main/art.asp?articlekey=16736 (accessed October 12, 2015).
2. Center for Medicare and Medicaid Services. 2014. National health expenditures by type of service and source of funds, CY 1960–2013. https://www.cms.gov/Research-Statistics-Data-and-Systems/Statistics-Trends-and-Reports/NationalHealthExpendData/NationalHealthAccountsHistorical.html (accessed October 11, 2015).
3. Organization for Economic Co-operation and Development (OECD). 2015. Health expenditures. http://www.oecd.org/els/health-systems/health-statistics.htm (accessed October 13, 2015).
4. US Debt Clock.org. 2015. US national debt. http://www.usdebtclock.org/ (accessed October 13, 2015).

5. Goins, C. 2012. Medicare faces unfunded liability of $38.6T, or $328,404 for each U.S. household. cnsnews.com, (April 23). http://www.usdebtclock.org/ (accessed October 13, 2015).
6. Kessler, G. 2013. Does the United States have $128 trillion in unfunded liabilities? *The Washington Post*, (October 23). http://cnsnews.com/news/article/medicare-faces -unfunded-liability-386t-or-328404-each-us-household (accessed October 13, 2015).
7. Rappleye, E. 2016. Healthcare outpaces social security spending for 1st time: Five things to know. Becker's: Hospital CFO, (January 25). http://www.beckershospitalreview .com/finance/healthcare-outpaces-social-security-spending-for-1st-time-5-things-to -know.html (accessed January 26, 2016).
8. Center for Medicare and Medicaid Services. 2012. National health expenditure high-lights. http://www.cms.gov/Research-Statistics-Data-and-Systems/Statistics-Trends-and -Reports/NationalHealthExpendData/downloads/highlights.pdf (accessed February 20, 2014).
9. World Bank. 2015. GDP (current US $). http://data.worldbank.org/indicator/NY.GDP .MKTP.CD (accessed October 13, 2015).
10. Wikipedia. 2015. List of motor vehicle deaths in the U. S. by year. https://en.wikipedia .org/wiki/List_of_motor_vehicle_deaths_in_U.S._by_year (accessed October 13, 2015).
11. Independent News. 2009. The man who saved a million lives: Nils Bohlin—Inventor of the seat belt. http://www.independent.co.uk/life-style/motoring/features/the -man-who-saved-a-million-lives-nils-bohlin-inventor-of-the-seatbelt-1773844.html (accessed October 15, 2015).
12. Wikipedia. 2015. Seat belt legislation in the United States. https://en.wikipedia.org /wiki/Seat_belt_legislation_in_the_United_States (accessed October 15, 2015).

Chapter 9

Improving Healthcare Strategy and Management

So far, the solution describes changing the role of patients so that they become the decision makers, the responsible parties, for their health and healthcare. Chapters 5 and 6 describe the most important issues, patient-centered care, wellness, and personal responsibility. The solution also proposes to alter health insurance plans so that patients, supported by their primary care physicians, can evaluate trade-offs and make good choices. Chapters 7 and 8 propose redesigning insurance plans and expecting patients to consider the full costs and benefits of the care they elect to receive. These elements of the solution go hand in hand as one reinforces the other.

Now, it is appropriate to consider providers, such as hospitals and healthcare professionals, who set the policies and procedures as well as design and proscribe the medical practices that define how healthcare is delivered. Hospital executives assemble and manage the resources needed to deliver care as they make decisions about facilities, equipment, and personnel as well as decide where and how to use those resources to satisfy patients' needs. Over the years, hospitals and healthcare professionals have responded effectively to patients' demands. Unfortunately, these demands have been distorted by a system that places too much emphasis on diagnosing and treating problems and pays too little attention to wellness and prevention. In fact, when healthcare insurance became popular after World War II, the primary purpose of insurance was to fix problems, and it often did not cover preventive testing let alone support wellness. In this environment, decisions were biased in favor of hospital stays, diagnostic tests, surgeries, drug therapies, and other treatments. Also, because patients often did not pay for services and therefore tended to ignore costs, providers paid little attention to cost control and efficiency.

Providers reacted by building more facilities, buying more equipment, and hiring more people.

If hospitals, clinics, and physicians are paid to treat sick patients rather than to create healthy ones, there is little reason to expect them to change how they behave. If the United States continues to pay more for healthcare, there is little reason to expect providers to control costs and increase efficiency. More recently, as third-party payers objected to unending cost increases, efforts began to control costs. As the changes described in Chapters 5 through 8 are made, providers will take additional steps to improve the healthcare delivery system so that it can respond both effectively and efficiently to these new priorities. A significant part of these efforts must address important strategic and resource management issues faced by healthcare organizations, especially hospitals. Other key parts of the solution are discussed in subsequent chapters, including the following:

1. Accelerating the use of information technology, Chapter 10
2. Making prescriptions drug costs more affordable, Chapter 11
3. Reducing the incidence of malpractice and legal liabilities, Chapter 12
4. Examining the roles of healthcare professionals and reconfiguring the provider network, Chapter 13

9.1 Nature of the Problem with Healthcare Organizations

A first question might be this: Why focus on healthcare organizations? Surely, there are other parts of the healthcare system that should be addressed. The logic for beginning with healthcare organizations, specifically hospitals, is clear. According to a Center for Medicare and Medicaid Services report, in 2012 hospital care accounted for about 31.5% ($882.3 billion divided by $2.8 trillion) of healthcare spending in the United States[1] (see Table 9.1). Physician and clinical services at 20.2% ($565 billion) was second. When administration is excluded, the prescription drug category at 9.4% ($263.3 billion) was third. When looking for savings, hospitals are a good place to start. Physician and clinical services as well as prescriptions drugs, topics of later chapters, are good places as well.

To understand the nature of the problems and the changes that need to be made, it is useful to review how hospitals evolved more than 100 years ago. At that time, hospitals were predominantly not-for-profit entities that were founded and supported by charitable institutions, usually religious groups, or by governments, usually cities, counties, or states. Their primary goal was to provide care, and they were often subsidized by these sponsors, which allowed the hospitals to provide charitable care. The words "profit" and "cost control" were not part of their vocabulary. Not-for-profit hospitals did not then and do not now pay property or income taxes because they are considered charities that are governed by trustees.

Table 9.1 U.S. Health Expenditures for 2012 (Billions of Dollars)

Type of Service	Amount	Percent
Hospital care	$882.3	31.5%
Physician and clinical services	$565.0	20.2%
Other professional services	$76.4	2.7%
Dental services	$110.9	4.0%
Other health, residential, and personal care services	$138.2	5.0%
Home healthcare	$77.8	2.8%
Nursing care facilities and continuing care retirement communities	$151.5	5.4%
Prescription drugs	$263.3	9.4%
Durable medical equipment	$41.3	1.5%
Other nondurable medical products	$53.7	1.9%
Administration	$322.3	11.5%
Structures and equipment	$115.7	4.1%
Total	$2798.4	100.0%

Source: The Center for Medicare and Medicaid Services. 2013. National healthcare expenditures 2012 highlights. http://www.cms.gov/Research-Statistics-Data -and-Systems/Statistics-Trends-and-Reports/NationalHealthExpendData/down loads/highlights.pdf.

Excess revenues are invested in improving hospital services. For-profit hospitals, a more recent phenomenon, are owned by private investors or shareholders of publically traded companies. Excess revenue or profits are reinvested in the hospital or returned to the investors.

As the U.S. population exploded in the late 19th and early 20th centuries, these facilities expanded rapidly. Population growth reaccelerated after World War II. Initially, hospitals could not build enough patient rooms, surgical suites, and delivery rooms to meet demand, but by the 1970s, the building boom had created excess capacity.

During the building boom and continuing today, medical technology improved markedly, and hospital length of stay has declined dramatically. An appendectomy that might hospitalize a patient for a week in the 1950s can now be done outpatient or with a one-day hospital stay. A meniscus surgery to repair a knee that once required a big incision and a lengthy hospital stay can be done easily and quickly without a night in the hospital. The patient is home only a few hours after surgery and is walking the next day. The hospital stay, therapy, medication, and complications from infection are reduced or eliminated.

Also, in the 1980s, the concept of a diagnosis-related group (DRG) began to be used when a patient had a particular condition, such as gall bladder surgery or pneumonia treatment. In essence, DRGs identify hospital-provided services and estimate the amount of resources needed to treat patients for their condition based on factors such as gender, age, and complications. DRGs are often used to reimburse hospitals and other healthcare providers at a standard rate rather than using the cost-plus approach, which was the previous practice.[2] The introduction of DRGs tended to decrease the length of stay as hospitals encouraged physicians to keep costs low.

A hundred years ago, and even today, healthcare providers operate in localized markets. Until the automobile became common, traveling long distances was not practical for the vast majority of the population. Most people did not have the financial means to travel, plus it was time-consuming and uncomfortable. To serve these small, localized markets, thousands of hospitals and other healthcare organizations emerged. Nearly every small city and many small towns had a hospital or clinic, and larger cities often had several. As a result, there are nearly 5700 registered hospitals in the United States, according to the American Hospital Association (AHA). Registered hospitals are those that meet AHA standards. Nearly 3000 are nongovernment, not-for-profit, community-based hospitals. There are about 1000 investor-owned, for-profit, community hospitals and about 1000 state and local government, community hospitals. Those remaining are federal government hospitals (about 200), psychiatric hospitals that are not part of the federal government (about 400), and less than 100 in other catagories.[3] Figure 9.1 has the breakdown.

Also, healthcare became more technical, requiring bigger facilities and more expensive equipment. The red tape from government regulations and complicated insurance reporting requirements forced hospitals to create larger bureaucracies with more managers. As a result, small hospitals faced exploding costs. They were unable to fund major equipment investments and had to absorb large increases in middle management costs without raising prices or receiving additional subsidies.

Fortunately for hospitals and other providers, as increases in demand and cost accelerated after World War II, many people in the United States did not pay for their healthcare. Coverage was provided by employer-paid health insurance that often had no copayments, no coinsurance fees, and very small if any deductibles. So the growing pains of hospitals were pushed into the future. The problems reemerged in the 1970s and 1980s as employers balked at paying ever-increasing costs and put pressure on providers to limit care and reduce costs through practices such as preapproval for treatments and cutting reimbursement levels. Employers began to ask employees to pay a share of their insurance premiums and healthcare costs.

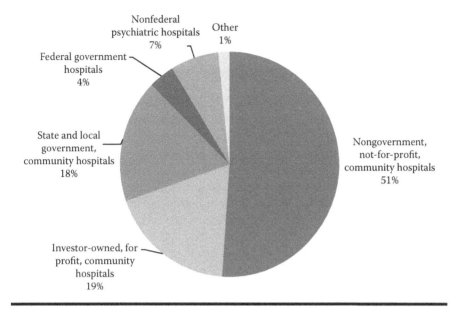

Figure 9.1 U.S. hospital types and percentages. (From American Hospital Association. 2013. Fast Facts on US Hospitals. http://www.aha.org/research/rc /stat-studies/fast-facts.shtml.)

To summarize, following is an overview of the issues facing hospitals and other healthcare providers as well as possible solutions.

1. Lack of scale in managing a complex organization: An evolving healthcare delivery system generated a large number of small hospitals and clinics, which were unable to invest in the latest technology or cope with high administrative costs. Even though some hospitals have closed their doors and others have merged or joined operating groups to share expenses, these problems still exist. More needs to be done in restructuring healthcare delivery. This includes mergers and acquisitions to increase scale; strategic and operating partnerships that allow hospitals to invest jointly in the latest technology both medical and managerial; and ways for rural, regional, and national medical centers to work together to provide full-service, top-quality care to every corner of the United States.

2. Mismatch between healthcare demand and capacity: Overbuilding, DRGs, and advances in medical technology have caused surplus capacity in some hospital services, most notably hospital beds. Idle beds are "perishable capacity" because they do not generate revenue and their unused time can never be recovered. The national bed occupancy rate in 2012 was only 61%, down from 64% in 2006.[4] On the other hand, advances in medical technology have required hospitals and clinics to add capacity in outpatient surgical care

even as beds are idle. Unused beds drive up costs, so hospitals must try to reconcile this difference between capacity and demand, yet they must invest capital in other parts of their business.

3. Tug of war between management and clinical staff: In the early days of hospital care, nearly all employees had hands-on contact with patients. Over time, hospitals got bigger and added sophisticated technology. They also faced regulatory, patient privacy, and insurance paperwork requirements. This drove the need for professional managers, experts in technical fields, such as information systems, as well as managers and workers who provide non-healthcare-services, such as housekeeping. Hospitals should assess the level of resources used to complete these nonclinical tasks and determine if these resources can be reduced by applying technology or be outsourced in cases in which suppliers have the expertise, lower costs, and/or better technology.

4. Coping with suppliers: The previous point suggests outsourcing as a way to address situations in which hospitals find it difficult to duplicate a supplier's expertise and/or cost structure. However, there is more to managing a supply chain than deciding to outsource or not to outsource. Effective supply chain management requires hospitals to (a) identify the criteria used to judge suppliers, which is likely to be different when outsourcing surgical maintenance compared to housekeeping, (b) determine a process to recruit and select suppliers, (c) develop a program to evaluate supplier performance and provide feedback to help them improve, and (d) ensure that suppliers are effective partners who understand how its actions impact the hospital.

5. Improving performance: Hospitals should find ways to enhance their clinical and managerial activities. Process improvement techniques, such as Lean thinking and Six Sigma quality, can be applied to clinical tasks to improve outcomes. These techniques can also be applied to administrative systems to reduce delays in paperwork processing and improve the comprehensiveness and accuracy of reporting systems. This provides managers with timely and accurate information for better and faster decision making.

The following sections discuss ways to address each of these important issues.

9.2 Restructuring Healthcare Organizations

Looking at the AHA data in a different way, there are approximately 2000 rural community hospitals and 3000 urban hospitals.[3] So the average state has about 100 rural and urban hospitals, a fairly large number. Texas has nearly 400, and Vermont has fewer than 10.[5] When the frequency distribution of hospitals based on bed size is examined, approximately 24% have fewer than 50 beds, about 47% have fewer than 100 beds, and only about 16% have 300 beds or more. So the United States has many hospitals and about half of them are small with fewer than 100 beds.[6]

These small hospitals, which are typically in rural areas or small communities, usually lack the size and scale to pay for the buildings, equipment, technology, regulatory reporting requirements, privacy laws, and health insurance processing practices, which are essential to deliver today's healthcare.

A way must be found to increase hospitals' ability, especially small rural hospitals, to invest in the latest equipment and technology and cope with regulatory and reporting requirements. An obvious part of the solution is to have mergers or acquisitions among hospitals to build economies of scale. When a merger or an acquisition involves closing one or more hospitals, this will take capacity out of the system, but it only works well in medium and large cities with multiple hospitals. A second way is to create strategic and operating partnerships that allow hospitals to share resources. A third part of the solution is to create tiered relationships among hospitals within the United States so that rural hospitals can partner with regional hospitals and national medical centers to provide a well-defined pathway so that their patients can receive the highly specialized care a rural hospital cannot provide. This is certainly not intended to reflect negatively on rural hospitals that provide excellent care. It is an acceptance of the fact that small hospitals do not have the resources to address all problems presented by their patients.

9.2.1 Mergers and Acquisitions

In many industries, mergers and acquisitions have been and are likely to continue to be ways that companies build economies of scale that allow them to cope with large capital investments in technology and equipment. These actions have worked well for manufacturers because goods can be produced in one part of the United States, or even outside the United States, and shipped anywhere. Most people are unconcerned about where the good is produced as long as it is competitively priced and convenient to purchase: online with home delivery, at a dealer's showroom, or at a local retail store.

A merger is a legal combination of two or more entities that form a single company, and an acquisition is one company purchasing another. Hospitals engage in mergers and acquisitions to increase size and financial strength, which allows them to cope with high levels of fixed costs, invest in high-technology equipment, meet specialized needs, and deal with compliance requirements. Mergers and acquisitions can also help hospitals build a brand and attract the best healthcare professionals. They result in multihospital healthcare systems, such as Kaiser Permanente, which is a nonprofit group headquartered in Oakland, California, that has 38 hospitals and serves more than nine million people in eight states and the District of Columbia.[7]

One question to consider is the following: How do mergers and acquisitions impact access to care? Although patients may be willing to travel for special needs, the markets for primary and emergency care are local. When mergers or acquisitions involve closing a hospital, remaining hospitals can more fully utilize their existing resources, including hospital beds, surgery rooms, information systems, and other fixed cost assets. The closing leads to reductions in middle managers because the managerial workforce at the closed facility will no longer be needed. It is likely that the physicians and other hands-on medical staff will still be needed because demand for care has not changed, but many of the people who plan, manage, and schedule the medical staff are likely to be eliminated.

Closing a hospital and having its patients use other facilities is an effective way, maybe the most effective way, to reduce costs because it takes unneeded capacity out of the system. However, mergers or acquisitions may not work well in rural areas and small communities where there is only one facility.

9.2.2 Strategic and Operating Partnerships

Operating partnerships are agreements among two or more organizations to share resources used to produce the goods and services that customers demand. It has many of the same advantages as mergers and acquisitions but does not require consolidating ownership. For hospitals, it is likely to involve the following:

1. Sharing access to equipment and facilities
2. Sharing physician specialists and other highly trained personnel, who would be underutilized if employed by one hospital
3. Using common systems to manage information and paperwork
4. Creating a joint purchasing function to save operating costs and to earn volume discounts on prices for products purchased by the hospitals plus shipping discounts for these products

Operating partnerships allow hospitals to have better systems and services, improve management and information technology, and lower purchasing costs and prices paid. Strategic partnerships normally involve the elements of operating partnerships but go further. They could also include the following:

1. Joint marketing programs to attract new patients
2. Joint fund-raising efforts to deal with capital needs
3. Joint financial planning and investment to ensure that capital is well spent and investments achieve the best returns while keeping the costs of these activities low
4. Joint accounting and billing systems to reduce the costs of these clerical activities
5. Joint human resource development and recruiting activities to attract and retain the best managers and clinical staff

Strategic and operating partnerships allow hospitals to invest in and share the latest technologies, both medical and managerial. They can be used effectively to unite rural hospitals with regional and national medical centers to provide full-service, top-quality care to patients in every corner of the United States.

9.2.3 Creating Tiers among Hospitals

As shown in Figure 9.2, assume that hospitals operate at three levels. Tier 1 is rural hospitals and hospitals in small cities and towns. For convenience, these are labeled rural hospitals. Tier 2 includes hospitals in medium and large cities where there are multiple hospitals to serve the city and its suburbs. These are called regional medical centers. Tier 3 includes the top clinics, hospitals, and academic medical centers in the United States. These facilities have national and international reputations for high-quality care, such as the Cleveland Clinic or the Mayo Clinic. These are referred to as national medical centers. Although this classification scheme may not neatly accommodate all hospitals, it is useful for illustrative purposes.

Patients served by rural hospitals must have high-quality primary and emergency care close by as well as access to the best specialized care when needed. This requires working relationships that reach across these three tiers. These relationships could be the result of mergers or acquisitions, or they could be created by using the partnerships described in the prior section.

Rural hospitals would have a close working relationship with regional medical centers. They would share equipment and, as shown in Figure 9.2, would use the same electronic health record (EHR) system so that patient information could be passed back and forth in real time. They would also have the latest communication technology, so physicians at the rural hospital and the regional medical center could have virtual meetings to discuss a patient's condition at any time without the costs and delays of traveling. When physicians at a rural hospital consult with physicians at the regional medical center, the diagnoses and testing processes move forward seamlessly—that is, there are no delays, and outcomes are not impacted by distance. As shown in Figure 9.2, when patients are transferred to the regional medical center, appropriate arrangements are made, which could include moving the patient by personal vehicle, ambulance, or life-flight helicopter, depending on

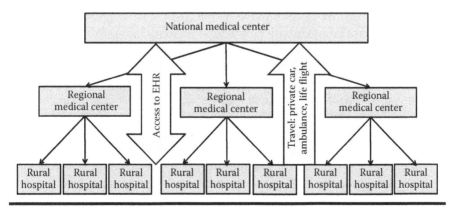

Figure 9.2   Linking rural hospitals, regional medical centers, and national medical centers to provide high-quality healthcare to every corner of the United States.

the patient's condition. Similar information, communication, and transportation links would exist between regional medical centers and national medical centers.

ProMedica is a locally owned, not-for-profit, multihospital system in Toledo, Ohio, that serves northwest Ohio and southeast Michigan. It has acquired rural hospitals and regional medical centers[8] to build economies of scale. Also, ProMedica's facilities are located in close proximity to the internationally known and well-respected Cleveland Clinic and the nationally known academic medical centers at the University of Michigan. It has recently signed a partnership with the University of Toledo's College of Medicine to invest in medical research and physician training through residency programs.[9] ProMedica is positioning itself to provide pathways to care for all the people living in the region.

9.3 Rationalizing Demand and Capacity

Related to the need for hospitals to build scale to keep costs low is the mismatch between capacity and demand for hospitals' basic service: patient beds. Some may ask, why is that important? After all, what harm is there in having extra capacity? In fact, some may argue that extra capacity is a good way to cope with unexpected events.

The harm should be clear; hospitals invest capital to acquire facilities, equipment, and beds whether they use them or not. They are also paying to heat, cool, clean, and maintain all the rooms, including the idle ones. The costs for idle rooms are not obvious on hospital bills because they are buried in other charges. Patients pay a portion of the costs for idle rooms, but third-party payers cover most of the costs. In the final analysis, taxpayers and consumers ultimately pay the lion's share of this cost through (a) taxes paid to the government, which funds Medicare and Medicaid, and (b) when buying products from the companies that pay the insurance premiums for their employees.

There is an element of truth in the notion that the United States should have some spare capacity to cope with emergencies. After all, healthcare should not be run like the airlines with nearly every plane crowded and full and, in some cases, customers being turned away because flights are overbooked. The question is, on the average, should 39% of the beds be unoccupied in order to have a comfortable cushion, or is a smaller cushion sufficient? Recall that the national occupancy rate for hospital beds in 2012 was 61% and has trended down from 64% in 2006,[4] so the problem of overcapacity seems to be getting worse.

Having 39 out of 100 hospitals beds idle as a safety factor seems excessive, and it is expensive. It is excessive because the ratio of unused to used beds is 39 divided by 61 or approximately 64%, meaning that demand for hospitals beds could be 64% higher than current average demand without running out of capacity. How expensive is it? Recall, hospitals costs were about 31.5% ($882.3 billion) of all U.S. healthcare costs in 2012. Hospital beds and the people, equipment, and facilities that support these beds are a major element in hospital costs. Evidence of this high cost is the average cost of a one-day hospital stay in the United States: Government hospitals at $1831 per day, nonprofit hospitals at $2214 per day, and for-profit hospitals at $1747 per day.[10] These costs are high, in part, because hospitals must cover the cost of unoccupied beds.

Statisticians would argue that the amount of extra capacity, called the safety factor, should be determined by the variation in demand as measured by the standard deviation of daily demand. Greater variation means a higher safety factor is required. Statistical techniques can be used to determine if it is reasonable to cut the percentage of unused hospital beds from 39% to 25%, 20%, 15%, or even lower. It is likely that the variance in daily demand for hospital beds differs from state to state and rural to urban areas. If so, the safety factors for different hospitals may be different. If healthcare is subject to market forces, the laws of supply and demand should guide decision makers to an appropriate safety factor. As the number of idle beds is reduced, it is essential to prepare contingency plans that enable hospitals to adapt their facilities and work together to face the most extreme emergencies.

The important question is how and where to reduce capacity. Market forces should decide which hospitals to close or have their capacity reduced. As a hospital's occupancy rate for beds drops, it should generate less revenue. In a free market, once revenue is insufficient to cover the hospital's full costs, management must decide to close it, reduce its capacity, or go bankrupt. Shedding capacity reduces the number of beds, thus allowing the remaining hospitals to improve their occupancy rate, increase revenue, and take advantage of economies of scale. The United States should not create a government plan that makes these decisions, and it does not want government policy or insurance reimbursement practices to incentivize hospitals to retain unneeded beds.

Also, the country does not need a government moratorium on hospital construction because there are parts of the United States that are growing rapidly and may need more capacity or at least do not need to reduce it. There are also cases in which it is necessary to replace old, outdated hospitals that have suffered through a dozen or more expansions and renovations. These facilities have jumbled, almost chaotic, layouts that are inefficient because managers as well as clinical and clerical staffs must take circuitous routes to do their work. Moving patients, equipment, and medical supplies around the hospital can be a herculean effort. These hospitals are hard to manage because people are scattered, making communication and coordination difficult. Plus, it is nearly impossible for patients to get from one point to another without continuous and expensive guidance from staff.

The question of where to reduce capacity should also be decided by market forces. The caveat is that adequate coverage for rural areas is essential. Healthcare is similar to other important services, such as mail delivery and primary and secondary education. Rural communities need access to basic healthcare as well as pathways to specialized care through partnerships with regional and national medical centers. This does not mean that every rural community must have a hospital. It does mean they need reasonable access to care. As with many issues, *reasonable* is a variable that is difficult to determine. A typical bureaucratic approach would be to set a standard that a rural community should be no more than 50 miles from a hospital, but such standards are arbitrary. For example, traveling 100 miles on interstate highways may be faster and easier than traveling 50 miles on country roads. Also, any policy needs to deal with exceptional circumstances. For example, Alaska has about 750,000 people spread across 663,268 square miles of land, including the remote Aleutian Islands, which extend hundreds of miles into the Bering Strait. This type of planning and decision making should be done at the state rather than the federal level, so differences can be effectively addressed.

There is another important element of capacity. Although there are too many hospital beds, there are other hospital services that are or will be in short supply. Demand for outpatient services is likely to increase, putting pressure on existing resources. By the way, this is likely to put more downward pressure on demand for beds. Also, if wellness and prevention are key elements of the solution, there must be ways to deliver wellness education, monitor patients' health screenings, and provide more preventive testing. This too should reduce the demand for hospital beds. The emphasis on wellness and prevention will require hospitals to reach into the community to gather, organize, store, and provide access to key data that will be collected at physician's offices, pharmacies, urgent care clinics, and other service providers. This may not require additional physical space, but it will require information systems and technologies, which hospitals are only now beginning to use effectively.

9.4 Addressing the Size and Scope of Middle Management

After World War II, demand for healthcare increased for a variety of reasons:

1. The birth rate increased dramatically as the baby boomer generation was born.
2. Advances in medical technology created new and innovative diagnostic and treatment options that stimulated demand.
3. More people had greater access to health insurance, which drove their out-of-pocket costs for care to zero or close to zero.
4. A more affluent society created greater healthcare expectations.

Hospitals responded by expanding facilities and services, and as hospitals grew, the need for professional managers became evident. Later, as mergers, acquisitions, and partnerships began, more managers were needed to plan and coordinate actions among multiple facilities that were spread across a region, state, or even the nation. In response, the management side of healthcare grew, resulting in large, expensive, hierarchical structures that competed for resources with clinical services.

Not only are these structures expensive, they tend to retard decision making and limit the hospital's ability to respond quickly to problems and opportunities. Issues and information move up the hierarchy for resolution until they find the right decision maker, someone who is willing to make a decision, hopefully a good one. The decision maker consults with other managers, makes a decision and sends it down the hierarchy, and details are added by subordinates to facilitate implementation. These details often take time to discuss and resolve. In most cases, the process takes too long, and even if the decision is a good one, it is often too late, so problems fester and opportunities are missed.

Many organizations in other industries, such as automotive, insurance, and banking, faced these problems decades earlier, and they responded by reducing hierarchies and pushing decision-making authority and responsibility down the organizations. These organizations struggled with the following question: What is the right balance between managers and workers? In manufacturing, it is the balance between supervisors and operators; in insurance, it is between managers and agents; and in investment banking, it is between managers and stockbrokers. The tendency has been to streamline middle management; reduce direct supervision; and expect the operators, agents, and brokers to make decisions and take responsibility. This requires well-trained and educated workers with the skills that allow them to understand the overall goals and objectives of the company, see how their part of the work impacts the desired outcomes, and execute accordingly.

This is happening in the automotive industry when assembly line workers are taking on much more responsibility for their workspace and equipment, including process improvements, maintenance and machine repairs, and reshaping their work to enhance safety and product quality. These duties were once performed by supervisors, technicians, and engineers. These specialists still exist, but there are fewer of them, and their role is now supportive, supplying specific expertise and helping to overcome bureaucratic and technical barriers associated with creating and implementing change.

Hospitals have a head start on implementing this approach because they have a well-educated clinical workforce:

1. Physicians know the strengths and weakness of existing processes, can articulate the desired outcomes, and can generate ideas to improve those outcomes.
2. Nurses, therapists, and technicians are highly educated, and they understand their work as well as the impediments to doing it better.

Involving these workers in process and quality improvement efforts should be standard operating procedure. Hospitals should encourage, incentivize, and empower their clinical workforce to have a greater role in designing, organizing, and managing the processes that deliver care. The clinical workforce understands patients' concerns, and their knowledge is vital in many applications, including creating and implementing ways to collect and disseminate patient data. They understand a broad range of problems from admitting patients to releasing patients and most everything in between.

Involving clinical staff is important for another reason: securing their buy-in for change. When clinical staff participates and leads efforts to improve the way work is done, not only are the solutions more likely to address the underlying problems, but the clinical staff has a vested interest in achieving success. When a process is evaluated and a new one is designed and implemented by consultants, there is a tendency for clinical staff to push back and seek reasons why the new approach won't work, especially at the first sign of trouble. A likely response to patients who complain about a new process is the following: "This wasn't my idea." The response is not unique to healthcare. It is human nature. One thing that is different about healthcare from other industries is the power physicians have, so if they are on the outside looking in, there is little chance for success. On the other hand, when the clinical staff is involved and committed, they will look for ways to succeed.

Also, hospitals should carefully examine activities being done by hospital staff that could be done more effectively and efficiently by outside experts. Some are nonmedical activities, such as food, laundry, and janitorial services. The savings can come in two parts. When performed inside the hospital, these activities require managers to plan and schedule the work. It is possible, maybe even likely, that the management costs in the hospital are more than the management cost incurred if suppliers plan and oversee the work. Second, there may be operational savings as suppliers apply their technology and expertise to do the job better, faster, and cheaper. In addition, there may be medical activities that require special knowledge and equipment, such as maintaining surgical suites, which hospitals may choose to outsource because acquiring the expertise and the sophisticated tools to do the work is too expensive.

9.5 Designing and Building Effective Supply Chains

When hospitals consider outsourcing, they face two important decisions: Which activities should an organization outsource? How should an organization design and manage its suppliers? There are entire books[11] written on when and how to outsource because this decision has many strategic and operational considerations, which are discussed briefly here.

9.5.1 Deciding What to Outsource

This decision is not based solely or even primarily on lowering labor costs because labor costs are only one small part of the decision. The decision to outsource should include considering whether a supplier is better across the following set of factors, including costs, than the organization itself. Which options to consider are whether it

1. Offers high-quality, reliable, and consistent service
2. Delivers the service in a timely manner
3. Has expert knowledge
4. Develops innovations that improve performance
5. Holds patents on proprietary technology
6. Has sufficient volume to achieve economies of scale and lower costs

To begin, outsourcing is a strategic decision in any organization, and hospitals are no exception. A company like Apple outsources all of its manufacturing activities but holds tight to product design and marketing to protect the Apple brand. GE Aviation has a tight grip on product design and maintains ownership of production because these factors determine the safety, quality, and performance of its jet engines, and these outcomes are critical for long-term sales growth. These companies do not outsource work that determines their reputation with customers or is central to accomplishing their mission.

For hospitals, outsourcing can begin with things, such as food, laundry, and janitorial services, that are readily available commodities. Here, poor performance, such as a bad meal, which many patients have actually come to expect, may be annoying, but a bad meal is not a serious or life-threatening error, such as leaving sponges inside patients after surgery or giving patients the wrong medication. Once hospitals understand the outsourcing process and its risks, they can move toward outsourcing medical services that can be routinized and are not part of the hospital's brand, such as laboratory testing and pharmacy management. They may carve out activities such as emergency room (ER) services for suppliers to run. Hospitals may want to think twice before allowing suppliers to own and operate their surgical centers or respiratory treatment facilities. If suppliers perform these key functions, what gives the hospital its competitive advantage? The hospital's reputation is in the hands of a supplier, and one significant error could damage its reputation and increase its legal liability. This means that outsourcing is a multifaceted decision based on a variety of criteria and not a search for cost savings alone.

Outsourcing is a high-level management tool that allows organizations to position themselves for success. Outsourcing makes sense when it does the following:

1. Enables hospitals to focus resources: When hospitals outsource an activity, they do not have to invest in the skills, equipment, technologies, and managers needed to run this area or improve its performance. As a result, hospitals have more capital dollars and management time to spend on activities that help them build competitive advantages and separate themselves from their competitors. But hospitals must work with suppliers to set performance goals

related to quality, safety, and costs; collect data to assess progress toward those goals; and provide feedback to suppliers so that outcomes improve. This goal-setting, assessment, and feedback cycle should also be used when working with internally managed activities.

2. Increases innovation: When hospitals outsource a service to a supplier who specializes in this activity, the supplier should be able to spot opportunities to improve performance in various ways, including changing equipment, improving the skill level of its workforce, or applying new practices to reduce costs and improve quality. Because it serves many hospitals, the supplier is likely to have a critical mass of experts who have the knowledge to drive innovation. Plus, the supplier can spread the cost of pursuing innovation across all of the hospitals it serves, so it has more resources to invest in innovation than a single hospital or even a small group of hospitals.

3. Fills missing expertise: A hospital may simply lack knowledge in a specific area, and the best way to cope with the deficiency is outsourcing. For example, hospitals are working with outside experts to design and implement EHRs and other important information technology (IT) projects. They are also beefing up their internal IT staffs to provide basic capabilities, advise top management on IT needs, and work with these external IT providers. Hospitals often outsource maintenance and repairs of sophisticated and expensive equipment because they lack the knowledge and technology to do it themselves.

4. Gains access to proprietary technology: In other cases, suppliers have proprietary technology that hospitals cannot duplicate even if they wanted to. The only option is to outsource.

5. Allows suppliers to achieve economies of scale: Looking at this from the suppliers' perspective, they have the opportunity to combine the demand from several hospitals and build economies of scale to provide services at much lower costs than an individual hospital. In this situation, suppliers achieve higher utilizing of their equipment, facilities, and workforce. Suppliers pass along part of these savings to hospitals in lower service fees.

When the benefits of outsourcing, such as a clearer focus on creating competitive advantage, more innovation, better quality, and access to proprietary technology, are combined with lower costs, outsourcing may be the right choice. Outsourcing must be carefully examined and selected only when it makes sense across multiple criteria. It is not just a cost-saving tool.

9.5.2 Designing and Managing the Supply Chain

Supply chains and outsourcing involve important decisions that may require high-level inputs from an executive steering committee. This committee provides top management with a mechanism to form policies and procedures that govern outsourcing as well as an oversight role that assesses the performance of outsourcing.

After deciding to outsource an activity, success depends on designing and managing the relationship with the supplier, which begins by understanding how the outsourced activity affects the hospital's ability to meet patients' expectations. Based on the following steps, hospitals should work hard to transform these expectations into an effective, efficient, workable relationship with its suppliers:

1. Understanding patient expectations
2. Determining supplier capabilities
3. Identifying one or more metrics to measure each capability
4. Picking a target for each metric
5. Designing and implementing plans and programs to increase supplier performance
6. Providing feedback to suppliers
7. Starting again by reviewing this process to achieve continuing improvements

The process for designing and managing a supply chain begins when hospitals engage in their strategic planning processes where they identify what factors are most important to their customers and set overall goals and objectives for customer satisfaction and hospital results. From these goals, hospital leadership must determine what capabilities suppliers should have to work effectively to meet patients' expectations. For example, food service affects patients in at least three ways: good taste and presentation, on-time delivery, and appropriate nutrition that promotes healing. These capabilities must be converted into metrics, such as scores on a patient survey that assesses food quality and timely delivery plus an appraisal of the food's nutritional value. For ER care, the capabilities would be things such as response time, patient safety, and quality. Response time can be measured by collecting time stamps when a patient arrives and at each point in the care process. Patient safety and quality of care can be measured by things such as complications and return visits for the same issue.

The first three steps—patient expectations, capabilities, and metrics—should be established prior to identifying a pool of suppliers. With this information, hospitals can begin a proactive program to recruit suppliers rather than a passive one that relies only on those who seek out the hospital's business. If the pool is created prior to knowing patient expectations, capabilities, and metrics, the supplier selection process will be without direction and will likely end up focusing on what the pool of suppliers does well.

To begin supplier evaluation, a hospital sourcing team determines the importance of each metric and rates the potential supplier on the metric, using a 10-point scale or something similar. Not every metric, and its underlying capability, has the same importance. For example, the nutritional value of the food may be more important than timely delivery. An importance rank is multiplied by the rating for each metric to determine a score. When these scores are summed for the supplier, each one has a total score that is used to determine the supplier's relative performance. Based on the total score and information gathered through interviews and site visits, a decision is made.

Now, steps 4 through 7 can begin as the hospital and the supplier may use benchmarking and other tools to set a target for each metric. The supplier must be committed to reach the target, so achieving supplier buy-in is essential. The supplier working with the hospital establishes a set of plans and programs to continuously improve performance. The hospital collects performance data and periodically provides feedback to the supplier about its performance. Review meetings with the supplier can be used to determine if decisions about capabilities, metrics, targets, or other elements of the hospital–supplier relationship should be changed. The essence of the interaction with the supplier is to provide continuing feedback that drives the supplier to meet the needs of the hospital.

9.6 Improving Managerial and Clinical Processes

Many people outside of healthcare and some insiders suggest that hospitals should become strong advocates of process improvement aimed at enhancing business functions, such as handling insurance claims and hospital admissions, and clinical tasks, such as dispensing medicine and providing respiratory therapy. Some hospitals have embraced process improvement, and others have tried it without building commitment and achieved mixed results; still others have not begun. In some instances, there is resistance from healthcare professionals who believe that applying these techniques, which were developed and tested in manufacturing, cannot work well in healthcare because hospitals deliver highly personal, customized care.

When these techniques, originally called just-in-time and statistical quality control, were successfully implemented by the Japanese to turnaround its automotive industry after World War II, U.S. automakers were slow to embrace these ideas. They claimed that there were fundamental, cultural differences between the United States and Japan, and those differences explained why these techniques could not work in the United States. History shows that U.S. companies were wrong. The Japanese automakers opened efficient and profitable plants in the United States making high-quality, low-cost cars and took market share from U.S. companies. For more than three decades, U.S. companies have been fighting back, implementing newer versions of these techniques called Lean thinking and Six Sigma quality. After decades of work, the design, quality, and costs of U.S. cars are competitive with the Japanese and other global producers.

The point of this digression is that new ideas, especially those that involve radical changes, meet resistance, and the resistance is the greatest when the company or industry facing the change is doing well. For many years, hospitals, like the U.S. automotive industry after World War II, could pass along costs to consumers without negative consequences. There was little global competition. This created an attitude or culture that did not value cost reduction and process improvement.

Well-designed processes and procedures carry less risk, meaning there is a smaller chance of making a serious error. As an example, after removing a kidney from a donor, the clinical staff at a medical center accidently dumped the healthy kidney in the trash. What was the primary cause of this error? The existing procedures were not well understood by everyone in the surgery room. The checks and double-checks were insufficient. This was a patient safety issue that harmed both the donor and the recipient. It also hurt the center's reputation, impaired the psyche of the people in the surgery room, and cost the medical center a significant amount of money to find and implant another kidney and settle the legal claims. In this case, everyone lost. A better process would be safer and less costly.

Some leading-edge hospitals and clinics fully embrace these techniques. Their success has come not by hiring consultants to make changes but rather by hiring experts in systems engineering and process improvement who involve clinical experts not just as team members but as leaders. When this happens, the search for improvements focuses on improving patient safety, enhancing quality, reducing response time, and, oh by the way, cutting costs. There is ample evidence across many industries that doing a job right the first time and doing it quickly without mistakes leads to higher quality and lower costs.

As discussed in detail in Chapter 1, the Mayo Clinic used this approach to reduce dramatically the number of retained surgical items (RSIs), sponges in that case. A team, led by a surgeon and a systems engineer, studied the problem, considered the points of vulnerability, and tried different solutions. Eventually, a new system was developed and implemented with each sponge having a unique RFID tag. The surgical teams would scan each sponge as it was used and scan the sponges at the end of surgery to ensure that all were removed from the patient. The new method eliminated retained sponges over a three-year period.[12] The benefits are obvious.

University of Utah Health Care has made great strides, not only in understanding and measuring the costs of its services, but in finding ways to control those costs. As a result of these efforts, its costs over a one-year period have declined by 0.5%, and costs at other academic medical centers in the region have increased by 2.9%. Using cost data to understand and identify areas in which cost and care improvements can be made, the hospital has revised practices, cut unnecessary costs, and attained more effective and efficient care. Here are two examples:

1. Internal medicine physicians examined spending on routine lab tests and found that a large percentage were unnecessary. They implemented a policy requiring residents to justify lab tests. As a result, orders dropped and costs declined without negatively impacting care.
2. Cardiologists asked what caused differences in the costs and outcomes of bypass surgery. They standardized care after surgery and permitted nurses to give certain medicines and oxygen as the nurses saw fit. As a result of these changes, patients spent less time in the hospital, had fewer complications, and costs declined by 30%.[13]

At least three keys to success jump out: (a) physicians and other clinical professionals are involved in the process of determining and implementing change, (b) decision making is delegated to the "worker/nurse" on the "shop/hospital" floor (manufacturing terminology in quotes for emphasis), and (c) standardizing care makes a difference. Standardizing care obviously does not mean there are no deviations when circumstances dictate. It means that care begins with best practices, which for most cases leads to superior outcomes, and care is adjusted to meet changes in patients' conditions.

Even though healthcare and manufacturing are different, improving quality, reducing response time, eliminating wasteful activities, and making customers/patients safer and more satisfied are important in both industries. Differences can be addressed by the way these ideas are applied. As with the Mayo Clinic and University of Utah Health Care, other hospitals need to develop these skills in-house rather than hiring external consultants to tell them what to do. The clinic staff must be committed, supportive, and involved. *Committed* means they think it is a good idea. *Supportive* means they endorse spending hospital resources to hire full-time employees who understand how these techniques work. Most importantly, *involved* means clinicians participate actively, including leadership roles in selecting projects, redesigning processes, and implementing successful solutions. Once hospitals complete a few successful projects, clinical leaders become the best salespersons for expanding these efforts.

It is beyond the scope of this book to fully discuss the successful implementation of Lean thinking, Six Sigma quality, and other techniques, and why these techniques are important and useful in healthcare. For those who are interested, two books provide more details, including many examples: L. L. Berry and K. D. Seltman's *Management Lessons from Mayo Clinic* (2008, McGraw Hill) and J. Arthur's *Lean Six Sigma for Hospitals* (2011, McGraw Hill).

9.7 Driving Forces for Change

As with many of these changes, the power of the purse is usually persuasive in driving change. In most industries, the power is held by customers who describe what they want and pay the bill. In healthcare, third-party payers—government or insurance companies—pay most of the bill. So an important step is for these payers to set expectations for hospital behavior. They should work with hospitals to address the major items discussed in this chapter: building scale, matching capacity with demand, downsizing middle management when appropriate, creating effective relationships with suppliers, and engaging in process improvements to maintain or improve hospital performance while reducing costs. Ultimately, it is reimbursement that motivates hospitals to take actions.

Patients also have a role, and increasingly this role is based on self-interest as patients are being asked to pay an ever-increasing share of their healthcare costs. As with other products, patients should ask the price of the service, know how it may benefit them, understand its risks, and make an informed decision about purchasing it. Patients are on the front line of healthcare and should provide balance to the discussion about the benefits and the costs of services. Otherwise, the decision is biased in favor of saying yes to the test, procedure, or treatment.

There are other entities that are relevant in helping hospitals make these changes. The American Hospital Association (AHA) has a program called "Hospitals in Pursuit of Excellence" that offers educational webinars and provides guidance for performance improvements. It also has a certificate center that designs and administers certification programs to confirm mastery of important topics in healthcare management. The AHA could play an important role in helping hospitals improve performance. The Accreditation Commission for Health Care (ACHC) is a national organization that accredits hospitals. The ACHC can set standards that direct hospitals toward policies and procedures that will improve the hospital's operations. The American College of Physician Executives (ACPE) provides education and certification through its certified physician executive program. This becomes an important training ground for future leaders.

9.8 Impact of Improving Healthcare Strategy and Management on Healthcare Outcomes

Rethinking healthcare strategy and management has multiple and, in some cases, conflicting outcomes. In some cases, it involves shuttering capacity; in other cases, outsourcing activities; and in still other cases, building new facilities. Process improvement can also enhance hospital performance by better utilizing existing resources so that fewer resources are needed to do the same amount of work. Following is a summary of the impacts of these ideas on the relevant root causes, which are discussed in Chapter 2.

1. Unused facilities and equipment: Improving healthcare strategy and management should have an interesting impact on facilities and equipment. It should bring into closer alignment the demand and capacity for hospital beds, most likely by reducing the number of beds. It may also drive some small and inefficient hospitals to close while building new hospitals that are better designed to meet current needs, including more outpatient services. With process improvement, it is possible to better use existing facilities and equipment, freeing resources to treat other patients and eliminating resources that are not needed (root cause #3).

2. Poorly designed policies and procedures: The essence of better management is to improve policies and procedures to have safer, higher quality services that cost less and can be delivered in a timely manner (root cause #4).

3. Excessive legal liability and malpractice insurance costs: When hospitals and clinical staff have well-designed policies and processes, they make fewer mistakes, leading to less legal liability and lower malpractice insurance costs (root cause #7).

4. Shortage of healthcare professionals: Activities that make healthcare professionals more productive allow them to care for more patients and cope with the current physician shortage, which is expected to get worse (root cause #8).

9.9 Summary of Recommendations

Following is a listing of the key recommendations contained in this chapter.

1. Several important changes should be made to improve the strategy, structure, and management of healthcare organizations.
   a. Engage in mergers and acquisitions that allow hospitals and hospital groups to share equipment and other resources to build economies of scale and lower costs.
   b. Build strategic and operating partnerships among hospitals so that they can share resources, reducing investment and lowering costs.
   c. Create a tiered system of hospitals that involve electronic information linkages and transport mechanisms so that rural hospitals are linked to regional medical centers and regional medical centers are linked to national medical centers. This enables people from every corner of the United States to have the finest care.
2. Match capacity and demand so that the number of hospital beds available is in line with the number of beds needed with some safety factor for variation in demand.
3. Address the size and scope of middle management so that there is an appropriate balance between resources devoted to administration and resources for clinical activities. This involves delegating decision-making authority and responsibility to clinicians who do the work and involving them in activities to improve clinical processes.
4. Designing and building effective supply chains, including determining what activities to outsource and creating processes to build and manage relationships with suppliers.
5. Identifying and using management techniques to redesign clinical process so that quality of care is better and costs are lower.

References

1. The Center for Medicare and Medicaid Services. 2013. National healthcare expenditures 2012 highlights. http://www.cms.gov/Research-Statistics-Data-and-Systems /Statistics-Trends-and-Reports/NationalHealthExpendData/downloads/highlights .pdf (accessed February 2, 2014).
2. Office of Inspector General, Office of Evaluation and Inspections, Department of Health and Human Services. 2001. Medicare hospital prospective payment system: How DRG rates are calculated and updated. http://oig.hhs.gov/oei/reports/oei-09 -00-00200.pdf (accessed September 24, 2015).
3. American Hospital Association. 2013. Fast Facts on US Hospitals. http://www.aha .org/research/rc/stat-studies/fast-facts.shtml (accessed September 24, 2015).
4. Becker's Hospital Review. 2014. 8 Statistics on hospital capacity. http://www.beck ershospitalreview.com/capacity-management/8-statistics-on-hospital-capacity.html (accessed September 24, 2015).
5. American Hospital Directory. 2015. Hospital statistics by state. http://www.ahd .com/state_statistics.html (accessed September 24, 2015).
6. Dudden, R. F., Corcoran, K., Kaplan, J., Magouirk, J., Rand, D. C., and Smith, B. T. 2002. The medical library, association benchmarking network: Results. *Journal of the Medical Library Association*, 94(2) (April) http://www.ncbi.nlm.nih.gov/pmc/articles /PMC1435842/ (accessed September 24, 2015).
7. Kaiser Permanente. 2015. Who are we? http://www.kaiserpermanentejobs.org/who -we-are.aspx#loaded (accessed September 27, 2015).
8. ProMedica. 2015. Health connect. https://www.promedica.org/pages/home.aspx (accessed September 27, 2015).
9. Tuey, H. 2015. ProMedica announces partnership with University of Toledo. Fox 54 WFSG, (May 11). http://www.wfxg.com/story/29035563/promedica-announces -partnership-with-university-of-toledo (accessed September 27, 2015).
10. Realtor's Insurance Marketplace. 2013. How much does it cost to spend a day in a hospital? http://www.realtorsinsurancemarketplace.com/how-much-does-it-cost-to -spend-a-day-in-the-hospital/ (accessed August 14, 2014); Kaiser Family Foundation. 2013. Hospital adjusted expenses per inpatient day by ownership. http://kff.org /other/state-indicator/expenses-per-inpatient-day-by-ownership/ (accessed September 24, 2015).
11. Hugos, M. H. 2011. *Essentials of Supply Chain Management*, 3rd edition. Hoboken, New Jersey: John Wiley & Sons.
12. Cima, R. R. 2011. Application of safety technology in the operating room. Power point presentation, Mayo Clinic Conference on Systems Engineering and Operations Research (June 11); Berry, L. L. and Seltman, K. D. 2008, *Management lessons from Mayo Clinic*. New York: McGraw Hill.
13. Kolata, G. 2015. What are a hospital's costs? Utah system is trying to learn. *New York Times*, (September 7). http://www.nytimes.com/2015/09/08/health/what-are-a-hos pitals-costs-utah-system-is-trying-to-learn.html?ref=health&_r=1 (accessed September 8, 2015).

Chapter 10

Accelerating the Use of Information Technology

Information technology (IT) is the use of devices, such as computers, smartphones, and telecommunication equipment, to gather, organize, store, search, analyze, and transmit data and information. Among other things, IT can be used to identify and access information to support decision making, present important data in graphical or tabular form, perform sizeable and complicated calculations quickly, and display and manipulate complex shapes, including images of the human body in three dimensions.

Here, the focus is on IT as it applies to healthcare delivery and not to medical technology with which the United States has been and will likely continue to be the world leader. Medical technology is the design and use of devices and procedures to improve patients' health, increase their longevity, and improve their quality of life. Medical technology includes a wide variety of innovations, such as magnetic resonance imaging (MRI), cancer therapy, medications, new surgical procedures, implants, and organ transplants. IT is used to design drugs and state-of-the-art equipment and is imbedded in MRI, ultrasound, and other equipment.

Although there is great value in accelerating the use of IT for medical technology, this chapter focuses on how to use IT to deliver better care. IT provides patients and primary care physicians with the data and information they need to make good decisions, so IT is vital for implementing patient-centered care (PCC). IT is also critical for managing resources, including the facilities, equipment, and people who deliver healthcare. Ensuring that surgical suites, intensive care units, computed tomography (CT) scanners, and other resources are fully and effectively used is important for serving patients and lowering costs. The ability to track and locate equipment reduces the need to buy more equipment and allows providers to offer timely services to patients. Providing medical professionals with accurate and timely information leads to better care and improves productivity by eliminating wasted time.

10.1 Information Technology Use in Healthcare Delivery: Late to the Game

Healthcare delivery is a learning-intensive activity with which instant and reliable access to relevant data, information, and knowledge is paramount, yet healthcare delivery lags other industries in applying IT. Professional stock traders want to know as much as possible about the financial health of firms they trade, and they demand real-time quotes before buying or selling stocks.

As with these businesses, healthcare delivery needs a responsive information system to support decision making, achieve the highest level of wellness for patients, manage resources for effective and efficient use, and attain the best care. In fact, healthcare may have the greatest need for knowledge acquisition, knowledge sharing, and learning. Yet healthcare delivery is not leading when it comes to adopting and using IT. To illustrate this point, the concepts and technologies behind electronic health records (EHRs) have existed for decades, and working systems have been available for more than 30 years.[1] It would appear that a lack of interest from healthcare providers, who did not fully value the potential of EHRs, delayed their implementation. For evidence of the time lag, consider that Amazon and other retailers have for many years had reams of data about their customers' buying habits and use these data to present customers with items they might buy. Automotive service centers maintain electronic service records for their customers' vehicles. Retailers such as Costco have electronic purchase data, so when customers return items bought years ago, Costco can quickly locate the receipt electronically and process a refund.

The reasons for delays in EHR adoption are the following:

1. Unbalanced decisions: Patients pay little or none of the costs, yet they derive significant benefits from healthcare, so they are biased toward having care. Providers responded with a heavy emphasis on improving care and little emphasis on controlling costs. This explains, in part, the United States' exceptional performance in medical technology because it leads to better care and limited emphasis on IT projects that improve the efficiency and productivity of healthcare delivery.
2. Power of physicians: Physicians have been and will continue to be key players in healthcare, and many have been reluctant to adapt IT because they believe it gets in the way of working closely with their patients. Physicians are willing to try new medical technologies because they understand healing and

care, and they appreciate the benefits from new drug therapy or laparoscopic surgery. There are several other reasonable explanations for their reluctance to adopt IT in healthcare delivery:

a. Physicians are not trained in either the "value of" or the "how to" associated with efficiency, cost control, process improvement, or IT. They do not see the benefits of EHR or other IT applications, especially the cost-reduction benefits, because healthcare was a cost-plus business for a long time.

b. For many physicians practicing today, especially those in senior positions, IT was not part of their environment when growing up, and it was not part of their medical training, so they are unfamiliar with its use or capabilities. This is likely to change as a new generation of physicians, trained in IT and accustomed to its use, enter the field.

c. As with most people, physicians don't like change, especially when they have a limited understanding of the reasons for it or the value of it. This is true of IT, which for some seems almost magical, yet an eight-year-old feels comfortable and appears to master it.

d. The record-keeping, tracking, and controlling nature of IT seems clerical, something to be delegated to support staff.

In the past few years, progress has been made because EHR at physicians' offices is moving from the exception to the norm. This change is being driven, in large part, by incentive payments from the Center for Medicare and Medicaid Services (CMS) to hospitals that implement "meaningful use" of EHR. To meet this requirement, hospitals and physicians practicing at the hospital must store their patients' records in EHR and actively use this information, thus the term "meaningful use."[2]

10.2 Information Technology and Patient-Centered Care

The most important and best known IT application in healthcare is the EHR. To begin, it is useful to describe the differences between EHRs and electronic medical records (EMRs). Some define EMRs as the computerization of the patient's medical history—that is, the records physicians keep in their office. These records contain the patient's family history of disease and chronicle the patient's conditions, surgeries, diagnoses, and treatments. EHRs include all of this, plus it is designed to be portable outside of the practice, so information can be seamlessly shared with hospitals, specialists, pharmacies, laboratories, and other providers. EHRs should also be accessible by patients who actually own the data.[3] Information sharing is critical for electronic records, so the focus of this discussion is on EHRs.

There are other relevant aspects of IT. Medical simulation is emerging as a tool to study the human body, and for some applications, it is replacing cadavers as a teaching tool. Medical simulation can also be used to examine living patients by projecting a 3-D image of their body to help with diagnoses and determine treatment options. This emerging technology is only beginning to be understood and used.

A robust IT solution allows medical professionals to have unrestricted access to the latest diagnoses and treatment information as well as patient data, using smartphones and other devices. Recent information in *The New York Times* describes cases in which leading IT companies are addressing important health issues. SAP is focusing on digitizing information that can be quickly and easily shared so that medical professionals have real-time access to information. Intel is teaming up with medical researchers to reduce substantially the time to execute genome research and testing.[4] These and other technologies hold promise that future medical care will be better and cost less.

In addition, patients should be able to access their health information as well as learn about and implement wellness plans. They should be able to review their medical bills, which would help them understand the costs of healthcare and look for billing errors and fraud. Patients have a right to know about their health and a responsibility to (a) participate actively and meaningfully in the process and (b) ensure that value is received for the money spent even when spent by third-party payers.

10.2.1 Electronic Health Records

EHRs provide transportable information about patients, including a thorough medical history, all elements of a personal health plan, and an ongoing accumulation of medical information. EHRs should be quickly and easily accessible by patients, physicians, hospitals, and others as patients dictate. They should be designed so that physicians and patients have control over certain parts of the EHR. For example, patients could not change physician inputs about test results or diagnoses, and physicians could not change certain elements of a patient's medical history without their approval. EHRs could also signal patients when it is time for a preventive test or health screening.

10.2.1.1 Electronic Health Records and the Personal Health Plan

The foundation of EHRs and the personal health plan is the patient's medical history, which is discussed in Chapter 5 on PCC. The medical history has information on the following:

1. Current symptoms of the patient, which are updated at each visit
2. Immunizations received
3. Medications the patient is taking

4. Routine health screenings results, such as blood pressure and weight
5. Medical testing results, such as sonograms and MRIs
6. Personal medical history that includes patients' health, such as bronchitis or dizziness
7. Surgical history
8. Family medical history
9. Other health concerns relating to lifestyle choices, such as exercise and alcohol consumption
10. Personal information, such as marital status and hobbies[5]

After this information is entered initially, the EHR would be updated as part of a healthcare visit or by the patients as their condition changes.

In addition to the medical history, EHRs would include the other parts of the personal health plan: routing health screenings, preventive testing, wellness, and end-of-life plans. Results from executing the routine health screening plan and the preventive testing plan are included in the medical history. The wellness plan includes a set of actions and goals related to a patient's health and lifestyle that are designed to address problems, such as high blood pressure, osteoporosis, and smoking. The end-of-life plan contains relevant documents that describe how patients expect to be treated as they approach death, such as a living will or healthcare power of attorney.

10.2.1.2 Electronic Health Records and Data Collection

Data collection must be a comprehensive and continuous activity. EHRs would contain notes and reports in a digitized format for everything from each wellness visit to radiation and chemotherapy treatments. When patients have a knee replaced, the X-ray, MRI, therapy, lab work, prescriptions, and so on are part of the EHR. The EHR becomes a one-stop shop for information.

These data must be accessible by physicians, hospitals, and other healthcare entities involved in treating patients. The EHR is more than a patient-centric data repository; it is a document that can be shared seamlessly and in real time whether the patient is at home, across the country, or around the world (the last one may take a while). Patients at a hospital in a rural area who need attention at a regional medical center or patients traveling to the Mayo Clinic do not have to worry whether physicians at these locations have the latest data. They will when the EHR is fully implemented.

When physicians order tests, the results are submitted electronically and become part of the patient's EHR. When prescription drugs are needed, orders are sent to the pharmacy electronically. If there are questions, such as drug interactions, the pharmacist notifies the physician electronically. When the prescription is filled, an electronic order-fill is sent to the patient's EHR through the physician.

The computerized databases used to build an EHR system are capable of holding vast amounts of information and creating electronic hooks that allow people to organize and link information. So, as physicians search an EHR for all of the relevant information about a patient's condition, say a blocked coronary artery, the database is able to pull out and present useful information. Try doing that quickly and accurately with a three-inch-thick paper chart, which contains 25 years of data. Also, the paper chart most likely does not have all the information because the patient has seen multiple physicians, been tested at different labs, and been admitted to more than one hospital during treatment.

10.2.1.3 Linking Electronic Health Records

It is easiest to think of EHRs as having different levels, and these levels must be stitched together to create an effective system. An EHR begins with a patient's medical history, including his or her personal health plan. It continues with a hospital and related ancillary facilities, such as pharmacies and labs, eventually including other hospitals in the region. The final links are to hospitals and other treatment facilities across the country and around the world. Following is an overview of this hierarchy.

1. Patient's medical history at the physician level: The foundation for an EHR is a medical history, which is the responsibility of primary care physicians. The contents are described previously.
2. Hospitals as the driving force and building block for EHR success: As shown in Figure 10.1, hospitals are a key point of coordination and interaction because they possess a comprehensive set of resources and care options. They are central to EHR success because they work closely with physicians, are able to connect ancillary service providers, and can build multihospital systems and partnerships.
   a. Work with physicians: Hospitals strongly encourage and support physicians to engage in the "meaningful use" of EHR systems. Hospitals have the resources to implement EHRs, and physicians comply either because

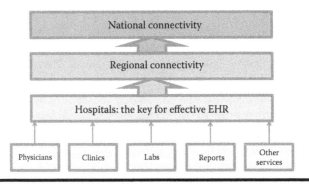

Figure 10.1   Hospitals are the driving force and building block for EHRs.

they are employees of the hospital or because they wish to retain admitting privileges at the hospital.

  b. Connect ancillary service providers: Hospitals are the hubs that link other service providers to this information highway. Medical clinics, urgent care centers, pharmacies, and many others must be able and willing to post information to the EHR and, in certain cases, extract information from it. If needed, hospitals must use leverage to get these suppliers to comply. At this point, hospitals have functional but limited EHRs because they only include physicians who practice at the hospital and ancillary service providers that work with the hospitals. If patients see physicians, fill a prescription, or have tests done using outside resources, the EHR will not collect these data.

  c. Build multihospital healthcare systems and partnerships: The first step to resolve this limitation is to ensure that all hospitals in a healthcare system are part of the same EHR system. Healthcare systems, such as Kaiser Permanente and ProMedica, are organizations that consist of multiple hospitals and clinics. Such organizations are formed through mergers, acquisitions, and strategic and operating partnerships. Regardless of how the alliance was formed, these hospitals, their physicians, and their ancillary service providers should have a common EHR system, so patients' information is accessible regardless of which hospital, physician, or ancillary service provider is involved.

3. Regional sharing: As shown in Figure 10.1, sharing in a region, which could be defined by state borders, depends on competing hospitals working together. Hospitals in the same region or state may be concerned that competitors could steal patients if access to data is unfettered. The most effective response is that the information in an EHR does not belong to hospitals. It is information about patients and is the property of patients. If patients choose to share information, they have every right to do so, and the hospital cannot restrict access. The basis for competition should be providing the safest, highest quality care at the lowest cost. In addition, withholding access to information to keep patients from seeking services they perceive as better is not consistent with the Hippocratic oath to do no harm.

4. National sharing: As shown in Figure 10.1, national sharing is based upon cooperation among the regions. National sharing may actually meet less resistance than regional sharing because most competition for healthcare is local. National sharing means that the health records of people traveling across the country would be available in case they encountered a problem. Nationwide sharing also provides access to EHRs when patients seek specialized help at a nationally known medical center. Although creating a national network to share EHR information may seem complex and difficult to do, recall that adults in the United States have credit scores that are based on information gathered about their purchasing and paying practices. This is hundreds of

transactions each year for hundreds of millions of people. If this can be done, creating a nationwide system to capture information about health and health-care is doable.

5. International sharing: International sharing is unlikely to happen soon, and the benefits are limited to those who travel outside the United States, but it is part of the logical progression.

An important prerequisite for achieving regional, national, and international connectivity is ensuring that medical codes are uniform and easy to use and that different computer hardware, operating systems, data configuration, software, and other details of the technology are compatible. This is likely to require leadership and incentives from government. For now, the focus is on building relationships among physicians, hospitals, and the ancillary service providers at the hospital level. This is likely to be accomplished to a great extent over the next three or four years. It will take time, but implementing a national EHR will succeed.

10.2.1.4 Benefits of Electronic Health Records

For an EHR, there are two distinct benefit categories: better care and greater effi-ciency. Fortunately, these two outcomes are strongly and positively correlated, meaning that efforts to create EHRs both improve care and increase efficiency. For example, when physicians can quickly access digital copies of patients' most recent MRIs through an EHR, patients avoid the delays and inconveniences as well as the risks and side effects from redoing the test. Plus, the cost of duplicate testing is avoided. This allows diagnoses and treatment plans to be prepared and implemented expeditiously.

Medical histories stored in the EHR are done once and are updated when new events take place. By contrast, when physicians ask patients to update their paper-based medical history, they hand patients blank forms to fill out from scratch. Over the years, there are likely to be a dozen or more medical histories in a paper-based system. In addition, patients complete one medical history for the primary care physician and are asked to fill out another one for each specialist. It is common for patients to see a handful of physicians, so there are likely to be three, four, five, or more paper-based histories floating around. And it is likely that each history will be different because patients prepare them hastily from memory while sitting in the physician's office, often making errors in this important document. If patients could access the medical history electronically, correct errors, and provide up-to-date information, they would take it more seriously, provide better data, and spend less time keeping it current and correct.

There are other benefits to using EHRs. EHRs are built using sophisticated data-bases, which have electronic links that allow the software to quickly create charts, graphs, and tables that display data about important medical conditions, such as blood pressure, cholesterol, or other health parameter, over a specific period of time.

Physicians can quickly and easily see trends or patterns that are useful. Physicians can rapidly access relevant information about a health condition such as diabetes, easily examine a list of pharmaceutical drugs a patient is taking, and quickly review the health conditions of parents or siblings. The EHR can be designed to automatically check for drug interactions. In a paper-based system, each of these actions would require thumbing through a ream of paper to find the relevant data.

The EHR should also contain the digitized results of diagnostic tests and laboratory procedures, and these can be easily and quickly accessed and viewed. So a test result, such as a CT scan taken two years ago, can be compared to one done recently to see how conditions have changed. An X-ray done by the primary care physician can be used by the orthopedic physician, so a retake is avoided. EHRs allow information to be shared easily and quickly among all interested parties whether they are local primary care physicians, specialists in Boston or Seattle, hospitals in the same town, rural hospitals, or national medical centers that are hundreds of miles away. A paper-based system requires someone to identify what is needed, fax it or scan it, and hope that critical information is not lost in the process. This leads to delays and miscommunications that could have negative impacts on patients.

There are also substantial costs to a paper-based system that can be avoided by using EHRs. Here is a look at how a paper-based system works. Visualize a traditional health record room in a large physician practice or clinic. There are rows and rows of patient records stored in alphabetic order in storage racks that extend from floor to ceiling. This space is usually one large area, and it may be in the basement. Managing the paper is an expensive and time-consuming task, and there are significant problems because patients' charts are physically moved and can be easily misplaced or lost. Also, there are a number of important actions and possible errors that take place each day. Most patients never see and usually don't think about them. Follow the letter by number designations on the arrows in Figure 10.2 for an overview of this complex and expensive process. Here are some of the activities:

1. Patient appointments: Each day, staff members review the list of incoming patients, go to the chart storage room prior to the patient's scheduled arrival (see arrow A1), find each patient's chart, pull it, and take it to patient check-in (A2). The nurse for the physician takes the chart to the examination room (A3). The physician uses the chart, makes notes in it, and may return it to someone with instructions to put it in the chart storage room. As part of the process, the chart is returned to check-in (A4a), and it is eventually refiled (A5a). Or the physician asks someone to take the chart to the physician's office for additional review and documentation (A4b). The paper-based chart, which is returned to the physician's office, may stay there for a few hours, a few days, or more before it is returned to chart storage (A5b). It should be easy to see how much less clerical work is required if the charts are electronic and if physicians have computer access to them in each examination room.

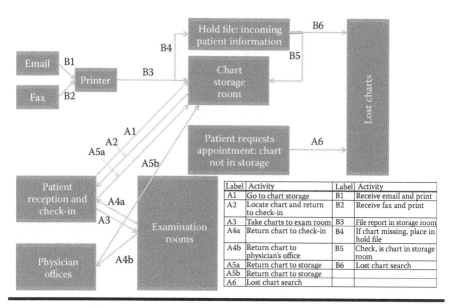

Figure 10.2 Schematic of a paper-based medical records system.

2. Incoming patient information: In a large physician practice or clinic using paper-based charts, information, and reports from pharmacies, labs, physician specialists, and others arrive hundreds of times each day either by email (B1) or fax (B2). The new patient information is printed and filed in the chart storage room (B3; see Figure 10.2). During the day or two or more that elapsed between pulling a patient's chart and returning it, no one knows for sure where the chart is, even when the system works perfectly. If the chart is not in the storage room, another process must be created to hold this information and check periodically to see if the patient's chart has been returned (B4). This process is invoked until the chart is returned and the new information is added (B5). If not found after several attempts over a few days, the chart will eventually be considered lost (B6), and someone will be assigned to look for it. Also, when a lab report or other information is waiting in a hold bin to be inserted into the patient's chart, the report could be misplaced. (In an effort to keep Figure 10.2 manageable, this issue is not shown in the figure.) These delays and problems are extremely unlikely to happen with an EHR. As long as the laboratory or other entity sending the electronic report has the right patient information, it will go directly to the patient's health records immediately whether the physician is using it or not.

3. Scheduling appointments and information requests: In addition to a scheduled patient visit, a patient's chart may be required for various reasons, such as setting a new appointment, refilling a prescription, or checking test results. Someone must fetch the chart, get the information, and eventually return the

chart. (When the physician is involved, this would be similar to activities A1, A2, A3, A4, and A5 in Figure 10.2.) However, the chart may not be in the central storage location, so there is another lost chart (A6). Some physician's offices have enough lost charts that a staff person is routinely assigned to search for them, spending several hours a week looking.

4. Simple filing errors: With a paper-based system, there is a substantial risk of misfiling the information. How many Smiths, Millers, or Joneses are in system? Even with a less common name, errors can occur when the clerical staff is rushed for time or unmotivated. An EHR provides seamless access to the chart and eliminates filing errors.

5. Keeping physicians informed: In a paper-based system, physicians may not know when new information arrives until the next patient visit. With EHRs, physicians receive electronic notifications, and they can review and take action as needed.

Implementing EHRs is the most important and immediate IT issue. As with most radical changes, it will take a few years to be accepted and to build a national network. When this happens, there will be a shift from the innovation, design, and implementation stage of EHRs to a second stage marked by continuous improvement through software enhancements, better equipment, and creative and new uses.

10.2.2 Medical Simulation

Medical simulation in one form or another has existed for many years, including the use of human cadavers to study anatomy and practice surgical procedures. It has advanced to the point at which medical students and residents use sophisticated mannequins that do the following:

1. Present symptoms and allow physicians to engage in diagnostic exercises
2. Replicate trauma so physicians can react quickly and correctly to emergency situations
3. Allow medical personnel to practice a lumbar puncture, suturing, and other treatments
   These tools offer substantial opportunities to improve teaching and the practice of healthcare, ultimately leading to better patient outcomes and enhanced safety.[6]

In addition to MRIs and CT scans, which use IT and imaging technology, medical simulation incorporates sophisticated 3-D imaging tools for surgical planning, 3-D volume analysis, and image rotation.[7] Three-dimensional imaging tools are able to create sophisticated medical avatars that physicians can use to map the entire body, including its vascular, nervous, muscular, respiratory, and skeletal systems. Using this technology, physicians can assess the functioning of these systems, identify potential problems, and propose and test solutions. It is as much a diagnostic and assessment tool as it is a teaching device. Surgeons can also use it to determine the best access for a surgical procedure. This technology, which is in early stage development, can be a hub for innovation as it helps industry, hospitals, and physicians work together.

Although it seems clear that these tools hold great promise in education, diagnoses, and treatment, it is not possible for even the most sophisticated users to predict the full potential. It would be like Alexander Graham Bell, who is credited with creating the first working telephone and was awarded a U.S. patent for it in 1876, predicting his work laid the foundation for future communications. In 1876 or any time up to his death in 1922,[8] if Mr. Bell had suggested that a person in the United States could take a photo and instantly send it to someone in China using a phone, he would have been ridiculed and thought to be insane.

10.2.3 Data and Information Access: Medical Professionals

Medical professionals need access to up-to-date information to make good decisions about health and healthcare. EHRs provide fast, easy, and reliable access to patient data that can be readily summarized and organized. However, these data are only one element in the healthcare equation. There are mountains of medical knowledge that can help physicians make the right diagnoses, prescribe the most effective medications, and apply the best treatments. Initially, a physician's learning takes place in medical school and residency, and it is updated through continuing education; reading medical journals; and acquiring knowledge from pharmaceutical companies, equipment makers, and other suppliers.

With medical knowledge exploding, it is difficult to keep up with new ideas and discard obsolete ones even with continuing education. Plus the sheer volume of knowledge makes it difficult to keep everything in immediate recall mode even for highly trained healthcare professionals. It is not a shortcoming to be unable to have an instant answer, but it is a shortcoming not to know how to find essential information. Healthcare professionals need fast, easy, and reliable access to knowledge and information about diagnostic and treatment options. The good news is that access is available in the form of smartphones, tablets, and other devices with connectivity to the Internet. The not-so-good news is that some medical professionals do not feel comfortable with the technology, and they don't have the skills to use it properly. Tough love may be needed—that is, to require medical professionals to become proficient users of these devices to search reliable websites for the latest information.

With access to well-designed websites, physicians could use knowledge-based support systems to provide diagnostic options given a patient's symptoms or to search easily and quickly for the best antibiotic for an infectious disease while also seeing its side effects and possible drug interactions. To be effective, these support systems are built around sets of questions that allow physicians and the systems to interact. This approach, sometimes called an expert system using artificial intelligence, is not intended to replace the medical professional but is designed to provide additional information and knowledge that they should consider before deciding on diagnoses and treatments.

Creating a database (the knowledge) and an inquiry engine (the set of questions or logic) that lead to the best decisions forces some questions to the surface. Who will build the system? How will the system be updated? What is the business plan to fund development and continuing operations—that is, who will pay for it? Individual companies who create new technology clearly have incentives to inform medical professionals about their technology, but they have little and possibly a negative incentive to keep medical professionals posted about other unrelated or competing technologies. There are health information systems offered by the Mayo Clinic (mayoclinic.org) and WebMD (webmd.com), but these tend to target patients who are interested in learning more about their own health problems.

There may be a role for the federal government in creating a medical diagnostic and treatment support system (MDTSS), but not as the builder. An MDTSS must be accurate, unbiased, and up to date, so its contents must be in the hands of medical professionals. As it did with EHRs, the federal government can, through the CMS, work with the healthcare industry to establish guidelines for developing an MDTSS and offer incentive payments for hospitals to use them. Hospitals will seek out vendors who are capable of creating these systems as they did with EHRs. Vendors will respond because there are opportunities to create a tool that hospitals will pay for. The Mayo Clinic and WebMD may choose to participate in developing such a tool. As hospitals, physicians, patients, and third-party payers see the benefits of these knowledge-based support systems, MDTSSs will become an integral part of healthcare delivery that pays for itself with lower costs and better care.

The ability to create this type of knowledge-based system has been around for decades. A system based on artificial intelligence, called MYCIN, was developed in the 1970s by experts at Stanford University. This computer-based system helped to identify the bacteria causing infections and recommended antibiotics. In head-to-head tests with physicians, MYCIN performed as well as or better than physicians. It was not used in practice because computers at the time were slower and much less responsive, plus there were concerns about legal liabilities if the computer's decision was incorrect.[9] Today, computer technology is much improved, and if the MDTSS is used only to provide information for the physician to consider, the legal liability should be easier to address.

10.2.4 Data and Information Access: Patients

Patients should have fast and easy on-line access to information about their health, healthcare records, diagnosis and treatment regimens, and medical bills. One problem is that the ability to access and use on-line information varies widely across the population. At one extreme, people have difficulty interfacing with electronic information because they do not have access to and/or do not feel comfortable with the technology, including computers, laptops, iPads, and smartphones. At the other extreme, a growing number of people thrive in this environment and use the technology frequently. They use their smartphones, smart watches, and fitness devices to monitor and even to upload their personal fitness data. Over time, the technology skill of the population should increase, and this can be accelerated by providing hands-on training to the general population through libraries and schools.

Following are the elements that patients should be able to access:

1. Wellness: Patients need access to information about the whys and hows of wellness. Reasons to be well should be clearly outlined, including the benefits, such as longevity and quality of life. The negatives outcomes of making poor choices, including diseases, physical limitations, and pain, must be understood. There should be programs that patients can customize and follow to address their problems whether they are related to smoking, alcoholism, drug dependencies, or eating disorders. There should be discussion of pros and cons for programs, such as hypnosis, to address addictions. The information should be organized and presented to patients so that they and their primary care physician can make good choices.

2. Healthcare records: Patients, for the most part, do not have access to their records. It takes a special request from them to receive copies of their blood work or other information in their paper-based chart. Why should patients be concerned about their health problems when they do not know their health status, such as blood pressure or cholesterol? Why should they take steps to address these concerns when they cannot see how changes they make impact these parameters? With EHRs, patients would have access to their health records and be able to assess status and progress. It is a fundamental human condition to set goals, make changes, assess progress toward those goals, and make adjustments when things are not working.

3. Diagnosis and treatment: Patients have a right and a responsibility to understand their health problems and to be a partner in fixing them. When patients understand their health and their ailments, they are more likely to provide physicians with the right information, and they may be more willing to undergo change to improve their condition. Mayoclinic.com and WebMD.com are important Internet sites for patients who are seeking information in preparation for a physician visit and to assess whether a second opinion is warranted.

4. Billing: Patients have a responsibility to verify that the healthcare services, for which they and their third-party insurer have paid, were actually received. This begins by giving patients on-line access to their itemized healthcare billing statements. This fact alone will encourage hospitals and others to improve the accuracy of their bills.

10.3 Information Technology and Resource Management

Resource management is the effective and efficient deployment of an organization's assets to reach its goals. For hospitals, physician practices, clinics, and other healthcare entities, a patient-centered, resource management perspective implies a dual mandate: high-quality, safe, and timely care as well as efficient processes that keep costs low. In addition to the benefits of EHRs, simulation, and fast access to information, IT is a central part of running the business functions of healthcare organizations, such as personnel, scheduling, inventory control, and dozens of others. There are hundreds of books and articles that describe these and other applications in detail, so these topics are not pursued here. Suffice it to say that healthcare firms can do the following:

1. Learn about best practices in these functions from other industries
2. Assess how these practices could be used in healthcare
3. Adapt and implement the practices to work well
4. Strive to continuously improve their performance

If they are successful, healthcare organizations can use resources more effectively and reduce costs in these functional areas. Lower costs, in turn, may actually lead to better healthcare outcomes because resources freed by improving these functions can be directed toward the critical mission of delivering better care to more people. This is a win–win outcome that makes IT applications an important tool for healthcare organization.

IT is such an integral part of resource management in healthcare and other industries because nearly all activities are directly impacted by or supported by IT. In each of the major topics discussed in the prior chapter—evaluating mergers and acquisitions, partnerships, rationalizing demand and capacity, right-sizing middle management, building effective supply chains, implementing quality management programs, or engaging in process improvement efforts—IT plays a critical role. It is difficult to understand why executives, directors, managers, supervisors, or skilled workers in any organization would not have the IT training that allows them to access, evaluate, manipulate, and communicate information in the knowledge economy.

10.4 Dealing with Privacy (HIPAA) Concerns

Patients are concerned about retaining control over their health information, especially maintaining privacy. HIPAA, less commonly known as the Health Insurance Portability and Accountability Act, has several foci. The first is on healthcare access, portability, and renewability under Title I, which protects people in group insurance plans, people with preexisting conditions, and those transitioning between jobs. Title II, the second focus, aims to prevent healthcare fraud and abuse, simplify administration, and achieve medical liability reform. One element of Title II, called "the privacy rules," regulates the use and disclosure of protected health information. Although this rule is only part of HIPAA, privacy is the best-known element of the act. Other titles within HIPAA address medical savings accounts, tax changes involving insurance, and enforcement of group health insurance requirements, including clarifications of COBRA (Consolidated Omnibus Budget Reconciliation Act of 1985), which mandates the ability to continue health insurance coverage when changing jobs.[10]

There do not appear to be reasons why privacy concerns should preclude the development and deployment of EHRs or other IT applications. Currently, patients' health information is held by physicians, hospitals, clinics, pharmacies, and other entities. Patients have the right to control who accesses this information. In fact, when patients visit physicians and hospitals, they are presented paperwork to sign, which gives the entity permission to use and share this information.

Placing this health information in a digital format that is accessible electronically does not change, at least theoretically, the fact that patients have the right to control access to their health information. Patients still have this right. The practical difference is that the information is now in one place that might be accessed electronically by hackers who are seeking to gain some advantage.

This risk is no different than the financial risk from using a credit card or debit card, doing on-line banking or shopping, or accessing on-line investment accounts. Hackers may attack the information systems of the stores where people buy things and the banks and investment houses where they hold their money. Hackers can commit fraud and steal identities. These risks are ones that people are willingly to take in order to enjoy the convenience of using credit and debit cards and doing on-line financial transactions. Otherwise people would keep money in their mattresses or at local banks and would use cash or, if they were really adventurous, write checks to pay for goods and services.

Capabilities exist to protect government, industry, and financial information systems against cyber attacks. This expertise can be used to develop systems that prevent unauthorized access to EHRs. These protective measures are not perfect, and it is not likely that they will be perfect at some future time. As with other systems, the question is the following: Are people willing to accept this risk for healthcare information and be prepared with contingency plans to address data breaches?

Back to the point about what advantage the hacker might gain. In the world of finance, banking, and money, the advantages are clear. If hackers can commit fraud or steal a person's identity, they gain financially. There are hackers who seek government, military, or industrial secrets that can be used for their advantage by selling information to foreign governments or business competitors. There is another group, albeit a smaller one, who seems to enjoy hacking because it is the challenge that motivates them.

What advantage is gained from hacking an EHR system? The concern is not that health information is inherently valuable to hackers. It is difficult to see a financial motive. The problem is that health records can contain patients' social security numbers, birth dates, and other important pieces of personal information. The keys to preventing attacks are building defenses so that it is difficult to gain illegal access, developing tracing capabilities so that the likelihood of getting caught is very high, and setting severe penalties once hackers are convicted. The risk of a breach must be accepted. People do not stop shopping because of cyber attacks. They do not stop banking or investing because there might be identity theft. The United States cannot afford to say no to EHRs because there might be some privacy invasions.

10.5 Driving Forces for Change

Incentives offered by CMS have accelerated the use of EHRs. Hospitals are driving the transition from paper-based systems to EHRs and bringing physicians and other ancillary services along for the ride. The market position and power of hospitals make it relatively easy for them to convince physicians and ancillary service providers, such as medical labs and pharmacies, to participate. Hospitals are implementing EHRs and are working with physicians to overcome their reluctance to use them. Once physicians become comfortable with EHRs, they will be more likely to use medical simulation tools and access diagnostic and treatment options that are available on the Internet.

The next step is to incentivize hospitals to form regional and national networks of EHRs. To ensure these efforts move beyond islands of EHRs to nationwide connectivity, it is vital to have a common platform and protocol to support data interchange. In other words, a set of standards is needed so that the EHRs at one hospital can share information quickly and easily with others. This is filled with technical details that are beyond the scope of this book, but it is critical for success. Government through CMS may have to provide leadership and some incentives to overcome these technical barriers. CMS may also have a role in incentivizing the implementation of a system to support medical diagnosis and treatment, an MDTSS. This also requires convincing physician groups and hospital groups of the value of this tool.

IT initiatives are supported by physician groups, such as the American Medical Association and the American College of Physician Executives, and hospital groups, such as the American Hospital Association, who offer continuing education and certificate programs in medical IT. There are opportunities to work with physicians to illustrate that they can have effective and personal relationships with patients while using EHRs and other IT systems. For new physicians, this training should be built into their medical student and residency training. For existing physicians, it becomes part of their continuing education. A new generation of physicians should be receptive to IT as essential and integral to the medical profession.

10.6 Impact of Accelerating the Use of Information Technology on Healthcare Outcomes

IT is a powerful tool in other segments of the economy, such as retail, banking, and manufacturing, to improve performance and lower costs. Although it is not possible to simply pick up the IT from these areas and plop it down in healthcare, there are ways in which IT can have a substantial and positive impact on healthcare. Following is a summary of the impacts of this issue on the relevant root causes, which are discussed in Chapter 2:

1. Unused facilities and equipment: EHRs provide physicians with access to all the information about patients, making it unnecessary to duplicate testing, which should reduce the demand for equipment and people as well as reduce patient-days in the hospital. They should provide better care, leading to fewer complications, which lowers costs and reduces hospital visits and testing (root cause #3).

2. Poorly designed policies and procedures: IT offers a one–two punch that improves healthcare. (a) EHRs provide physicians with the right information quickly, and (b) physicians have access to the most up-to-date diagnostic and treatment options via high-quality on-line systems. This provides an atmosphere in which providing good medical care, efficiency, productivity, and rapid response are compatible goals (root cause #4).

3. Limited and ineffective information technology: EHRs, medical simulation, and access to information directly address the need to improve information technology. Physicians, pharmacists, and others have the information they need so that patients receive better and faster care, avoid unnecessary tests and treatments, and have lower healthcare costs (root cause #5).

4. Excessive legal liability and malpractice insurance costs: Better care leads to fewer mistakes, which, in turn, leads to less legal liability and lower malpractice insurance costs (root cause #7).

5. Shortage of healthcare professionals: Better and faster care and fewer mistakes mean that physicians have more time and can treat additional patients (root cause #8).

10.7 Summary of Recommendations

Following is a listing of the key recommendations contained in this chapter:

1. Ensuring the development and implementation of EHRs at the hospital or healthcare system level. Hospitals are the key to success as they include the physicians who practice there and the ancillary service providers that support them.

2. Extending EHRs beyond a single hospital or system of hospitals to achieve regional and national connectivity so that medical history is portable.
3. Pursuing new technology in medical simulation to improve care and lower costs.
   a. Sophisticated mannequins to present medical conditions to students and residents so that they can respond to life-and-death questions in a safe learning environment.
   b. Three-dimensional imaging tools to learn about the vascular, nervous, and other systems of the body and to assess their functioning. They are also used for surgical planning and other activities.
4. Providing medical professionals with access to the latest knowledge through a medical diagnostic and treatment support system (MDTSS), which could be quickly and easily accessed via the Internet. This would contain diagnoses and treatment information for a wide variety of medical conditions. Development and use of this tool would be incentivized by higher levels of reimbursement from CMS to hospitals that participate.
5. Providing patients with health and healthcare information so they can improve their wellness, be aware of their current health status, understand limitations and possible treatments for their health problems, and manage their medical bills to limit overbilling and possible fraud.
6. Addressing security issues for patients' electronic records by creating strong systems to restrict access, increasing the probability of catching hackers, and having severe penalties for the guilty.

References

1. HealthTechnologyReview.com. 2015. History of electronic medical records. http://www.healthtechnologyreview.com/art135_history_of_electronic_medical_records.php (accessed September 2015); Wikipedia. 2015. Electronic health records. https://en.wikipedia.org/wiki/Electronic_health_record (accessed September 17, 2015).
2. Center for Medicare and Medicaid Services. 2015. EHR Incentive program. http://www.cms.gov/Regulations-and-Guidance/Legislation/EHRIncentivePrograms/index.html (accessed September 17, 2015).
3. Differencebetween.com. 2011. Difference between EMR and EHR. http://www.differencebetween.com/difference-between-emr-and-vs-ehr/ (accessed September 17, 2015); Garrett, P. and Seidman, J. 2011. EMR vs EHR.—What is the difference? HealthITBuzz. http://www.healthit.gov/buzz-blog/electronic-health-and-medical-records/emr-vs-ehr-difference/ (accessed September 17, 2015).
4. Hardy, Q. 2015. SAP chief Bill McDermott embarks on healthcare mission after losing his eye. *The New York Times* (November 1). http://bits.blogs.nytimes.com/2015/11/01/sap-chief-mcdermott-embarks-on-health-care-push-after-losing-his-eye/?ref=business&_r=1 (accessed November 4, 2015).

5. Palo Alto Medical Foundation: A Sutter Health Affiliate. 2011. Adult health history for new patients. http://www.pamf.org/forms/143952_Adult_Med_Hx.pdf (accessed September 17, 2015).

6. Society for Simulation in Healthcare. 2015. Medical simulation. http://healthy simulation.com/medical-simulation/ (accessed September 21, 2015); Johns Hopkins Medicine. 2015. Simulation center. http://www.hopkinsmedicine.org/simulation _center/ (accessed September 21, 2015); Rutgers New Jersey Medical School. 2015. Simulation training for residents. http://njms.rutgers.edu/departments/anesthesiology /simulator.cfm (accessed September 21, 2015).

7. Association of American Medical Colleges. 2011. Medical simulation in medical education: Results of an AAMC survey. https://www.aamc.org/download/259760/data /medicalsimulationinmedicaleducationanaamcsurvey.pdf (accessed September 21, 2015); The University of Toledo. 2015. UT-Interprofessional Immersive Simulation Center (IISC). http://www.utoledo.edu/centers/iisc/index.html (accessed September 21, 2015); Anomalous Medical. 2015. Explore, create and share 3-D anatomy. http:// www.anomalousmedical.com/ (accessed September 21, 2015).

8. Biography.com. 2015. Alexander Graham Bell biography. http://www.biography .com/people/alexander-graham-bell-9205497 (accessed September 21, 2015).

9. Encyclopedia Britannica. 2015. MYCIN. http://www.britannica.com/technology /MYCIN (accessed September 21, 2015); Wikipedia. 2015. MYCIN. https://en.wiki pedia.org/wiki/Mycin (accessed September 21, 2015).

10. Center for Medicare and Medicaid Services. 2015. Health insurance portability and accountability act of 1996. https://www.cms.gov/Regulations-and-Guidance /HIPAA-Administrative-Simplification/HIPAAGenInfo/Downloads/HIPAALaw .pdf (accessed September 21, 2015); Texas Department of State Health Insurance. 2015. Health Insurance Portability and Accountability Act. http://www.dshs.state .tx.us/hipaa/default.shtm (accessed September 21, 2015).

Chapter 11

Making Drug Costs Affordable and Fair

According to a Center for Medicare and Medicaid Services report, U.S. healthcare spending reached $2.8 trillion in 2012, and the top three factors were hospital care at $882.3 billion (about 31.5%), physician and clinical services at $565 billion (slightly more than 20%), and prescriptions drugs at $263.3 billion (just under 9.5%). The expenditures for these three items were approximately $1.71 trillion or about 61% of the total.[1] In an earlier chapter, hospital costs are examined and suggestions are made to improve care and lower costs. In a later chapter, an approach is described to ensure that the United States has enough qualified physicians to provide high-quality care and contain costs. This chapter addresses the third largest element, prescription drugs.

The United States is a fertile environment for research in biotechnology and drug development. In a study of pharmaceutical innovations, the United States is shown to be the inventor country for 43.7% of the new molecular entities (NMEs) developed from 1992 to 2004.[2] NMEs are compounds that emerge from laboratory research and do not contain an active composition previously approved by the Food and Drug Administration (FDA). In the past five decades, the U.S. pharmaceutical industry has been a leader in innovations, such as blood thinners, acid inhibiters, HIV drugs, cervical cancer treatments, and many others.

This level of innovation must not only continue, it must accelerate if the United States is to improve health outcomes and take control of its healthcare costs. Often, drug therapy is an effective alternative to more expensive treatments, such as surgery. As an example, the cure for an ulcer was to remove the ulcerated portion of the stomach and hope that it did not return. Now, this can be effectively treated with acid inhibiters that achieve better results at a lower cost. Stents can be inserted into arteries quickly to improve blood flow, making coronary bypass surgery unnecessary in many cases.[3]

11.1 Drug Development Overview

Developing drugs is a complex process requiring many highly trained specialists who must work together to create innovative solutions to evolving medical problems. There are two major concerns:

1. The process from idea generation to marketable drug often takes many years, meaning that people suffer and die while they wait for potential cures.
2. Developing new drugs is very expensive; estimates vary widely from $43 million to $11 billion for each new drug.[4,5]

Such a wide range suggests that substantial disagreement exists about how this cost is calculated. A commonly used range for development costs is one to two billion dollars for each new drug reaching the market, which is a staggering amount that must be recovered once the drug is available for sale.

Contributing to this cost figure is a high failure rate. One study claims that drug makers investigate 5000 to 10,000 compounds to generate one FDA-approved drug. During development, costs are incurred by the successful drug as well as the other 4999 to 9999 compounds that were eventually eliminated. The successful drug must cover the cost of these failures. Also, marketing and sales costs are high, and there is a significant chance that drug makers may face legal action if their drugs have long-term negative consequences that are not apparent during clinical trials. This would seem to argue for longer trials, but these trials currently last six to seven years plus additional reviews that could add another year or more.[5]

11.2 Drug Development Process

Creating a new drug is a long and complex process that is fraught with uncertainty. What is presented here is a typical process. There are several stages in drug development: prediscovery, drug discovery and preclinical testing, clinical trials conducted as part of FDA oversight, FDA review and decision, and ramp up to full-scale manufacturing. The process follows a stage–gate approach, which is used for product development in many industries. Typically, drug development time is 10 to 15 years from drug discovery to patient availability. This does not include the time for the prediscovery stage, which could be months or several years or the ramp up to full-scale manufacturing stage, which could add six months to a year or

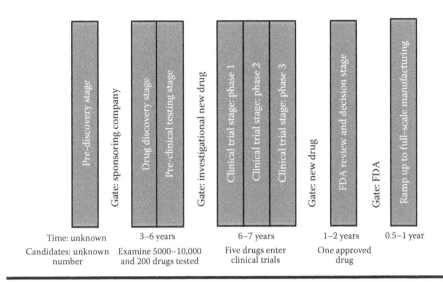

Figure 11.1 **Stage–gate model for drug development. (From PhRMA.org. 2015. Biopharmaceutical research & development: The process behind new medicines. http://www.phrma.org/sites/default/files/pdf/rd_brochure_022307.pdf.)**

more. An overview of the drug development process is provided in Figure 11.1 and is discussed in the following list[5,6]:

1. Prediscovery stage: Before scientists can create and evaluate chemical compounds to treat a health problem, they must understand the disease, the affected tissues, and how the disease impacts the patient. Efforts are made to ensure that the gene or protein in the affected tissue interacts with the drug. This stage is critical because it greatly increases the chance of success, thereby avoiding costly failures. As shown in Figure 11.1, the time for this step is unknown. The gate, which is used to decide whether or not to move to the next stage, is controlled by the sponsoring pharmaceutical company.

2. Drug discovery and preclinical testing stage: Drug discovery begins the search for compounds that can alter the disease. As shown in Figure 11.1, scientists may examine 5000 to 10,000 compounds during drug discovery to determine which ones might be effective treatments, easily absorbed, distributed to the diseased tissue, well metabolized, successfully excreted, and nontoxic. Early in the development process, scientists consider drug formulation (the other ingredients in the drug); delivery methods, such as an injection or orally; large-scale production concerns; and other issues. Next, the lead compounds, which may number more than 200, enter preclinical testing during which extensive tests are performed in the lab and on animals to assess the compounds' effectiveness and safety. Although this stage is under the control of the sponsoring company, much of the testing is mandated and defined by the FDA. At the end of

this stage, which typically takes three to six years, the company files an investigational new drug (IND) application with the FDA so that the candidate drugs, which have been winnowed down to five or so, can enter clinical trials. Pharmacological and safety results gained during testing on animals help to identify strategies for safeguarding human volunteers. The application, which is the next gate, includes rationale for testing on humans, the drug's chemical compound, its side effects, and how it works in the body. The application must have a plan for clinical testing. When the FDA has reviewed and approved the application, the sponsoring company can begin Phase 1 clinical trials. The process to this point is long and thorough with many safeguards along the way, but this is only the beginning.

3. Clinical trials stage: As shown in Figure 11.1, this stage involves testing on humans and has three phases. It must follow FDA procedures and protocols. The primary purposes of the trials are to measure effectiveness and to assess safety. The primary reason for having three phases is to ensure that candidate drugs do no harm, so the trials begin with a very limited number of healthy people to assess consequences. The trials progress to larger groups of people with the targeted health issue, at each stage measuring both safety and efficacy. The FDA and the sponsoring company can stop the trials at any time if problems arise. Under certain conditions, the FDA may stop the trial if the results are very good and there are few, if any, side effects because it would be unreasonable to withhold a promising drug from those who need it. During clinical trials, reporting requirements between the sponsoring company and the FDA are extensive. Typically, the clinical trial stage lasts six to seven years, and for every five candidate drugs that enter, approximately one will eventually be approved by the FDA.

   a. Phase 1 clinical trials focus on drug safety, and they begin with low doses of the compound administered to a small group of healthy people, usually less than 100. The trials assess how the drug is absorbed and metabolized, its side effects, and whether it has the desired outcome. The dosage may be gradually increased during the trial to assess the dosing range. The probability that a drug moves from Phase 1 to Phase 2 is about two chances in three.[7]

   b. Phase 2 clinical trials measure the effectiveness of the compound. There is still concern for safety, so the study size is kept as small as possible, typically 100 to 400 patients who suffer from the disease the drug is designed to treat. This phase provides additional information about negative side effects and safety, so the risk from taking the drug can be assessed. No drug has zero risk, so the FDA must determine whether the benefits of the drug justify accepting the possibility that some patients may incur significant complications. Phase 2 trials are also used to examine the effective dose, dosing interval, and method of delivery. The probability that a drug that makes it to Phase 2 advances to Phase 3 is about one chance in three.[7]

c. Phase 3 clinical trials are the largest (typically more than 1000 participants), longest, and costliest trials. Because of their size, Phase 3 trials collect statistically significant data about safety, including interactions with other drugs, effectiveness, and connection between risk and benefit. The sponsoring company is also preparing plans for full-scale production and the complex application required by the FDA. Once the data from all the trials are analyzed and explained, the new drug application (NDA), which can be 100,000 pages or more, is submitted for review and decision by the FDA. It should be noted that patent information must be submitted with all NDAs, so patent applications coincide with drug development. The probability that a drug in Phase 3 is approved by the FDA is about 80% or more, depending on the study.[7] Because Phase 3 testing is so expensive, companies are very careful about which candidate drugs to move forward.

4. FDA review and decision stage: Once the FDA receives the NDA from the sponsoring company, it identifies a team of experts, who carefully examine it. This team makes a recommendation to the FDA, which has final say on approval, denial, or seeking more information or additional studies, so this gate is controlled by the FDA. As shown in Figure 11.1, this stage can take from six months to two years—even more if additional testing is needed.

5. Ramp up to full-scale manufacturing stage: It is possible but not likely that the sponsoring company could decide not to produce a drug that is approved by the FDA because the company has a tremendous investment in development and is eager to gain a return on this investment. During ramp up, which can take from a few months to a year or more, the sponsoring company assembles the resources needed to produce the drug using the processes identified in the NDA. The company determines where to make the drug, secures the equipment and facilities to produce it, finds suppliers for the ingredients, and organizes and trains the workforce to make it. The company can wait for final approval before ramping up manufacturing. Or it can accept the risk of denial or a request for additional information and begin efforts to ramp up manufacturing while the FDA is deliberating, thereby reducing the time between approval and availability.

11.3 Can Drug Development Time Be Reduced?

There are two reasons why drug development takes so long, and neither is that pharmaceutical companies want to drag their feet. If anything, they want shorter review and approval times.

1. As illustrated by the prior discussion, discovery and approval are complex processes with investigators searching thousands of options until they find a drug that might work. The process requires two large teams of people: one at

the company and another at the FDA. Both teams have members from various disciplines, who have different perspectives and values. The size and heterogeneous nature of the teams as well as the intricacy of the process require large amounts of documentation, report writing, and communication.

2. It is only natural for people who supervise the approval process at the FDA to err on the side of ensuring drugs are safe and effective. No one at the FDA wants to face the headline, "Drug Approval Process by FDA Unsafe." Having a child, expectant mother, young adult, or others suffer irreparable harm or even death from an approved drug would damage the FDA and its administrators. Under these circumstances, efforts by the FDA to provide shortcuts may be viewed at the minimum as lax enforcement.

Little can be done to reduce the difficulty and complexity of the process, which are inherent in the task, but the process can become more efficient and faster. The FDA and the pharmaceutical industry must work together to streamline the development, review, and approval process. Discussing these efforts in detail is a herculean task that is beyond the scope of this book because the solution is one part science and technology, one part information and communication technology, one part interpersonal relationships, one part team building and organizational culture, and another part management structure.

The federal government has a role in convening a working group to tackle this important problem. These efforts would have pharmaceutical companies in the lead for the prediscovery, discovery, and preclinical testing stages because they control this part of the process. The FDA would lead during the clinical trial stage and review and decision stage because it controls this part of the process. The working group would consider how these two major segments in the process function and interact. It would look for ways to create synergies, eliminate redundancy, build more effective communication networks, enhance people and managerial skills, and improve reporting relationships that may reduce time.

Efforts to improve the process should not be about finding ways to increase drug company profits or even about reducing drug development costs, although it is likely that reducing development time will also reduce costs. Efforts should be about addressing the following important trade-off: On one hand, neither the FDA nor pharmaceutical companies want to unleash a harmful drug on patients for reasons involving losses in stature (FDA and pharmaceutical companies) and the potential for lawsuits and legal liabilities (pharmaceutical companies). On the other hand, when it takes 10 to 15 years for a drug to reach consumers, hundreds, thousands, maybe even millions of patients must wait to receive treatment, and during this time, they may suffer, and some may die. It is a delicate and difficult balancing act.

Figure 11.1 illustrates that prediscovery, discovery, and preclinical testing, which are undertaken by the pharmaceutical companies, account for about one third to one half of the time to developing a new drug. Because drug companies have a profit motive, it is in their best interest to make the development process as productive and as short as possible. They have strong incentives to avoid taking more time than needed to understand the disease and how it impacts the patient, to search for a compound that may be an effective treatment, and to complete preclinical testing. Some readers may say, "ah ha," these companies, driven by the profit motive, will do sloppy work to get the job done fast, not care about safety, and be unconcerned about obtaining good outcomes for patients. But that is simply not true.

The reason for the untruth is that when drug companies pick compounds that have serious side effects and/or marginal if any curative power, these flaws become apparent during the FDA's required clinical trials. The drug companies spend a lot of money for these trials and have no benefit or revenue when drugs are not approved. The best interest of the drug companies is served when they create effective drugs that have few side effects. It is reasonable to argue that the long and expensive review and approval process may actually discourage pharmaceutical companies from moving a drug that has "some" promise through FDA clinical trials because it costs too much to do so. It is difficult to know the number of drug compounds gathering dust at pharmaceutical companies that may help patients. In support of this claim, consider that the FDA has approved fewer new compounds each year since 1995, and drug companies are reluctant to move new compounds forward because of high cost and uncertainty.[8]

The larger part of the drug approval process, clinical trials, and decision, is controlled by the FDA. Here the FDA attempts to assess safety and effectiveness. In examining this process, it is important to understand and consider the following question. What is the right balance between safety and helping sick patients? This relatively simple question raises some important factors that should be considered including the following: What side effects has the drug shown, and how serious are they? How debilitating and/or life threatening is the health problem? What is the likelihood that the patient will survive until the trial is completed? If there are alternative treatments, how effective are these?

These questions seem to suggest that the approval process and, by association, the time required for approval should depend on several factors. It seems to be a "no brainer" that a patient suffering greatly and likely to die from a disease for which there is no known treatment should have access to medication that has few if any side effects and has demonstrated great success early in clinical trials. If they don't receive the medication, which offers some hope, the likely outcome is grave suffering and death. The real challenge is making these decisions when the line separating access or no access to the drug is not so bright. Suppose there are some, possibly even serious, side effects, or there is a current treatment, but it offers a cure in only a small percentage of the cases. What about a patient suffering from blindness or debilitating arthritis? These are not life-threatening conditions, but they can have a major impact on quality of life. How much risk would a patient be willing to take to find relief from these problems? It is likely that different patients may have different opinions about this.

To begin to address the safety versus effectiveness trade-off, the FDA created a breakthrough therapy classification in 2012 so that drugs designed to treat serious and life-threatening health problems can move through the approval process much faster. To get this designation, the drug must also show substantial improvement over existing treatments in the early phase of clinical trials.[9] The FDA also established an Office of Orphan Product Development with the mission of creating drugs to treat rare diseases or medical conditions as part of its efforts to design more drugs and get them in the hands of those who need them. Rare is defined as affecting fewer than 200,000 people in the United States. In some circumstances, this designation can be given if it impacts 200,000 or more.[10]

The FDA was created to protect the U.S. population from drugs that had no healing power or could harm them. In an ideal world, patients would be presented with all the facts about a particular experimental drug and would make the decision to take it or not. Promising drugs in clinical trials should be available to people facing death or serious debilitating health problems even when the risks are substantial or even fatal. Allowing patients greater access to experimental drugs seems reasonable if the patients, supported by their physicians, are rational and aware of the consequences from taking them. Expanding the notion of the breakthrough therapy classification, so that patients have a choice, gives them more access to treatment. This idea would also be part of the working group's mission.

11.4 Can Drug Costs Be Reduced?

The $263.3 billion spent on prescription drugs in 2012[11] is driven by both the amount of drugs consumed and the selling price for the drugs. To effectively address overall drug costs in the U.S. economy, it is essential to examine both volume and price.

11.4.1 Impact of Usage on the Overall Costs of Prescription Drugs

There has already been much discussion about how the consumption of drugs may change. The details are not repeated here, but a brief summary of these points follows:

1. Wellness: If people can improve their health through better lifestyle choices, they will consume fewer drugs.
2. Effective trade-offs: If the United States implements patient-centered care and reforms insurance so that patients face a balanced trade-off, they are more likely to make better decisions about whether or not to use prescription drugs. This would likely reduce drug consumption.

3. Aging population: Drug consumption is likely to increase as the baby boomer generation ages.
4. Increased access: As more people have access to care through the Affordable Care Act, the consumption of drugs is likely to increase.
5. Innovations in prescription drugs: Innovations in drug research will likely increase use. Plus, drug therapy may replace other more expensive and riskier forms of treatment, such as surgery.

The net effect of these countervailing forces is unclear at this time, but patients will make better choices about whether they should take prescription drugs and how much to take and for how long. Whether U.S. consumers buy more or fewer drugs, they will spend wisely and have better health outcomes.

Another key issue is fraud. Criminals employ various techniques to bill Medicare for services, including prescription drugs, which are unnecessary or are written for patients who do not exist. The General Accounting Office and CBS News have estimated annual Medicare fraud at $48 billion and $60 billion, respectively.[12] In other cases, unscrupulous physicians are using their ability to write prescription as a way to traffic drugs.[13] One way to deal with these drug abuses is to require physicians and pharmacists to check a prescription drug database to verify the appropriateness of prescriptions and check patients' patterns of use. This would help catch drug-dealing doctors and doctor-shopping patients. Several, but not all, states have these databases in place. If every state had such a system and these systems were connected, catching criminals and lowering prescription drug costs would be much easier.

11.4.2 Impact of Price Paid on the Overall Costs of Prescription Drugs

The other part of the cost equation is the price paid. People often claim that prescription drugs are too expensive. If only greedy drug companies would be satisfied with lower profits, drugs would cost less. At its simplest level, lower profits should lead to lower drug costs. But if profits are reduced or eliminated: How much less would drugs cost? The other side of the question is this: Would individuals, pension funds, and others with capital to invest be willing to risk it to develop new drugs? In a free market, capital moves to projects that pay returns (capital repayment and a profit) that are commensurate with investment risk. To spur innovation, drug companies must be attractive places for investors.

To spur the creation of new medicines in response to declining research productivity by pharmaceutical companies, the federal government has plans to create a billion dollar drug research center. The new center would do as much research as necessary to attract drug company investment and turn the commercialization over to the private sector.[14] This tactic is likely to stimulate less investment by pharmaceutical companies as they step back and let government do more work and accept more risk. On top of that, the federal government has difficulties running agencies, such as Veterans Affairs (inability to provide timely care and covering up these problems), the IRS (targeting conservative groups), and the U.S. Postal Service (financial problems). Government has demonstrated over and over that it is incapable of picking winners and losers in the private sector. The most likely outcomes from this planned endeavor are fewer new and innovative drugs, longer development times, and higher costs.

11.4.2.1 Putting Drug Company Profits into Perspective

It is helpful to examine the income statement of two prominent drug companies, Pfizer[15] and Merck,[16] shown in Table 11.1. They were picked at random from

Table 11.1 Income Statement for Pfizer and Merck

	Income Statements (All $ in Millions)			
	Average for 2011, 2012, and 2013			
	Pfizer Inc.		*Merck*	
	Amounts	*% of Revenue*	*Amounts*	*% of Revenue*
Revenue	$55,759	100.00%	$10,449	100.00%
Cost of sales	$10,536	18.90%	$2929	28.03%
Gross margins	$45,223	81.10%	$7520	71.97%
Research & development	$7614	13.66%	$1510	14.45%
SGA	$15,702	28.16%	$2922	27.96%
Other expenses	$9104	16.33%	$2109	20.18%
Income before tax	$12,803	22.96%	$979	9.37%
Taxes	$3383	6.07%	$177	1.69%
Income after tax	$9420	16.89%	$802	7.68%

Source: Pfizer Inc. 2014. Pfizer annual report 2013. http://www.annualreportowl.com /Pfizer/2013/Annual%20Report?p=18 (accessed January 16, 2015); Merck Group. 2014. Merck annual report 2013. http://reports.merckgroup.com/2013/annual -report/financial-statements/income-statement/print.html (accessed January 16, 2015); Merck Group. 2013. Merck annual report 2012. http://reports .merckgroup.com/2012/ar/financialstatement/incomestatement/print.html (accessed January 16, 2015).

Note: SGA, selling general and administrative expenses.

among the well-known companies. Income statements were averaged over a three-year period (2011, 2012, and 2013) to smooth out impacts from one-time events. Research and development (R&D) costs were 13.66% and 14.45% of revenue for Pfizer and Merck, respectively, and SGA (selling, general, and administrative) expenses were 28.16% and 27.96%, respectively. The majority of SGA expenses were for marketing. When R&D and SGA are added, they account for about 42% of revenue for each firm, a remarkably similar number, which provides some idea about the order of magnitude for these expenses throughout the industry.

Pfizer and Merck had income after tax (profit) of 16.89% and 7.68% of revenue, respectively. To compare these profits with other well-known companies, Apple's average income after tax was about 23% of revenue,[17] JP Morgan Chase's average income after tax was slightly more than 19.5%,[18] and Google's average income after tax was about 23%.[19] These companies were picked prior to knowing their profits, because they are well-known service providers. Now, the question is this: Which company should financial advisors recommend as an investment to a pension plan? On profits alone, the pharmaceutical companies are the least attractive. Certainly, there is more to consider than profit, but profit is certainly an important factor. This analysis provides evidence that profits made by pharmaceutical companies are not out of line with other firms. In fact, one could argue that the profits, especially for Merck, may be too low to attract new investment. The next step is to examine the cost side of drug development, specifically R&D and marketing, which consume about 42% of revenue for both Pfizer and Merck.

11.4.2.2 Shortening Development Time Reduces Drug Costs

Part of the reason that drugs are expensive is the long time from prediscovery until availability, and drug companies begin spending money from the first day. Funds come from two sources, bondholders and stockholders, and each want a fee to use their money. Bondholders require periodic interest payments and the return of capital. Stockholders share in the company's success through dividend payments, which usually come quarterly, and stock appreciation that is realized when the stock is sold. These returns to the bondholders and stockholders combine to form what financiers call the cost of capital for the company, which varies depending upon the risk associated with the company's endeavor. The risk for pharmaceutical companies is slightly above average as measured by their "beta," which is used by equity investors to assess risk. Higher beta means more risk. The cost of capital for pharmaceutical drug companies as of January 2015 was slightly more than 7.24%.[20]

This means that every dollar invested by a drug company costs the firm 7.24 cents each year. So, a dollar invested in R&D at the beginning of year 1 incurs an additional 7.24 cents in capital costs for a total investment of $1.0724 at the end of year 1. There is no income until there are sales of the new drug, which is years in the future, so capital costs become part of the investment. By the end of year 2, this one-dollar investment has increased to $1.150042 because the firm's investment at the beginning of year 2 is $1.0724, so the capital charge for year 2 must be higher at 0.077642 (1.0724 times 0.0724). The cost of capital increases the investment at a compound rate of 7.24% a year until there is a revenue stream from the investment to repay the capital plus the cost of using the capital.

For the sake of discussion, assume a drug takes 12 years to make this journey. As shown in column 2 of Table 11.2, every dollar invested at the beginning of the first year of this journey becomes $2.313565 when the charges for using the capital are included. For each dollar invested in year 2, which is 11 years prior to launch, the amount becomes $2.157371. Each dollar invested in subsequent years generates a slightly smaller amount until the dollar invested in the year prior to launch, which is year 12, has a cost of 1.0724. The sum of column 2 is $19.456725, which means investing $1 per year for 12 years, actually costs the firm $19.46, not $12. For each investment of $1 million per year, column 3 shows that the actual cost to the firm is $19,456,725 over a 12-year period, not $12 million. If development time could be cut to 10 years and development costs reduced to $10 million, the total investment as shown in column 4 would drop to $14,985,789, which is $4,470,936 less than column 3—a decline of about 23%. As shown in column 5, even if the amount of R&D expense remains at $12 million but the time is reduced to 10 years, the total investment would drop to $17,982,947 for a savings of $1,473,778 or about 7.6%.

Another factor driving up costs is a high dropout rate. As described earlier, companies may examine 5000 to 10,000 compounds to identify 200 or so drugs to consider in preclinical testing. They winnow this down to about five drugs to submit to clinical trials, and this typically leads to one revenue-generating drug. This drug must earn enough to support all of the R&D expenses incurred by the failed attempts. Plus, development expenditures accelerate as a drug moves through the process, explaining why companies put a lot of effort into reducing the number of candidate drugs before going to clinical trials.

11.4.2.3 Marketing and Sales Cost Reductions

Marketing and sales are another major cost, and the most controversial part is direct-to-consumer (DTC) advertisement, which represents about 12.5% of marketing costs.[21] Critics argue that DTC advertising, which often involves TV commercials, is an expensive way to inform consumers about treatment options and leads to increased drug use as consumers pressure physicians for prescriptions. For these reasons, several states have created legislation regulating DTC advertising.[22] Supporters, on the other hand, argue that patients have a right to know about treatment options and to be involved in decision making. Many would agree with this latter point of view, so it is important to find better ways to provide high-quality, unbiased information so that patients and their physicians can make good decisions.

Table 11.2 Capital Cost for Investing in Drug Development

	Cost of $1 Invested in the Beginning of Year X at the End of Year 12	Cost of $1 Million Invested in the Beginning of Year X at the End of Year 12	Cost of $1 Million Invested in the Beginning of Year X at the End of Year 10	Cost of $1.2 Million Invested in the Beginning of Year X at the End of Year 10
Year 1	$2.313565	$2,313,565	$2,011,722	$2,414,067
Year 2	$2.157371	$2,157,371	$1,875,907	$2,251,088
Year 3	$2.011722	$2,011,722	$1,749,260	$2,099,112
Year 4	$1.875907	$1,875,907	$1,631,164	$1,957,397
Year 5	$1.749260	$1,749,260	$1,521,041	$1,825,249
Year 6	$1.631164	$1,631,164	$1,418,352	$1,702,022
Year 7	$1.521041	$1,521,041	$1,322,596	$1,587,115
Year 8	$1.418352	$1,418,352	$1,233,305	$1,479,966
Year 9	$1.322596	$1,322,596	$1,150,042	$1,380,050
Year 10	$1.233305	$1,233,305	$1,072,400	$1,286,880
Year 11	$1.150042	$1,150,042		
Year 12	$1.072400	$1,072,400		
Total	$19.456725	$19,456,725	$14,985,789	$17,982,947

Another major element of marketing costs is promoting drugs directly to physicians, which is about 25% of the total.[21] Most often, this involves sales representatives providing information, encouragement, and incentives for using the company's drugs during visits to physicians' offices and hospitals. These representatives are often paid a commission and are well compensated. An often-used incentive is providing free drug samples, which is the largest part of marketing costs at more than 55%.[21] Making substantial changes in the way drugs are marketed and sold could reduce costs and give patients and physicians the information they need to select the best treatment option.

A solution, at least a partial one, is to create a prescription drug information clearinghouse (PDIC) that describes what the drug treats as well as its side effects, interactions, and costs. For those who are interested, links would be available to the results of the drug's clinical trials. This database would be searchable by anyone, including physicians and pharmacists, in various ways, including but not limited to drug name and medical condition. The PDIC would be part of the medical diagnostic and treatment support system (MDTSS) discussed in the previous chapter. As part of the FDA drug approval process, companies would be required to post information to the PDIC in a standard format and in language that is understandable to typical patients.

11.4.2.4 More Physician Education

Many physicians and patients are unaware of the cost of prescription drugs, especially when patients have insurance that pays most of the cost. Sales representatives typically present expensive, patent-protected drugs to physicians with information touting the drug's capabilities. Patent-protected means these drugs cannot be copied and produced at a low cost. This protection is the chance for companies to recoup their R&D costs. Drugs that are not patent-protected, commonly called generic drugs, are much cheaper because there is no R&D cost and minimal advertising. Recall from Table 11.1 that production costs, shown as the "cost of sales," is a small part of the costs, so generic drug are usually much cheaper than patented-protected ones. Typically, salespeople do not stop at physicians' offices to sell generic drugs, so the path of least resistance for many physicians is to prescribe these more expensive drugs.

Patients and physicians need information about drug costs and alternative treatment options, and the PDIC is a start. In addition, beginning in medical school, physicians need to develop the attitude that providing value is important. Value means giving high-quality treatment and keeping costs low. Physicians should have continuing education opportunities that reinforce this attitude and describe ways to find less expensive treatments including less expensive drugs. The role of pharmacists may expand because they are a good source for information about drug treatment options and costs, so they may be able to suggest less expensive medications that are just as effective.

11.4.2.5 The Pharmaceutical Company–Physician Relationship

When the issue of marketing drugs to physicians is discussed, the question about payments from drug companies to doctors for using certain medications is raised. It is illegal and certainly unethical for pharmaceutical companies to offer and for physicians to accept direct payment to prescribe their drugs.

However, pharmaceutical companies can and do pay substantial sums of money to some physicians to speak at medical conferences. The obvious question is this: Does a quid pro quo exist between the parties—that is, the physician who prescribes the company's drug and the company that hires the physician? Although there may be a need for qualified physicians who have experience in using a drug to speak about it at conferences, it is quite clear that a conflict of interest exists for the physician. Under the new healthcare law, companies had to begin disclosing these payments by 2014.[23] This does shed some light on the practice, but it is unlikely that patients would access this information unless it is readily available, such as being part of the PDIC. The preferred option would be to eliminate the practice of hiring physicians as speakers.

11.5 Setting a Fair Price

There is another important element in selling drugs at a fair price in the United States, and it has to do with how the fixed costs in drug development, such as R&D and advertising, are allocated. Going back to Table 11.1, both Pfizer and Merck have a very low "cost of sales" at 18.9% and 28.0% of revenue, respectively. This is the cost to produce the drugs sold by the companies. The rest of the deductions from revenue are primarily fixed cost, things that do not change, depending on production. In other words, if sales and production go up or down by 10% or 20%, these costs do not change. For Pfizer and Merck, that is R&D, SGA, and other expenses, which are approximately 58% and 63% of revenue, respectively.

As discussed earlier in the book, drug companies charge a lower price in Canada and Western Europe and even a lower price in underdeveloped countries than they do in the United States. It is understandable and acceptable for humanitarian reasons for U.S. companies to offer prescription drugs at lower prices in underdeveloped countries. The Trade-Related Aspects of Intellectual Property Rights (TRIPS) agreement administered by the World Trade Organization grants low-income countries the opportunity to receive licenses from high-income countries to manufacture life-saving drugs for consumption in their countries. For example, Sovaldi, a Hepatitis C drug, costs $1000 a pill in the United States, but a Bangladeshi pharmaceutical company received a license under the TRIPS agreement, and it is manufacturing the drug in Bangladesh and selling it for $5 a pill.[24]

On the other hand, it is not acceptable for U.S. companies to sell prescription drugs at a much lower price in developed countries. As an example, the Pharmacy

Checker website indicates that a 30-day supply of Lipitor (40 mg) costs $310.80 or $10.36 per pill from a U.S. pharmacy. The same pill from a Canadian or other non–U.S. pharmacy can cost as little at $0.72 per pill for 90 pills or $1.17 per pill for 30.[25] A report by *60 Minutes* reveals that some drugs cost 10 times more in the United States than they do in parts of Western Europe.[26] Purchasing U.S.–made drugs from foreign pharmacies, which is sometimes called drug reimportation, is illegal in the United States. However, U.S. government officials have made it clear that individuals who order noncontrolled drugs for their personal use will not be prosecuted if the supply is for 90 days or less. Unfortunately, reimported drugs are not eligible for health reimbursement accounts or flexible spending accounts. Reimported drugs may not be eligible for reimbursement from traditional employer-based insurance plans.[25]

The obvious questions are the following: What is the justification for this large difference between U.S. drug prices and Canadian and Western European drug prices? Why would drug companies want to lose money on drugs sold in Canada and Western Europe? The answers to these questions are based on understanding two fairly technical accounting terms called *full accounting costs* and *contribution pricing*.

In Figure 11.2, the full accounting cost for a drug, which is designated as D1, includes its variable costs per unit plus a share of fixed costs, which includes R&D, SGA, and other fixed expenses. This share is determined by dividing the fixed costs assigned to drug D1 by D1's expected sales volume. If the company has five drugs, labeled D1 through D5, and a similar process is followed for all five drugs, selling the expected volume of each drug at a price that equals its full accounting costs means the company covers all of its fixed and variable costs. In other words, it breaks even. As indicated by the equation at the top of Figure 11.2, to make a profit the selling price for drugs D1 and the other four drugs is set higher than their full accounting costs. At this higher price and selling at the expected volume, the

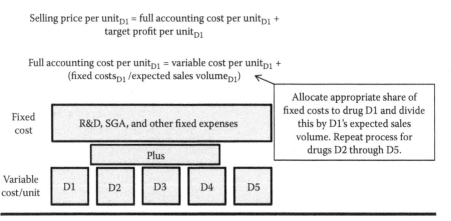

Figure 11.2 Determining full accounting costs and selling prices for drugs.

revenue covers the company's costs and tax liability, and it provides a profit (see the income statement in Table 11.1).

So how does a company charge different prices in different countries? It does so by allocating all or most of its fixed costs to the drugs sold in one country, the United States in this case, and allocates none or very little of the fixed cost to drugs sold in another. Under this scenario, U.S. consumers pay the production costs and all or most of the fixed costs plus they generate profits for drug companies. Foreign buyers pay production costs while paying nothing or very little toward fixed costs because all or the vast majority of the fixed costs are paid by U.S. consumers. As a result, foreign sales still contribute to profitability.

As illustrated in Figure 11.3, this is contribution pricing with foreign buyers paying more than the variable cost per unit but less than the full accounting cost. As shown in Figure 11.3, the selling price can be set along a continuum with the first point of interest being D1: Variable cost per unit. If the selling price for D1 for all customers is set here, no matter how much is sold, the company has a loss because fixed costs are not covered. As explained earlier, setting a selling price for all sales of D1 that equals the full account cost per unit and selling the expected sales volume will cover the variable and fixed costs but not yield a profit. What drug companies appear to be doing is setting the selling price for drugs sold in the United States at D1: U.S. selling price, which covers the variable and all or most of the fixed costs and generates a profit. At the same time, they set the selling price for drugs sold in Canada and Western Europe at a much lower level, a level that is above the D1: Variable cost per unit and much below D1: Full accounting cost per unit. The latter sales do

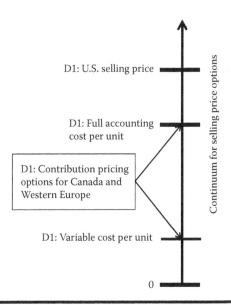

Figure 11.3 Understanding contribution pricing for drug D1.

contribute toward profits because all or most fixed costs are covered by U.S. sales. So U.S. consumers are subsidizing consumers in Canada and Western Europe. In an industry such as pharmaceuticals, the difference between a price set above a drug's full accounting costs and a contribution price can be substantial because variable costs are small compared to fixed costs (see Table 11.2 for confirmation).

In terms of a solution, some may suggest that drug companies should be forced by law to sell drugs in the United States for the same low price paid in Western Europe. If that happened, drug companies would lose money because their fixed costs would not be covered. They would be unable to attract investors and would go out of business. In general, government price controls are not only ineffective, they are counterproductive, even disastrous. The solution is to allocate fixed costs to all drug sales, and U.S. prices would decline while prices in Canada and Western Europe would increase.

The problem of differential drug pricing was created by government regulation, and the best way to address it is to remove the regulation. As noted early, buying U.S.-made drugs from pharmacies in Canada, Western Europe, or other countries is prohibited by federal law. Even though this law is not enforced for small purchases for individual use, there are other stipulations involving reimbursement that make these purchases from foreign pharmacies difficult. Government should first remove these stipulations, which would make drug reimportation legal, and second, instruct the FDA to work with and sanction entities in foreign countries that sell drugs to U.S. consumers, thereby offering assurance that reimported drugs are authentic and safe. This makes it possible for U.S. consumers to have lower prices. This solution uses market forces to inform pharmaceutical companies that they must transfer a fair share of their fixed costs to foreign buyers. U.S. drug prices would decline, and Canadian and Western European prices would increase.

Getting back to the question as to why drug companies have chosen to set different prices, the answer appears to be that Canada and most countries in Western Europe have single-payer, socialized medicine where the government negotiates prices. Negotiators in foreign countries have access to the financial statements of pharmaceutical companies, so they know their cost structure. A foreign government can pressure pharmaceutical companies to offer lower prices if they want to sell their drug in that country. To complete the picture, drug companies lobby the U.S. government to make drug reimportation illegal. Making reimportation legal is the way to put market forces and competition back into drug pricing. It also provides drug companies with leverage in negotiating selling prices in other countries.

11.6 Driving Forces for Change

Reducing drug development time requires the FDA and pharmaceutical companies to work together to streamline the development process. The federal government has a critical role in forming an effective working group that includes these participants and in creating a platform that allows them to work toward the goal of reducing drug development time. In addition, drug costs are influenced to a great extent by R&D and marketing. R&D costs are influenced by the length of time and level of complexity in the drug-development process. Because of this connectivity, it makes sense to roll issues regarding the cost of drug development into the duties of this working group.

Marketing and advertising costs are another matter. These are discretionary costs that have virtually no impact on the effectiveness, efficiency, or timing of the company's most important activity, drug development. Pharmaceutical companies working with the FDA should carefully examine marketing costs to see how the companies benefit. Some part of the costs is absolutely necessary as it provides patients, physicians, pharmacists, and other healthcare professionals with basic information about the drug. However, this portion is only about 5% of marketing costs.[21] Another part of marketing involves direct sales to physicians, when company representatives visit physicians, provide free samples, and seek to persuade physicians to prescribe the company's drugs. Although this may lead to more sales, it is very expensive, accounting for more than 80% of the marketing costs.[21] There must be better and more cost-effective ways to interact with physicians. These two marketing initiatives are within the purview of the pharmaceutical companies, but they may benefit from insights from the FDA.

The third element is direct-to-consumer advertising, which has come under scrutiny. Many people feel, at a minimum, it is an unnecessary expense, and in the worst case, it exerts excessive pressure on consumers, driving up prescription drug use and stimulating demand for expensive drugs. One approach would be working with pharmaceutical companies to greatly reduce or eliminate direct-to-consumer advertising. The companies may be hard to convince because they seem to believe that advertising stimulates demand. However, it wasn't until the middle of the 1990s before the FDA issued rules on how companies could advertise on TV,[27] so prior to that, TV advertising was very limited. Another way is to educate patients and physicians, so they understand treatment options and are not susceptible to this advertising. Letting consumers know that they can get the same high-quality outcome at a lower price is a powerful tool. This is the essence of the PDIC. As a last resort, legislation can be passed to limit drug advertising to consumers. This is not without precedent as tobacco advertising is severely restricted.

Creating a PDIC would involve participation from a variety of organizations, including the American Pharmacists Association (APA); nationwide pharmacies, such as Wal-Mart and CVS; pharmaceutical companies; the FDA; and representatives from top-level hospitals, such as the Mayo Clinic and Cleveland Clinic. The pharmaceutical companies would provide information about the drug, including side effects and potential cures, and various pharmacies would provide local pricing data. The APA, hospitals, and the FDA would provide oversight to ensure accurate, timely, and easily searchable information. With leadership from the FDA, government would mandate the creation of this database. Funding for a PDIC could be handled similarly to funding for the Federal Deposit Insurance Corporation (FDIC) where banks pay a very small percentage of revenue into this insurance fund. Here drug companies would pay a very small percentage of their revenue to support the PDIC.

Educating physicians about drug cost requires efforts from groups such as the American Medical Association and the American College of Physician Executives who control curriculum and provide continuous education. If the United States is to have high-quality care and affordable costs, it is vital to education physicians about the importance of considering costs when selecting treatment options.

Finally, drug reimportation should be made legal, and the prime mover is the federal government. The current restriction on buying U.S.–produced drugs from another country is the antithesis of free markets and free trade. For decades, the United States and its presidents have been in favor of free trade. It seems hypocritical to block U.S. citizens and residents from buying drugs from Canada or Western Europe. Blocking drug reimportation is about government control that benefits one industry and a small group of lobbyists to the detriment of its citizens and residents.

11.7 Impact of Fair and Affordable Drug Prices on Healthcare Outcomes

At just under 9.5%, prescription drug cost is the third largest healthcare expense after hospital care and physician and clinical services.[1] Whether the expense increases or decreases is much less important than reforming the system so that patients make better choices about whether and which drugs they use and the price they pay for those drugs. Following is a summary of the impacts of this issue on the relevant root causes, which are discussed in Chapter 2:

■ High drug costs: It is unclear whether the forces impacting drug usage will cause drug costs to increase or decrease. But when drug usage is determined by a full and complete set of information, the usage should be reasonable and appropriate for the needs of patients. At the same time, addressing the drivers of drug costs should lower the price paid by consumers for their medications. Even though the net effect of these changes on costs is unclear, the overall cost should be lower than if the status quo is maintained. The idea is to ensure that drug prices are fair and reasonable and at the same time high enough to generate a profit and ensure future investment in drug development. This should address the high costs of drugs (root cause #6).

11.8 Summary of Recommendations

Following is a listing of the key recommendations contained in this chapter.

1. Reducing drug development time.
   a. The FDA and the pharmaceutical industry must work together to stream-line the drug development process with the dual mandate of reducing time and maintaining safety. Pharmaceutical companies would lead improvements for prediscovery, discovery, and preclinical stages, and the FDA would lead during the clinical trial stage and review and decision stage.
   b. Empower patients with serious health problems, supported by their physicians, to make decisions about taking drugs that are in FDA clinical trials when available treatment options either do not exist or have proven to be ineffective.
2. Reducing drug development cost.
   a. In prior chapters, two important elements are discussed that reduce the consumption of drugs: having patients focus on wellness, leading to less demand, and having patients face a balanced trade-off that considers both the benefits and costs of taking drugs.
   b. Reduce prescription drug fraud by creating a national database and requiring physicians and pharmacists to check prescriptions to verify their appropriateness and check patients' patterns of use.
   c. Reduce the price paid for drugs by reducing the amount of time it takes to develop and win approval for new drugs. This reduces research and development costs and generates revenue more quickly, thereby lowering capital costs.
   d. Reduce marketing and sales costs by cutting back or eliminating direct-to-consumer marketing, direct marketing to physicians, and free drug samples.
   e. Create a prescription drug information clearinghouse (PDIC) that would provide patients and their physicians with a drug's potential uses, side effects, interactions, and costs. This would replace direct-to-consumer advertising and direct marketing to physicians.
3. Currently, drug companies charge a much higher price for drugs sold in the United States compared to those sold in Canada and Western Europe. This is discrimination against U.S. consumers and can be resolved by allowing drug reimportation.

References

1. Center for Medicare and Medicaid Services. 2012. National health expenditure highlights. http://www.cms.gov/Research-Statistics-Data-and-Systems/Statistics-Trends-and-Reports/NationalHealthExpendData/downloads/highlights.pdf (accessed February 20, 2014).

2. Keyhani, S., Wang, S., Hebert, P., Carpenter, D., and Anderson, G. 2010. US Pharmaceutical innovation in an international context. *Am J Public Health*, 100(6), (June): 1075–1080. http://www.ncbi.nlm.nih.gov/pmc/articles/PMC2866602/ (accessed January 1, 2015).

3. Gregory, P. R. 2012. Obama care will end drug advances and Europe's free ride (unless China steps in). *Economics and Finance*, (July 1). http://www.forbes.com/sites /paulroderickgregory/2012/07/01/obama-care-will-end-drug-advances-and-europes -free-ride-unless-china-steps-in/ (accessed January 9, 2015).

4. Herper, M. 2012. The truly staggering costs of inventing new drugs. (February 10). *Forbes*, http://www.forbes.com/sites/matthewherper/2012/02/10/the-truly-staggering -cost-of-inventing-new-drugs/ (accessed January 9, 2015); PLOS Medical Journal's Community Blog. 2012. Pharmaceutical R&D costly myths. (March 7). http:// blogs.plos.org/speakingofmedicine/2012/03/07/pharmaceutical-rds-costly-myths/ (accessed January 28, 2015); Morgan, S., Grootendorst, P., Lexchin, J., Cunningham, C., and Greyson, D. 2011. The cost of drug development: A systemic review. *Health Policy*, 100(1) (April). http://www.ncbi.nlm.nih.gov/pubmed/21256615 (accessed January 27, 2015).

5. PhRMA.org. 2015. Biopharmaceutical research & development: The process behind new medicines. http://www.phrma.org/sites/default/files/pdf/rd_brochure_022307 .pdf (accessed November 5, 2015).

6. Pharmaceutical and Healthcare Association of the Philippines. 2015. The R&D process. http://www.phap.org.ph/index.php?cid=3 (accessed November 5, 2015); Wikipedia. 2015. Drug development. https://en.wikipedia.org/wiki/Drug_development (accessed November 5, 2015).

7. Hay, M., D. W. Thomas, J. L. Craighead, C. Economides, and J. Rosenthal. 2014. Clinical development success rate for investigational drugs. *Nature Biotechnology*, (January) 32:1:40–51.

8. Boyle, R. 2011. Federal government to develop its own drugs in effort to spur pharmaceutical industry. http://www.popsci.com/science/article/2011-01/feds-open-new -drug-research-center-effort-spur-pharmaceutical-industry (accessed November 10, 2015).

9. Healthline.com. 2014. FDA strikes a balance between access and safety with 'breakthrough' drug program. http://www.healthline.com/health-news/fda-breakthrough -drugs-072914 (accessed January 15, 2015).

10. FDA.gov. 2005. Developing products for rare diseases & conditions. http://www.fda .gov/ForIndustry/DevelopingProductsforRareDiseasesConditions/ucm2005525.htm (accessed January 15, 2015).

11. The Center for Medicare and Medicaid Services. 2013. National healthcare expenditures 2012 highlights. http://www.cms.gov/Research-Statistics-Data-and-Systems /Statistics-Trends-and-Reports/NationalHealthExpendData/downloads/highlights .pdf (accessed February 2, 2014).

12. Merrill, M. 2012. Medicare and Medicaid fraud is costing taxpayers billions. *Forbes*, (May 31). http://www.forbes.com/sites/merrillmatthews/2012/05/31/medicare-and -medicaid-fraud-is-costing-taxpayers-billions/ (accessed September 25, 2015); CBS News. 2009. Medicare fraud: A $60 billion crime. (October 23, 2015). http:// www.cbsnews.com/news/medicare-fraud-a-60-billion-crime-23-10-2009/ (accessed November 10, 2015).

13. Consumer Watchdog. 2015. Arrest of substance-abusing "pill mill" doctor shows need for mandatory use of prescription drug database. (January 15). http://www.consumerwatch dog.org/newsrelease/arrest-substance-abusing-%E2%80%9Cpill-mill%E2%80%9D -doctor-shows-need-mandatory-use-prescription-drug-d (accessed November 10, 2015).

14. Boyle, R. 2011. Federal government to develop its own drugs in effort to spur pharmaceutical industry. http://www.popsci.com/science/article/2011-01/feds-open-new -drug-research-center-effort-spur-pharmaceutical-industry (accessed November 10, 2015); Harris, G. 2011. Federal research center will help develop medicines. *The New York Times*, (January 22). http://www.nytimes.com/2011/01/23/health /policy/23drug.html (accessed November 10, 2015).

15. Pfizer Inc. 2014. Pfizer annual report 2013. http://www.annualreportowl.com /Pfizer/2013/Annual%20Report?p=18 (accessed January 16, 2015).

16. Merck Group. 2014. Merck annual report 2013. http://reports.merckgroup .com/2013/annual-report/financial-statements/income-statement/print.html (accessed January 16, 2015); Merck Group. 2013. Merck annual report 2012. http:// reports.merckgroup.com/2012/ar/financialstatement/incomestatement/print.html. (accessed January 16, 2015).

17. Apple Inc. 2015. Apple annual report 2014. http://investor.apple.com/secfil ing.cfm?filingID=1193125-14-383437&CIK=320193#D783162D10K_HTM _TOC783162_11 (accessed November 10, 2015).

18. JP Morgan Chase &Co. 2012. Income Statement 2011. http://investor.shareholder.com /jpmorganchase/secfiling.cfm?filingID=19617-12-163 (accessed November 12, 2015).

19. Google Income Statement. https://investor.google.com/pdf/20131231_google_10K .pdf (accessed November 12, 2015).

20. New York University, Stern School of Business. 2015. Cost of Capital by Sector (US). http://pages.stern.nyu.edu/~adamodar/New_Home_Page/datafile/wacc.htm (accessed January 15, 2015).

21. Wikipedia. 2015. Pharmaceutical marketing. http://en.wikipedia.org/wiki/Pharma ceutical_marketing (accessed January 29, 2015).

22. National Conference of State Legislatures. 2013. Marketing and direct-to-consumer advertising (DTCA) of pharmaceuticals. http://www.ncsl.org/research/health/market ing-and-advertising-of-pharmaceuticals.aspx (accessed January 27, 2015).

23. Smyser, K., and Kwan, N. 2013. Docs paid thousands to promote drugs they prescribe. *NBC Chicago*, (May 15). http://www.nbcchicago.com/investigations/doctors-prescrip tion-drugs--207652001.html (accessed November 23, 2015); NPR. 2011. Doctors often receive payments from drug companies. (September 14). http://www.npr.org/templates /transcript/transcript.php?storyId=140438636 (accessed November 23, 2015).

24. Barton, J. H. 2004. TRIPS and the Global Pharmaceutical Market. *Health Affairs*, 23(3), (May/June): 146–154.

25. PharmacyChecker.com. 2015. Compare drug prices. http://www.pharmacychecker .com/drug-price-comparisons.asp (accessed November 12, 2015).

26. Senior Health Insurance. 2015. Prescription drug costs in the U.S. and Canada. http://www.seniors-health-insurance.com/drug-costs-compared-us-canada.php (accessed January 27, 2015).

27. Zimney, E. 2006. A history of drug advertisement on TV. EveryDayHealth.com, (August 24). http://www.everydayhealth.com/columns/zimney-health-and-medical -news-you-can-use/a-history-of-drug-ads-on-tv/ (accessed November 12, 2015).

Chapter 12

Reducing the Incidence of Malpractice and Reforming the Legal System

The most effective way to reduce legal liabilities and malpractice insurance costs is to reduce the number of medical errors. Several components of the solution discussed so far should drive the incidence of malpractice lower by creating healthier patients, driving better decision making, and improving the quality of care. There are other ways to improve care that are discussed later in this chapter.

The logic for reforming the legal system is not to prohibit filing or even to make it difficult to file malpractice lawsuits. Everyone has the right to legal redress when they suffer injuries or damages at the hand of another even when the incident is not a criminal offense. These are civil lawsuits. As a country of laws, people have the right to seek reparations for their injuries whether they are caused by medical malpractice, vehicle crash, slip and fall accident, or libelous or slanderous comment. These and other similar situations are classified as personal injury cases because the injury is to an individual rather than to his or her property. Plaintiffs must prove both the extent of their injury and that the injury was caused by the defendant's negligence. A successful prosecution leads to compensation based on damages.

In most personal injury cases, including medical malpractice, the plaintiff's lawyers are compensated on a contingent fee basis, which means they are paid a percentage of the settlement, typically 33% to 40%. In addition, defendants are responsible for expenses, such as postage, filing fees, and expert witnesses. In some cases, expenses are paid by defendants while the case is underway, and in others, expenses are deducted from the defendant's portion of the settlement, so defendants receive less than 60% to 67% of the settlement.[1] If damages are not awarded, plaintiffs do not pay attorney's fees but may be responsible for expenses. Plaintiffs have little if any financial risk, so pursuing a lawsuit is often an easy choice.

12.1 Impact of Malpractice on Healthcare

Malpractice lawsuits impact healthcare in at least three ways:

1. All healthcare costs, including the cost of malpractice, are paid for by patients and third-party payers, so U.S. consumers and taxpayers ultimately pay these costs. These costs show up in the healthcare system as higher malpractice insurance costs.
2. Over the years, the healthcare system responded to lawsuits with what is commonly called "defensive medicine," where tests and treatments are ordered to protect physicians and hospitals in case a lawsuit is filed. These tests and treatments are legal safeguards, not medical necessities.
3. When sued, physicians change their routine in the short term as they and their staff take time away from their practice to gather information and respond to the lawsuit. This reduces their productivity and efficiency and increases costs. In the long term, physicians may react by taking early retirement or changing careers to avoid future litigation, which exacerbates the physician shortage discussed in the following chapter.

It is interesting to note that malpractice costs, as measured by insurance premiums, are the costs that people hear about the most, but these expenses have a much smaller impact on healthcare costs than defensive medicine.

12.1.1 Malpractice Costs

It is very difficult to know the cost of malpractice because out-of-court settlements are usually not public for a variety of reasons. Attorney's fees and other court-related costs are also difficult to estimate. One way to estimate the legal aspects of malpractice costs is to consider what physicians and hospitals, the two primary defendants, pay for malpractice insurance. Physicians often purchase malpractice insurance, but in a growing number of instances in which physicians are employees of hospitals, malpractice insurance is provided by the hospitals. To further complicate matters, hospitals are often self-insured and may have only catastrophic insurance coverage, which funds the portion of a payout that exceeds a certain threshold. So malpractice insurance premiums may underestimate the legal aspects of malpractice costs.

Malpractice premiums paid by physicians vary widely by specialty and by state. In 2010, the high and low rates were $48,245 to $3200 for internists, $192,982 to $11,306 for general surgeons, and $204,864 to $13,400 for Ob-Gyns. Parts of Florida and New York had the highest premiums, and California was among the lowest.[2] Another study showed similar differences.[3] Typically, states with smaller premiums required plaintiffs to have their case certified by a medical expert who practiced in the same field as the accused physician and/or the states capped jury awards. One source claims that a reasonable guideline for malpractice insurance costs for internal medicine doctors to be $4000 to $6000 annually, general surgeons about $10,000–$15,000, and Ob-Gyns about $15,000 to $20,000.[4] This supports a claim that Florida and New York are outliers for malpractice insurance premiums. These and the other high-cost states should consider changing their laws to address their high malpractice insurance costs.

One study estimates the cost of medical malpractice in the United States for 2010 to be $55.6 billion. The report estimates the cost of defensive medicine at $45.6 billion, which leaves about $10 billion for medical malpractice costs.[5] If changes could cut this cost by 20%, the saving would be $2 billion, which is small compared to total healthcare spending, which was about $2.8 trillion in 2012. Of course, it is only in the context of government when a couple of billion dollars is "small potatoes." In the real world, saving $2 billion is worth the effort. Remember that the average cost of healthcare in the United States was $8917 per person for 2012. So each $1 billion saved would allow the United States to treat 112,145 people who currently go without healthcare. Try telling these people that it is not worth the effort. Plus, reducing the incidence of malpractice lawsuits should greatly reduce the practice of defensive medicine.

12.1.2 Defensive Medicine: Extra Testing and Treatments, Just to be Safe

The second and larger impact of malpractice lawsuits on costs is defensive medicine, which is hidden from view. Defensive medicine is a reaction to litigation and the high cost of malpractice insurance premiums; it is a deviation from sound medical practice to address the threat of a lawsuit. Physicians engage in defensive medicine when they make decisions that protect them from lawsuits rather than giving patients what they need. Tests or procedures, whether they are given for defensive medicine or diagnostic and treatment purposes, have complications, which can harm patients. In addition, high-risk specialists often order unnecessary tests, such as CT scans, biopsies, and MRIs, and they prescribe more antibiotics than dictated by sound medical practice. The estimate for defensive medicine is substantial, $45.6 billion in 2010 or about 1.6% of total healthcare spending. In theory, all costs for defensive medicine are unnecessary and could be eliminated, but if these costs could be cut in half, more than 2.5 million patients ($45.6 billion multiplied by 0.5 divided by $8917) who do not currently have healthcare could be treated.

One option is to employ a standard of care that defines actions that should be taken in different medical situations. There are diagnosis-related groups (DRGs) that identify hospital "products," such as a gall bladder removal or coronary bypass surgery. The intent is to define the care needed and the resources required to deliver the care and then to use this as the basis for reimbursement. This concept could be expanded with the intent of identifying which tests and procedures are appropriate when patients present with certain medical conditions. If a test or procedure falls outside of these guidelines, it would require justification before the physician and hospital would be reimbursed.

12.1.3 Impact of Malpractice on Physicians

It is even more difficult to put a price tag on the impact that malpractice has on physicians because it impacts many things. Over the next decade, nearly everyone projects a shortage of physicians in the United States caused by a variety of factors, including an aging population and expanding care through the Affordable Care Act.[6] This shortage is being exacerbated by medical malpractice lawsuits. In the short term, lawsuits disrupt physicians by taking time away from their practice to prepare for the case, attend meetings, and be involved in the trial.

In addition, physicians who are confronted with a malpractice lawsuit face a challenge to their self-worth, their ego, because they are accused of substandard work that led to patient suffering. In some states and some medical specialties, these psychological challenges are compounded by extremely high malpractice insurance costs and the risk of lawsuits. Florida, a state with very high malpractice insurance costs, is facing a severe shortage of physicians.[7] Malpractice insurance costs and the fear of lawsuits contribute to the shortages as physicians take early retirement or switch careers. There are also indications that well-qualified people are choosing not to become physicians for several reasons, including the possibilities and the consequences of medical malpractice lawsuits.

Physicians who have been involved in malpractice lawsuits or have colleagues who have been sued may view their patients as potential plaintiffs and feel uneasy around them. These physicians may consciously or subconsciously treat patients differently and choose to avoid high-risk patients altogether.

12.2 Reducing the Incidence of Medical Malpractice

The most effective ways to reduce the incidence of malpractice are to reduce the need for healthcare, thereby reducing the potential for errors, and to improve the quality of the care. Several elements of the solution discussed so far should help to accomplish this, and they are summarized here. In addition, changes can be made to the continuing education process to strengthen it, which should further improve service quality and reduce the incidence of malpractice.

12.2.1 What Has Been Discussed So Far

Several ideas have been discussed and are summarized here:

1. Implementing patient-centered care (PCC) and emphasizing wellness should improve the overall health of people, reduce the incidence of disease, and allow people who need medical attention to have fewer complications.
2. Rethinking and redesigning health insurance and viewing healthcare trade-offs positively allows patients and their primary care physicians to make better decisions—decisions that will likely lead to reductions in testing, diagnosis, and treatment, including fewer prescription drugs.
3. Improving managerial and clinical processes as part of an effort to improve healthcare strategy and management should lead to the application of Lean thinking and Six Sigma techniques that, when properly implemented, reduce medical errors and improve patient outcomes.
4. Accelerating the use of information technology, including electronic health records, should provide better information more quickly, thereby enabling better decision making.

12.2.2 Enhancing Continuing Medical Education

More can and should be done to improve the quality of healthcare and reduce the number of medical errors. All medical professionals, including physicians, are required to participate in continuing medical education (CME). There are dozens of websites offering CME classes, including some that emphasize price and list courses from which physicians can select more or less at random[8] and others that allow physicians to earn CME "Credits While You Cruise."[9] Although these offerings are most likely high-quality and effective learning tools, the process for selecting CMEs seems haphazard. There must be a better way to update the knowledge of these most important service providers.

One approach is to provide an organizing structure for CMEs that is designated as 5 × 1. The long-term view, five years seems like a reasonable period, identifies a set of learning goals, and outlines a plan to get there. The short-term focus, a one-year time frame, creates a learning agenda for the coming year. The five-year plan and its goals are dynamic because the plan is reviewed and updated each year. So the five-year plan rolls forward year after year, adjusting the five-year goals as needed and creating a new one-year plan for each annualized planning cycle. Even though the discussion focuses on physicians, this approach could apply to all healthcare professionals.

The process for setting goals is based on gap analysis. Each year, physicians and their employers identify the skills and knowledge needed to be successful. These needs are compared to the current knowledge and skills of the physician to determine the gaps between needs and capabilities. Learning goals are determined based on these gaps, and they become the basis for creating a customized CME program for each physician, so he or she ultimately closes the knowledge gap.

Even though hospitals are moving toward employing physicians, the majority of physicians are still independent contractors who seek admitting privilege at hospitals. These physicians must also be required to prepare such a plan, using the hospitals to which they admit the most patients or through a panel of colleagues who could provide input into the process of creating a customized CME program. It is in the best interest of the physicians, hospitals, and patients to have a focused and effective CME program. It should be self-evident that the content of the learning modules should be well designed and demanding and that the mandatory assessment should be rigorous.

Another facet of CME planning is to link it to a peer-review program that takes place regularly. Peer review can take a variety of forms, including a routine assessment in which one or more physicians review and comment on the charts of patients who are under the care of another physician. These comments should help to identify areas in which physicians would benefit from CME.

In addition, there is a process, which takes place as needed, to examine and learn from medical errors. Here, cases are reviewed by a team of physicians to understand what happened, learn from the errors, and take action so that it does not happen again. There could be several outcomes, including changing hospital processes and procedures, employing different treatment regimens and using different medical devices. Physicians, among others, have suggested that physicians should police themselves through this type of process. When physicians are identified who are not performing at a suitable level, they would move through a process, which includes extra CME classes, to help them get better. If this fails, physicians could have their license to practice rescinded. It is in the best interest of physicians to assure high-quality care. The biggest problems with self-policing are ensuring that processes are fair and protecting the physicians who are part of the peer-review team from retaliatory lawsuits.

12.3 Understanding the Legal Process

It is important to have a consequence for negligent behavior. Giving those who are negligent a free pass for bad behavior reduces the incentives to strive for better outcomes. The intent is not to stifle worthwhile lawsuits but to rid the legal system of lawsuits that have little or no chance for success. They clog the courts, delay settlements in legitimate cases, waste legal resources, and increase costs. Although the discussion focuses on medical malpractice lawsuits, the issues are applicable to other types of personal injury cases. In personal injury cases, four groups, in addition to the court, are involved:

1. Plaintiffs who allegedly have suffered from poor medical services
2. Plaintiffs' lawyers who are seeking damages for plaintiffs and compensation for themselves

3. Defendants who have allegedly rendered substandard care
4. Defendants' lawyers who develop and execute a defense and are usually compensated by the hour

Working through the legal system, these four groups determine the proceedings, including how long it takes. The following sections examine these groups to see what motivates and inhibits their behaviors.

12.3.1 The Plaintiffs' Predicament

Plaintiffs who were under the care of physicians and/or had services at a hospital or surgical center allegedly suffered negative consequences from their treatment. Plaintiffs are upset, hurt, confused, and possibly angry about the outcome. Plaintiffs hear stories from various sources about large settlements in personal injury cases. They are aware, even encouraged through television and other advertisements, to file lawsuits. The ads often claim that law firm X or lawyer Y can get settlements for plaintiffs to ease their suffering. There are testimonials from successful litigants about how a law firm or lawyer fought hard to get them the settlements they deserved.

The plaintiffs are suffering, feel someone else is responsible, and have a good chance to receive a substantial settlement. These forces motivate plaintiffs to contact an attorney and file a lawsuit because of the following reasons:

1. Plaintiffs have no upfront costs
2. Plaintiffs may have little to no out-of-pocket costs even if the case goes to trial
3. The plaintiff's lawyer is paid only when they are successful

12.3.2 The Plaintiffs' Lawyers' Predicament

Plaintiffs' lawyers are taking a calculated risk. Like the plaintiffs, these attorneys are risking their time, but more than that, they are risking their livelihood, their job. Plaintiffs' lawyers have expenses for office space and support staff, so there are biweekly and monthly obligations they must pay long before receiving a settlement check. Once their practice is up and running, their cash flows become easier as past victories allow them to pay their obligations to support current cases.

On the other hand, there are positives for the plaintiffs' lawyers. Although there are risks, the rewards are substantial. It does not take many victories each year to have a successful practice when the fee is 33% to 40% of the settlement—plus the settlement pays other expenses. Plaintiffs' lawyers must work hard to identify and select cases that are most likely to be successful, especially for out-of-court settlements. Defendants are incentivized to settle out of court because, unlike the plaintiffs, the defendants' legal expenses begin when the suit is filed. When plaintiffs can sit back and wait, and defendants feel pressure to settle, a low bar is set for what cases are winnable.

12.3.3 The Defendants' Predicament

Physicians in medical malpractice lawsuits are placed in an uncomfortable position. They face a legal challenge that could be very expensive to resolve, including attorney's fees, court costs, and a settlement if the case is lost. Some part of these costs may be covered by malpractice insurance and by funds from hospitals or surgical centers where they work. However, insurance is not free, so any amount paid by insurers is reflected in physicians' malpractice insurance premiums, which, in turn, become part of their fees. Hospitals' malpractice premiums, their portion of any settlements, and their financial support for physicians are not free either. These costs are embedded in the fees patients pay for hospital services.

Beyond these costs, plaintiffs and their lawyers have challenged the quality of the physicians' work as well as their reputation. This is a psychological blow that may cause physicians to question their value and competence, and it may be difficult for them to accept. Physicians face a second fiscal hardship as they take time away from their practice to meet with lawyers, gather information, and spend time in court if the case goes to trial. Damage to their reputation may translate into fewer patients and lower incomes. Medical facilities, like physicians, also face the consequences of damaged reputations.

Hospitals, surgery centers, and other healthcare entities are likely to be defendants or codefendants in medical malpractice lawsuits. If the incident occurred at a hospital, the physician and the facility will almost certainly be sued. Lawyers don't want to file suit against a physician and go through the legal process only to learn that the physician did nothing wrong and the hospital was negligent. If lawyers sue the physician and the hospital, they can collect from one or the other or both, depending on the findings. Having other defendants affords multiple sources of funds to pay potentially larger settlements, plus medical facilities are likely to have deeper pockets than physicians.

12.3.4 The Defendants' Lawyers' Predicament

In some ways, defendants' lawyers are in the best position of the four. They are not being sued, they assume no financial risk because they are paid whether they win or lose, and they have not suffered a serious injury. In many cases, they do not even have to go to court because defendants, plaintiffs, and plaintiffs' lawyers often prefer to settle out of court.

Defendants prefer to settle out of court because they avoid the cost of going to trial and the possibility of a much larger settlement from a sympathetic jury. Also, defendants can keep the details quiet, prohibit plaintiffs from discussing the case, and admit no wrongdoing, which may help them avoid damage to their reputation. Plaintiffs may prefer out-of-court settlements even though the settlement is usually less than a jury may award because plaintiffs get the money much more quickly, which is important for paying medical bills and living expenses. Estimates vary widely, but the average jury award is about twice as large as an out-of-court settlement.[10] Plaintiffs' lawyers like out-of-court settlements because they are paid more quickly and avoid the risk of going to trial and getting nothing.

Although the defendants' lawyers may earn more by going to trial, their reputation is damaged if they encourage defendants to do so and then lose. Defendants are very unhappy when this happens because their attorney and legal fees are higher, and they may have to pay a much larger award than could have been negotiated with an out-of-court settlement. When this happens, defendants are likely to seek different counsel for future cases. In addition, defendants' lawyers are well compensated for out-of-court settlements because the time and effort required to craft settlements can be substantial, taking months or even years. Plus, when lawsuits are settled out of court, defendants' lawyers have the capacity to handle more cases.

The defendants' lawyers can justify their large fees for out-of-court settlements by claiming how much more defendants would have to pay for a trial—never mind a much larger cash award. A reputation for settling out of court at a fair price may actually bring the defendants' lawyers more clients as long as they use good judgment about when defendants want to go to trial and when the lawyers feel they can win. After all, the job of the defendants' lawyers is to keep the damages, both financial and reputational, as low as possible. They are sitting in the "catbird seat."

12.3.5 The Dynamic: A Process Favoring Out-of-Court Settlements

When these four groups interact in a process that is both long and uncertain, it is reasonable to predict that many of the cases will be settled before going to trial. Defendants often need or want the money as soon as possible, and they could lose at trial. Unfortunately, there is no definitive data on the percentage of cases settled out of court with various studies showing 60% at the low end and more than 95% on the high end. These data support a claim that the majority and possibly the vast majority of these cases are settled out of court.

When a case does go to trial, the plaintiffs win only about 20% of the time.[11] One way to look at this low success rate is that the system is biased in favor of the defendants. However, the points made here seem to indicate this is not true. The other, and probably more accurate, explanation for the low success rate is that defendants and their attorneys work very hard to settle meritorious cases before they go to trial. As mentioned before, defendants want to keep attorney's costs low, and a jury award is typically much larger than an out-of-court settlement. In fact, it is likely that defendants and their attorneys will bend over backwards to avoid going to trial, meaning they settle cases out of court that they could win at trial. This is the bias in the current system. This bias encourages lawsuits because insurers, physicians, and hospitals want to settle cases to avoid a trial and its negative publicity and costs. As a result, more lawsuits are filed by plaintiffs and their law-yers because the odds are high for out-of-court settlements.

The tendency to pursue settlements is encouraged by the courts and a legal pro-cess that requires filing motions and going through discovery during which infor-mation is gathered and exchanged and that includes hiring expert witnesses who consult on the merits of the case. As the process moves forward, courts continue to encourage settlement talks.[12] Although discovery and information exchange are important and useful parts of the process, they provide another push toward out-of-court settlements.

12.4 Changing the Legal System

The legal system is biased in favor of plaintiffs because they have little or no upfront costs if they lose, and their lawyers are paid a percentage of the settlement only when they win. However, the solution is not to take away the contingency fee arrangement for malpractice and other personal injury cases nor is it to make it more difficult to reach out-of-court settlements, forcing plaintiffs to trial. These would be dramatic changes that would turn the table and bias the process in favor of defendants who have deep pockets and would attempt to delay and complicate the process. Most plaintiffs don't have resources for a long legal fight, especially if the incident has incapacitated them and they are unable to work. In addition, there certainly are cases in which malpractice has occurred and defendants deserve a settlement.

The adjustment must be more subtle so that plaintiffs' lawyers make better decisions about which cases to prosecute. With the current circumstances, it is in the best interest of the plaintiffs' lawyers to take any case for which they believe an out-of-court settlement is possible. With defendants' concern about high legal fees and not knowing how juries might react, defendants often settle cases that they would almost certainly win at trial. Settling for $50,000 or even $100,000 may make sense because the defendants' legal fees at trial may be more than that—plus one never knows about a jury award.

One way to adjust the process is to have penalties for plaintiffs' lawyers who bring lawsuits that, among other things, lack basic legal merit, have no underly-ing justification in fact, and/or ask for extreme remedies. This stipulation does not mean that plaintiffs' attorneys are liable for bringing a well-reasoned lawsuit and losing at trial. It means that the suit was egregious because it lacked the fundamen-tal underpinnings of a lawsuit. It could mean, among other things, that the plain-tiffs' lawyers did not do their due diligence regarding the factual basis for the claim. Action also could be brought if the plaintiffs' attorney repeatedly submits the same motion to the court or deluges the court with meaningless or trivial motions. This tactic is designed to drag out the process and further pressure defendants to settle as their legal fees rise. In effect, facing a potential lawsuit for legal malpractice, the plaintiffs' attorneys must now balance the reward from winning a lawsuit with the risk of being sued by defendants for unnecessary or frivolous lawsuits.

In addition, some states have specific requirements in place that address these points. Pennsylvania requires lawyers who file a malpractice case to prepare a certificate of merit signed by a licensed medical professional. The certificate must assert that the medical treatment in question did not meet accepted standards of care. They also prohibit venue shopping by which plaintiffs' lawyers file suit in a location they feel would be sympathetic to the case. This has led to reductions in the number of medical malpractice cases filed.[13] Other states, including Ohio, have placed caps on the amount of noneconomic damages. This limit does not apply to payments for medical expenses, lost wages, or other economic losses.[14] Recall from an earlier discussion that California has among the lowest malpractice insurance costs in the United States. This is attributed to California's 1975 landmark medical liability law, the Medical Injury Compensation Act, which among other things, capped noneconomic damages.[15]

12.5 Streamlining the Legal Process

Plaintiffs who suffered from the injury must suffer again because the process for personal injury lawsuits is long and convoluted. Even lawsuits that are relatively straightforward and involve small amounts of money require many months to resolve—even longer if they go to court. Delays are costly and hurt the plaintiff, who may have medical bills and may not be able to work. Although it is clear that individuals should be entitled to due process, there is something to be said for resolving issues quickly and moving forward.

Part of the solution for reducing the length of time required to resolve malpractice lawsuits is to eliminate frivolous lawsuits, which chew up legal resources and court time, thereby delaying more well-reasoned ones. If there is a requirement that a malpractice lawsuit has a certificate of merit as discussed earlier, there is some assurance that the lawsuit has legal credibility. Then, if the case is small and relatively simple and if the defendant and the plaintiff are interested in a settlement, it should be possible to reach one quickly by categorizing and standardizing cases so that amounts can be easily determined. Formulas and established practices can make it fast and simple to determine lost wages and other economic damages. Noneconomic damages, including pain and suffering and punitive damages, can be handled as well. For these cases, pain and suffering can be capped and set in relation to medical expenses. Punitive damages, which are usually reserved for cases involving egregious or outrageous conduct, would be set at zero for these small and relatively simple cases.

For these types of cases, defendants who feel comfortable working without a lawyer may be able to move through this simplified process without hiring attorneys and sharing a large portion of their settlement with them. As magistrates in the legal system learn from engaging in this process and defendants feel more comfortable with it, the process may be expanded to include larger and more complicated cases. It is a win:

1. For defendants who want to settle because their legal costs will be lower
2. For plaintiffs who want to settle because they will get their money quickly and may not have to share it with their attorney
3. For healthcare because the costs of settling malpractice cases and the cost of malpractice insurance should decline

Some cases will have substantial damages, complex medical issues, and considerable uncertainty about who is responsible for the injury. These complicated cases will most likely take a long time to reach a settlement and may eventually go to court, and the solution to streamlining the legal process is not obvious. The first step is to organize, at a national level, an interdisciplinary study team composed of magistrates, plaintiffs' lawyers and defendants' lawyers, malpractice insurance specialists, and representatives of healthcare. They would describe the current system, examine its strengths and weaknesses, and make recommendations to improve it. It is important to ensure that deserving plaintiffs have their day in court, but the day needs to be sooner rather than later.

12.6 Driving Forces for Change

Many of the steps needed to reduce the incidence of malpractice are discussed in prior chapters. This chapter discussed changing the CME process so that it is more focused and better planned. CME should emphasize closing the gap between the knowledge and skills physicians need to do their jobs and their current capabilities. This change may be opposed by physician groups, so it is important that the groups, such as the American Medical Association, are brought on board to build support for this change. Hospitals and hospital groups are also key participants so that groups, such as the American Hospital Association, must be involved. Hospitals benefit if there are fewer malpractice lawsuits and lower malpractice insurance costs.

There have been a number of attempts to reform the personal injury process, and all have met firm and sometimes overwhelming resistance from the trial lawyer lobby. Some reforms have been achieved, but more are needed. It is clear that future changes to malpractice laws will face similar resistance. This is a particular problem as many who serve in state houses and senates as well as the U.S. House and Senate are attorneys and may be sympathetic toward trial lawyers. So it is essential to present malpractice reform as part of a solution in which all players, physicians, hospitals, insurers, pharmaceutical companies, etc., share the responsibility for making better outcomes for patients. The key is to make it clear to all reasonable people that what is being proposed is fair and balanced and not an attempt to tilt the table in favor of the plaintiffs or defendants. This will require building constituents in state and federal governments, who will support this reform and move it forward as part of a comprehensive and integrated plan to improve healthcare. Streamlining the legal process should also be a part of this conversation, so defendants and plaintiffs get swift and fair outcomes.

12.7 Impact of Reducing Malpractice and Reforming the Legal System on Healthcare Outcomes

Medical malpractice increases healthcare costs by increasing malpractice insurance premiums and increasing the funds spent on defensive medicine. It also has an impact on the current physician shortage as physicians take early retirement and switch careers. Following is a summary of the impacts of this issue on the relevant root causes, which are discussed in Chapter 2:

1. Excessive legal liability and malpractice insurance costs: By improving patients' health, quality of care, and CME programs, the incidence of malpractice should decline. Making changes to the legal system will also reduce the legal liability, reduce malpractice insurance premiums, and cut dramatically or eliminate the cost of defensive medicine. These factors should reduce the costs of malpractice claims and improve patient outcomes (root cause #7).
2. Shortage of healthcare professionals: The current shortage of physicians, which is likely to be exacerbated by the high incidence of malpractice lawsuits and the correspondingly high cost of malpractice insurance, can be relieved to some extent by reducing malpractice claims (root cause #8).

12.8 Summary of Recommendations

Following is a listing of the key recommendations contained in this chapter:

1. Several recommendations from prior chapters describe ways to reduce the incidence of medical malpractice. They are the following:
    a. Implementing PCC and emphasizing wellness
    b. Rethinking and redesigning health insurance and viewing trade-offs positively
    c. Improving managerial and clinical processes
    d. Accelerating the use of information technology
2. Creating a standard of care that would identify which tests and procedures are appropriate for certain medical conditions and requiring explanations for deviating in order to be reimbursed.

3. Improving CME by providing structure and focus. This involves a five-year plan that sets learning goals and a one-year plan that identifies CME classes taken in the current year. New five-year and one-year plans are created each year. Physicians and other healthcare professionals should do the following:

   a. Link results from regular peer-reviewed assessments to the CME plan
   b. Link periodic reviews of medical errors, as appropriate, to the CME plan

4. Changing the legal system to eliminate frivolous lawsuits and balance the playing field between plaintiffs and defendants by doing the following:

   a. Having penalties or legal liabilities for attorneys who bring lawsuits that lack legal merit, use unreasonable tactics to draw out the process, or ask for extreme remedies
   b. Requiring the plaintiff to have a certificate of merit before proceeding
   c. Capping noneconomic damages

5. Streamlining the legal process by doing the following:

   a. Categorizing and standardizing small and simple lawsuits so that they can be settled quickly and easily, possibly without attorneys
   b. Creating a national, cross-disciplinary group to examine the legal process and simplify it for cases that are too large and too complex to be categorized

References

1. Goguen, D. 2015. Lawyers' fees in your personal injury case. AllLaw. http://www.all law.com/articles/nolo/personal-injury/lawyers-fees.html (accessed August 19, 2015).
2. Greenwood, B. 2015. How much do doctors pay for insurance? http://work.chron .com/much-doctors-pay-insurance-7304.html (accessed February 7, 2015).
3. Quora. 2010. How much, on the average, does doctors' malpractice insurance cost in the US? http://www.quora.com/How-much-on-the-average-does-doctors-malpractice -insurance-cost-in-the-US (accessed February 16, 2015).
4. InsuranceQnA. 2015. What is the average cost for malpractice insurance? http:// www.insuranceqna.com/liability-insurance/average-cost-for-malpractice-insurance .html (accessed September 15, 2015).
5. Lott, J. 2010. Malpractice liability costs U.S. $55.6 billion: Study. *Reuters*, (September 7). http://www.reuters.com/article/2010/09/07/us-malpractice-usa-idUS TRE6860KN20100907 (accessed February 7, 2015); HealthDay News. 2010. Cost of medical malpractice tops $55 billion a year in the US. *U.S. News and World Report*, (September 7). http://health.usnews.com/health-news/managing-your-healthcare /healthcare/articles/2010/09/07/cost-of-medical-malpractice-tops-55-billion-a-year -in-us (accessed February 9, 2015).
6. Sataline, S., and Wang, S. 2010. Medical schools can't keep up. *The Wall Street Journal*, (April 12). http://www.wsj.com/articles/SB10001424052702304506904575 180331528424238 (accessed September 15, 2015).

7. Budryk, Z. 2014. Report: Florida has worst physician shortage. Kaiser Family Foundation. http://www.fiercehealthcare.com/story/report-florida-has-worst-physician -shortage/2014-11-19 (accessed February 9, 2015); Greenwood, B. 2015. How much do doctors pay for insurance? http://work.chron.com/much-doctors-pay-insurance -7304.html (accessed February 7, 2015); Quora. 2010. How much, on the average, does doctors' malpractice insurance cost in the US? http://www.quora.com/How -much-on-the-average-does-doctors-malpractice-insurance-cost-in-the-US (accessed February 16, 2015).

8. NetCE Continuing Education. 2015. Ohio MDs and PAs… get 30 CME credits for only & $79—Fast. http://www.netce.com/ohiophysicians?utm_source=bing&utm _medium=cpc&utm_campaign=Physicians%2BOhio (accessed September 15, 2014).

9. Credits While You Cruise. 2015. Continuing Education, Inc. http://www.continuing education.net/?utm_source=bing&utm_medium=cpc&utm_campaign=BingAds (accessed September 15, 2015).

10. OnLine Lawyer Sources. 2015. Medical malpractice settlements. http://www .onlinelawyersource.com/malpractice-settlements/ (accessed September 15, 2015); Goguen, D. 2014. What is the average medical malpractice settlement? NOLO. http://www.medicalmalpractice.com/legal-advice/medical-malpractice/medical -malpractice-introduction/average-settlement.htm (accessed February 7, 2015); LawFirms. 2015. Length and process of a medical malpractice suit. http://www .lawfirms.com/resources/medical-malpractice/medical-negligence-lawsuits/length -process.htm (accessed February 7, 2015).

11. Goguen, D. 2014. What is the average medical malpractice settlement? NOLO. http:// www.medicalmalpractice.com/legal-advice/medical-malpractice/medical-malprac tice-introduction/average-settlement.htm (accessed February 7, 2015); Gever, J. 2012. Docs win most malpractice cases at trial. *Practice Medicine*, (March 15). http://www .medpagetoday.com/PracticeManagement/Medicolegal/32692 (accessed February 7, 2015).

12. LawFirms. 2015. Length and process of a medical malpractice suit. http://www .lawfirms.com/resources/medical-malpractice/medical-negligence-lawsuits/length -process.htm (accessed February 7, 2015).

13. Administrative Office of Pennsylvania Courts: Office of Communication. 2012. Background on Medical Malpractice. (November) http://www.pacourts.us/assets /files/setting-2236/file-1736.pdf?cb=ee37a5 (accessed September 15, 2015).

14. Medical Malpractice. 2015. Ohio Medical Malpractice: Statute of Limitations and Award Limits. NOLO. http://www.medicalmalpractice.com/statute-of-limitations/OH /Ohio-Medical-Malpractice-Statutes.htm (accessed February 1, 2015).

15. Marcelis, R. interview of Fred J. Hiestand. 2015. *Business Law Journal*, (February 26). http://blj.ucdavis.edu/archives/vol-11-no-1/interview-fred-j-hiestand.html (accessed September 15, 2015); Greenwood, B. 2015. How much do doctors pay for insurance? http://work.chron.com/much-doctors-pay-insurance-7304.html (accessed February 7, 2015); Quora. 2010. How much, on the average, does doctors' malpractice insur ance cost in the US? http://www.quora.com/How-much-on-the-average-does-doc tors-malpractice-insurance-cost-in-the-US (accessed February 16, 2015).

Chapter 13

Rebuilding the Provider Network

This chapter focuses on healthcare professionals, specifically on physicians who are currently in short supply. It also examines nontraditional methods to deliver healthcare with emphasis on an expanded role for pharmacies. Hospitals are a key part of the provider network, but an earlier chapter discussed how hospitals may change, so those ideas are not repeated here. For many decades, pharmacies have provided essential services. With approximately 159,000 highly educated pharmacists operating at 75,000 locations in the United States,[1] pharmacies are an underused community resource that can play a key role in delivering knowledge about wellness, collecting health screening data for patients, and even providing routine healthcare services onsite. Pharmacies can be a hub for delivering healthcare to neighborhoods.

On the people side of healthcare, it seems clear that the current and potentially growing physician shortage is the most pressing issue because it takes a long time to educate physicians. When high school graduates decide to become physicians, they typically need four years in a premedicine or similar program to earn their bachelor's degree, four years in medical school, and three to six years in a medical residency program to be eligible for board certification (see Table 13.1 for the length of residencies by specialty). In addition, many specialties offer advanced fellowship training after residency that may take one to three years more. Without a fellowship or additional subspecialty training, it takes physicians 11 to 14 years after high school to complete the journey.[2]

Registered nurses (RNs) require four years after high school to earn a bachelor of science in nursing (BSN) or three years to earn either an associate degree in nursing (ADN) from a college or university or a diploma of nursing through a hospital-based

229

Table 13.1   Physician Residencies and Primary Care versus Specialists

Specialty	Minimum Residency Length (Years)[a]	Primary Care or Specialist
Family practice	3	Primary care (always)
Internal medicine	3	Primary care (often)
Pediatrics	3	Primary care (often)
Anesthesiology	4	Specialist
Cardiology	6	Specialist
General surgery	5	Specialist
Obstetrics-gynecology	4	Specialist
Oncology	4	Specialist
Ophthalmology	4	Specialist
Orthopedic surgery	5	Specialist
Pathology	4	Specialist
Plastic surgery	6	Specialist
Psychiatry	4	Specialist
Urology	5	Specialist

Source: Washington University School of Medicine in St. Louis. 2015. Residency road-map. http://residency.wustl.edu/Residencies/Pages/LengthofResidencies.aspx.

Note: List is illustrative and not exhaustive.

[a] In some cases, lengths vary because of fellowship and additional requirements of subspecialties.

program.[3] Each of these alternate paths allows graduates to become RNs when they sit for and pass the National Council Licensure Examination (NCLEX). Table 13.2 provides an overview of the requirements and timing to educate physicians and RNs as well as physician assistants and nurse practitioners, which are discussed later.

The time difference among these alternatives begs the question: Why take the BSN route to become an RN as it requires more time? There is a belief and some evidence to support the claim that more education helps BSNs to be better at their work. According to a study by the Association of Colleges of Nursing, RNs with a BSN education achieve better patient outcomes, lower mortality, and lower failure to rescue rates.[4] Also, the Institute of Medicine's report on the future of nursing recommends that the proportion of RNs with four-year degrees should increase to 80% by 2020.[5]

Table 13.2 Educational Pathways and Timings for Physicians, Registered Nurses, Physician Assistants, and Nurse Practitioners

	Physician	*Registered Nurse (RN)*	*Registered Nurse (RN) with Bachelor's*	*Physician Assistant*	*Nurse Practitioner*
Undergraduate degree	Bachelor's degree, typically in premedicine (4 years)	Associate degree (often 3 years) hospital-based diploma (3 years)	BSN (4 years)	Science-based bachelors (4 years)	BSN (4 years)
Graduate degree	Medical Doctorate or Doctor of Osteopathy (4 years)	None	None	Masters in Physician Assistant Practices, Masters in Health Sciences, or Masters in Medical Sciences (2–3 years)	Doctorate of Nursing Practice (DNP) or Master of Science in Nursing (MSN) (4 years typically; change is underway to combine BSN and DNP programs)

(Continued)

Table 13.2 (Continued)   Educational Pathways and Timings for Physicians, Registered Nurses, Physician Assistants, and Nurse Practitioners

	Physician	Registered Nurse (RN)	Registered Nurse (RN) with Bachelor's	Physician Assistant	Nurse Practitioner
Post-graduate residence	3–6 years, possibly more	None	None	None	None, but RN practical experience is required
Licensure/board certification	Required	Required	Required	Required	Required
Minimum time after high school	11–14 years	3 years	4 years	6–7 years	8 years
Continuing medical education	Required	Required	Required	Required	Required

Regardless of whether it takes three or four years after high school to educate RNs, it takes far less time to address a nursing shortage than a physician shortage. Plus, educators have developed ways to respond even faster. Many programs accept applicants who are licensed practical nurses and provide them with additional education so that they can earn an associate degree or diploma. There are many programs that accept RNs with associate degrees or diplomas and offer them the opportunity to earn a BSN. In addition, there are programs that accept applicants with degrees in fields other than nursing and educate them so that they can take the RN licensing exam. This is an example of what happens when there is demand and an open and free market: Organizations can respond with solutions. Standards are maintained by accreditation agencies that ensure high-quality, rigorous programs and by boards and licensing groups that ensure high-quality outcomes through independent testing.

As a profession, nursing is well positioned to cope with current and future shortages. This statement is not intended in any way to minimize the importance of nurses nor to diminish the trend toward RNs that have earned a BSN. It is merely a statement of fact that there are innovative programs that train high-quality RNs in a relatively short time.

Other types of healthcare providers, such as physical therapists, pulmonary therapists, and other technicians, don't appear to be in short supply. Even if they are, the time required to educate these professionals is relatively short, so a quick response to shortage is likely. It seems clear that the biggest personnel problem is not having enough qualified, well-trained physicians to deliver healthcare.

13.1 Future Needs for Physicians

According to many sources, there is a shortage of physicians, and it will only get worse. The causes are several:

1. The aging population will require more care. There were 76.4 million births from 1946 to 1964, the baby boom years, and nearly 11 million deaths so far. This leaves 65 million baby boomers, which is a conservative estimate because it does not include immigrants following the Immigration Act of 1965. When immigrants are included, the number increases to about 76 million, nearly one-quarter of the U.S. population.[6]
2. More people will have access to healthcare as a result of the Affordable Care Act (ACA). If even half of the 45 million people without care take advantage, the ACA alone will increase demand for physicians, significantly. There are about 269 million people in the United States with access to health insurance (314 million in the population minus 45 million without insurance). Providing insurance only to one half of this amount, 22.5 million people, would increase demand for physicians by about 8.4% (22.5 million divided

by 269 million). The American Medical Association (AMA) estimates that there are about 923,000 physicians practicing in the United States.[7] To maintain the same level of service, the number of physicians would have to increase by about 78,000 (0.084 multiplied by 923,000).

3. Medical technology will make advances that offer new diagnostic and treatment options. As in the past, this is likely to generate more demand for care that saves lives and improves living.

An article in *USA Today* expects the physician shortage to be 91,500 and 130,000 by 2020 and 2025, respectively.[8] The Association of American Medical Colleges (AAMC) anticipates a shortage of 150,000 physicians by 2026 and other predictions approach 200,000. The Bureau of Labor Statistic predicts the need for 145,000 new physicians by 2018.[9] If the most conservative estimate is used, that would suggest an increase of about 14% (130,000 divided by 923,000 physicians) or about 1,053,000 physicians by the year 2025. This assumes no losses for other reasons, such as retirement or career changes for various reasons, including high malpractice insurance costs. Over the next 10 years, nearly one third of all physicians, approximately 307,000, are expected to retire.[10] So not only will demand for services grow, but replacement must be found for a silver tsunami of retirements.

How can the United States deal with the projected shortfall and coming retirements? For 2013, the AAMC reported 18,154 graduates from MD-granting medical schools. In 2014, the number dropped to 18,087.[11] For 2013, the Osteopathic Medical Profession Report from the American Osteopathic Association (AOA) showed 5,154 graduates from Doctors of Osteopathic (DO) medical schools.[12] For this discussion, it is important to distinguish between MDs who graduate from schools associated with the AAMC and DOs who graduate from AOA schools. Combing the number of graduates from both groups, there were 23,308 graduates in 2013.

To reconcile the expected losses from retirements and the newly educated physicians, consider the data in Table 13.3. Beginning with 923,000 physicians, the

Table 13.3 Analysis of Physician Availability and Need for 2025

Circumstance	Number of Physicians
Status quo	923,000
Retirements by 2025	307,000
New physicians educated by 2025 (23,308/ year multiplied by 11 years)	256,400
Physicians available in 2025	872,400
Physicians needed in 2025	1,053,000

United States is expected to have 307,000 retirements by 2025. If 23,308 physicians are educated each year for 11 years, the United States will have only 872,400 physicians by 2025. This is determined by subtracting the number of retirements from the status quo and adding back the newly educated physicians. Educating 23,308 physicians each year is a generous assumption because most of the newly educated physicians for the next three to six years are currently serving their residencies. These numbers fall short of 23,308. To raise the total to 1,053,000 by 2025, the United States would have to educate about 437,000 new physicians (130,000 for unmet demand plus 307,000 for retirements) or about 39,700 physicians each year for 11 years. This issue is compounded by delays in the educational process. If medical schools decided to increase admission immediately, it would take four years of medical school plus three to six years of residency, or a total of seven to 10 years, to see the impact of this change.

It is fair to ask the question: Why have the responses from the MD-granting and DO-granting schools not been sufficient to meet the growing demand for services and cope with physician retirements? After all, the march of the baby boomer generation toward senior status and the age profile of physicians have been known for many years and could be projected with reasonable accuracy. The only somewhat recent change was the passage of the ACA in 2010, which extended health insurance to those without coverage. The number of graduates from MD-granting schools increased about 7.5% from 2010 to 2014, which is 1.8% per year (16,836 in 2010 and 18,087 in 2014).[11] Between 2002 and 2014, the number of graduates from MD-granting schools increased about 13% in total or 1% per year (15,676 in 2002 and 18,087 in 2014).[13] The number of graduates from DO-granting schools increased about 37% from 2010 to 2013 or 11% per year (3752 in 2010 and 5154 in 2013). Since 2000, DO graduates have increased by 124% or 6.4% (2298 in 2000 and 5154 in 2013).[12]

The growth in the DO schools is coming primarily from increasing class size rather than adding schools. It is clear that DO schools anticipated the shortfall and responded aggressively, and MD schools have lagged. The question is why? It should be noted that DOs have the same rights, privileges, and responsibilities as MDs. They can compete for the same medical residency programs and are subject to rigorous testing and certification requirements, which are similar to those required of MDs.[14]

13.1.1 Restricting Admission to MD-Granting Medical Schools in the United States

DO-granting schools are ramping up admissions, and MD-granting medical schools are late to the game. What is the rationale for limiting admissions to MD-granting medical schools, and how is this taking place? The AMA is often credited or blamed, depending on one's perspective, with opposing the development and construction of new MD-granting medical schools and limiting enrollment in existing ones.[10] In *Freedom to Choose*, Milton Friedman argues that the AMA has attempted to increase physicians' wages by using its power to limit the supply of physicians and to contain nonphysician competition, including efforts to restrict chiropractors and osteopathic physicians to as small an area of practice as possible.[15] Others charge the AMA with limiting the supply of physicians and inflating the cost of medical care in the United States by restricting the number and size of medical schools as well as the curriculum through its relationships with state licensing boards.[16]

Evidence of higher salaries for U.S. physicians compared to their foreign counterparts is clear. Even when salaries are adjusted for purchasing power, general practitioners and specialist in the United States earn more than twice as much as physicians in other developed countries.[17]

In essence, central planners in the U.S. government determine physician supply, which is a key part of the work force for more than one sixth of the U.S. economy. The number, size, and curriculum of MD-granting medical schools are set by state licensing boards that are influenced by state medical societies, which are associated with the AMA.[16] Government controls the number and types of medical residencies through funding support and other mechanisms. Accreditation is also under government control as the Liaison Committee on Medical Education, which is sanctioned by the U.S. Department of Education and Congress, must review and approve new medical schools. This process can take eight or more years.[10] Canada also faces a physician shortage that is likely to grow worse, and its shortage may also be a result of the government policies that restrict physician training.[18]

More recently, the AMA has acknowledged a growing physician shortage and has supported modest growth in admissions to MD-granting medical schools. It is only after the problem became clear that steps were taken. As reported earlier, graduates from MD-granting schools increased at about 1.8% per year from 2010 to 2014.[11] Unfortunately, the size of the increase is too small to make a significant dent in the shortage, and the timing is poor as the 2014 graduates will finish their residencies in 2017 through 2020, depending on their field of study.

13.1.2 International Medical Graduates (IMG)

The physician shortage is actually bigger than discussed earlier because the United States depends heavily on international medical graduates (IMG) to deliver healthcare. IMGs are physicians who graduate from a medical school outside of the United States (except for Canada).[19] In some cases, IMGs are U.S. citizens, but for the most part, they are not. All IMGs, whether U.S. citizens or not, must satisfy well-articulated steps to practice in the United States. These include earning certification from the Educational Commission for Foreign Medical Graduates, completing residency training in the United States or Canada, and earning a state license.[20]

In 2006, the AMA reported that approximately 25% of all physicians practicing in the United States were IMGs.[21] In 2007, 25% of the applicants for residency and 15% of the matches were non–U.S. citizens who graduated from international medical schools.[22] In 2010, 15% of the residency matches were from this group.[10]

Using IMGs allows the United States to understate its physician shortage. The growth in demand for healthcare services and pending retirements are visible, but the shortage covered by the IMGs is hidden from view. The use of IMGs means that for many years, decades in fact, the United States has not been graduating enough physicians. Consequently, the United States turns to IMGs to fill slots in medical residency programs and ultimately to practice medicine in the United States. In effect, the use of IMGs can be thought of as a mechanism to control the number of practicing physicians. Enough IMGs are accepted to fill the medical residency programs, effectively controlling and limiting the supply of physicians. Unfortunately, it may be necessary to rely more heavily on IMGs to address the coming shortage of physicians.

Why is this unfortunate? There is no evidence that IMGs perform poorly. The unfortunate part is that IMGs take opportunities from U.S. citizens and U.S. permanent residents (commonly known as green card holders). Some argue that IMGs are needed because there are few, if any, unemployed MDs and DOs who hold U.S. citizenship or permanent resident status. On its face, the argument is correct. However, the control point for limiting the number of physicians is admission to medical school. So that raises the question: Are there enough qualified applicants to U.S. medical schools?

The truth is that there are far more qualified applicants to U.S. medical schools than admitted students. For 2014, the AAMC reported that there were 731,595 applications to U.S. MD-granting medical schools, which were generated by 49,480 individual applicants. Applicants were highly motivated because each one, on the average, completed 15 different applications. Of these 49,480 individuals, 20,343 were accepted and matriculated to one of the schools.[23] These successful applicants are scheduled to graduate in 2017 and will finish their residencies in 2020 to 2023. The ratio of applicants to available slots in medical schools for 2014 was 2.43. This ratio has increased since 2003 when it was 2.1 (34,791 applicants divided by 16,541 matriculants).[24] There are more than enough qualified applicants from U.S. citizens and U.S. permanent residents to increase admissions to U.S. medical schools.

Some might argue that increasing admission to U.S. medical schools for U.S. citizens and permanent residents is unfair to IMGs, but that perspective is not correct. In fact, foreign workers cannot legally take a job in the United States, including being physicians, unless there is clear and well-documented evidence that no qualified U.S. citizens or permanent residents are available to fill the position. By limiting admissions to medical schools, the shortage is ensured. It should be clear that IMGs who are U.S. citizens or permanent residents, and a few IMGs are, cannot be discriminated against in hiring, but they must follow the process described earlier for IMGs to practice medicine in the United States. U.S. labor law makes it not only acceptable to discriminate in hiring based on U.S. citizenship and permanent resident status, but the law makes it a legal requirement to do so.

13.2 Revising the Education System for Physicians

Revising education is a huge task with many components, including the curriculum, admission standards, number of medical schools, number of students admitted to the program, and selecting residents. Although it is beyond the scope of this book to discuss curriculum in detail, there are important elements that are related to the solutions offered in this book that deserve attention. With an increased reliance on computer systems to manage patient data and access diagnoses and treatment information, physicians require a basic understanding of information technology (IT). This would include general knowledge about IT systems and their capabilities, the power of databases, and the ability to find and organize relevant information as well as mundane skills, such as keyboarding. As voice recognition software is implemented, physicians must develop skills to use it effectively so that they can speak rather than type orders, data, and information into the computer system and the patients' electronic health record.

Physicians need knowledge in economics that emphasizes the value of productivity, efficiency, and cost control in the practice of medicine. This must be practical, hands-on knowledge in a medical context that allows physicians to understand why and how to improve the systems in which they practice. It should also involve understanding trade-offs between the value and cost of medical care, and the patients' role in evaluating these trade-offs. Who would buy or sell a couch or any other good or service and not know if it cost $300, $3000, or $30,000? Healthcare is the only transaction in which neither the buyer/patient nor the seller/physician usually knows the cost of the service.

Physicians should have fundamental knowledge about quality and process improvement activities so that they can be involved in project teams that focus on improving important outcomes, such as service quality, patient satisfaction, response time, capacity utilization, and cost. To be effective, they not only need a basic understanding of these ideas; they need to know how to work as part of a team.

Not all of these skills must be part of a four-year medical school curriculum. For example, some of the knowledge about improving processes and teamwork would be best learned in medical residency programs. Things such as basic IT knowledge and skills could be part of a premed undergraduate program, and the basics of keyboarding could be a skill learned in grade school or high school.

Most importantly, physicians must understand and participate in patient-centered care (PCC), wellness, and prevention. As health problems arise, primary care physicians will still be the starting point for diagnoses and treatment, but their primary job will be to keep patients healthy. Even specialists must understand and appreciate this emphasis. General knowledge about these three important elements should be included in medical school, and knowledge related to its implementation and practice should be a central focus for the residency programs for primary care physicians.

Before continuing, it is important to clarify differences between primary care physicians and specialists. Primary care physicians provide first contact with patients who have an undiagnosed health concern and give continuing care for various medical conditions, not limited by cause, organ system, or diagnosis.[25] Primary care physicians have residencies, often called specialties, such as family practice, internal medicine, and pediatrics, which is primary care for children. When people use the term *specialist*, they are referring to physicians who focus on organ systems, such as urologists and cardiologists; diagnoses, such as oncologists; and surgery, such as plastic surgeons and orthopedic surgeons (see Table 13.1). Other specialists, such as anesthesiologists, have very specific skills. When the terms *primary care physician* and *specialist* are used, they refer to this distinction. When the terms *resident* or *residencies* are used, they refer to the learning experience for both primary care and specialist physicians.

13.2.1 Allowing Enrollments in Medical Schools to Adjust to Market Needs

Speaking broadly, central planning and control of labor markets has been ineffective, creating either surpluses or shortages, and healthcare is no exception. Central planners are slow to respond to changing demand, and they take a long time to make and implement decisions. It is vital to allow the healthcare marketplace, rather than central planners, to determine physician supply. Medical schools, using estimates of demand for physicians and forecasts of the number of qualified applicants they might receive, would be free to make decisions about how many and which applicants to admit. When medical schools are state funded, leadership would work with officials to check state coffers and reconcile demand for graduates, applicants, and available funds.

It is important to place the decision to open additional medical schools in the hands of the entities that provide the funds to build and operate the schools and not in the hands of the federal government. In some cases, states provide this support, and in other cases, funds are provided by private school endowments, donations, and foundations. These entities must look at the long-term needs of the state, region, and nation to determine if additional facilities are required. This decision is likely to vary from state to state and from region to region. For example, Ohio has six MD-granting schools and one DO-granting school and a relatively stable population. If Ohio needs more physicians, it may make sense to increase enrollment at existing medical schools rather than to build another one. There is no need for investments in additional assets and a duplicative administration to train more physicians. On the other hand, the state of Washington has only one MD-granting school and one DO-granting school, and it is considering a new MD-granting medical school on the Washington State University campus. Another medical school may make sense for Washington, but let the university and state leaders decide if they should invest in one to cope with an anticipated physician shortage in the state and the region.

Although the decision to increase enrollment or invest in new schools should be made by the entities that control the funds, it is essential that these programs graduate high-quality physicians. This requires independent bodies to accredit medical schools to ensure their curricula are well designed and properly delivered and to test and license physicians to verify that they meet these high standards. These bodies, which currently exist, must be autonomous, and they do not have to be government entities.

13.2.2 Allowing the Number of Medical Residencies to Adjust to Market Demand

Central planning and control of residency programs present similar problems to those identified and discussed for medical schools. Letting markets determine the number of residencies offered as well as admissions to medical school should facilitate coordination between these two important decisions. Clearly, an increase in demand for physicians that causes medical schools to increase admissions and have more graduates should have a corresponding increase in residents. Hospitals and other healthcare entities seeking residents should be free to offer the number of residencies they need to meet current and future demand. To the extent these residences are funded by state and federal governments, government needs to be part of the process for responding to market demand.

Looking back, it seems clear that central planning for residencies, especially for specialists, such as ophthalmologists and neurologists, for whom compensation tends to be high, has led to shortages. It could be argued that the decisions to limit the number of residencies has restricted supply and elevated wages. Patients can often get appointments with their primary care physicians in a few days, but once patients are assigned to specialists, it can take many weeks to see one. Because delays to see specialists are common, patients accept them, but there is no reason why waiting must be part of healthcare delivery—occasionally maybe but not routinely. Free markets should help to balance supply and demand, making it easier and faster to see specialists as well as enhance competition among physicians.

This brings us back to the IMG issue. One could argue that IMGs are used mostly to alleviate a shortage of primary care physicians. If several weeks or months were required to get appointments with primary care physicians, there would be overwhelming pressure to increase admissions to medical schools and expand the number of residencies in all fields. This supposition is supported by data that shows many IMG physicians practice in primary care, which includes internal medicine, family practice, and pediatrics. By the way, these also tend to be the lowest paid physicians, making about half of what specialists make. The AMA reports that there are 57,029 IMGs practicing in internal medicine, which represents 37% of all internal medicine physicians. The numbers for family practice and pediatrics are 22,250 at 23.8% and 20,318 at 28%, respectively. There are approximately 100,000 IMDs practicing in these three primary care areas.[26]

13.2.3 Dealing with an Imbalance between Demand and Supply

Even free markets can have an imbalance between supply and demand, but free markets work instinctively to rebalance. When supply exceeds demand, wages fall, and physicians leave the profession seeking better opportunities. When demand exceeds supply, wages increase, encouraging people to become physicians. Although this creates some dislocations, markets respond more quickly and more effectively than centralized planners, so the dislocations are fewer and less disruptive.

Although dealing with an oversupply of physicians is not without pain, the solution is manageable. Some physicians may want a part-time practice for various reasons, from spending more time with a young family to being semiretired and enjoying more leisure time. Physicians who are 65 or older may find it easy and convenient to retire as they see their patient load and income decline. Physicians who are close to retirement may decide to retire early. Other physicians may secure employment outside of healthcare, where they can improve their income. Primary care physicians who work in a network or a group practice can easily transition their patients to other physicians if they want a new career. If these efforts to reduce supply fail to balance it with demand, physicians can work less until demand increases. One benefit of having supply exceed demand is that the cost of medical care is likely to remain steady or even decline as other goods and services do when they are oversupplied.

When demand exceeds supply, wage increases encourage people to become physicians. Unfortunately, even when the marketplace controls the supply for physicians, it is difficult to build supply quickly because it takes a long time to train new physicians. Free markets will respond more quickly than centrally planned ones, so the imbalance between supply and demand will be less severe.

There are ways to cope with a shortage of physicians. It is possible that some physicians who have given up their practice may return. Physicians who are working part time may decide to practice full time, and others who are working full time may decide to work more than the standard workweek. Physicians at retirement age may postpone retirement to build a bigger nest egg. Well-trained military physicians may find working as civilian doctors to be very attractive. Addressing the problems of high malpractice insurance costs and frivolous malpractice lawsuits, discussed in the prior chapter, may reduce the number of physicians who leave the profession prematurely. Another way to extend the capacity of physicians is to use physician assistants and nurse practitioners, who are discussed in more detail later in this chapter. It takes far less time to train these professionals and prepare them to work.

The physician shortage can also be addressed by actions discussed in this book. Implementing PCC, wellness, and prevention are likely to reduce the need for healthcare. Reexamining health insurance and viewing healthcare trade-offs positively are likely to lead to better decision making as decisions are less biased in favor of having care. Accelerating the use of IT is likely to make physicians more productive and enable them to make better diagnoses and treatment decisions, leading to fewer return visits.

It is also possible to address the shortfall by using IMGs. If it will take medical schools too long to ramp up capacity and the other measures discussed here are not sufficient to cope with demand, then adding to the IMG pool could be part of the solution. However, adding to the IMG pool should be the last alternative because doing so makes a long-term commitment as each new IMG is likely to work for many years. This postpones the point in time when a graduate from a U.S. medical school, who is a U.S. citizen or permanent resident, is needed to meet demand.

13.3 Leveraging Physician Resources

As patients visit their physicians, they are seeing "new" professionals called physician assistants and nurse practitioners doing work formerly done by their physicians. Although these professionals may seem new, they have been around for decades. Table 13.2 provides an overview of the requirements as well as the time needed to train physicians, registered nurses, physician assistants, and nurse practitioners.

Physician assistants (PAs), which originated in the 1960s, have a science-based bachelor's degree plus two to three years of graduate studies, leading to a master's degree in physician assistant studies, health science, or medical science. PAs provide a broad range of services, such as conducting physical exams, ordering tests, prescribing drugs, and performing procedures. They can diagnose and treat health problems and may assist in surgery. PAs must work under the supervision and license of physicians, either primary care or specialists. The physicians are not required to be present when the PA sees the patient. In fact, the physicians can be at a different location.[27]

Practice nursing began in the 1940s with nurse anesthetists and nurse midwives. It continued in the 1950s with the advent of psychiatric nursing. The current concept of an advanced practice registered nurse, commonly called a nurse practitioner (NP) was introduced in the 1960s in response to, as one might suspect, a physician shortage. NPs must do the following:

1. Have a BSN degree
2. Earn an RN license
3. Practice as an RN
4. Have a master of science in nursing (MSN) or a doctorate of nursing practice (DNP)

NPs can cope with a broad range of acute and chronic medical problems, and their scope of work is at least as comprehensive as PAs. NPs, for the most part, function as primary care physicians, and they are able to practice independently in some states in the United States.[28]

In the future, healthcare will come to rely more heavily on these well-trained professionals for two reasons. First, as the physician shortage grows, demand for these professionals will increase. PAs and NPs can be educated and trained in only a few years because there is a large pool of potential applicants who (a) have science-based undergraduate degrees, the requirement to become a PA, or (b) have a BSN, the requirement to become a NP. These professionals are capable of treating patients autonomously, plus they are able to work with physicians to leverage their time and help them be more productive.

Second, PAs and NPs are well paid but are paid substantially less than primary care physicians. The average salary for PAs in the United States is about $84,000 with a range between $68,800 and $109,000.[29] NP earnings are similar, about $85,500 annually with a range between $66,500 and $106,000.[30] According to Forbes, primary care physicians earn more than $200,000 per year, and specialists earn nearly $400,000, so treatment by PAs and NPs should be much less expensive.[31] As PAs and NPs become bigger parts of the treatment network, their lower salaries should reduce the cost of healthcare.

It is interesting to ponder how many people would choose a PA or NP for routine healthcare if they had to pay these medical costs out of their pockets rather than have them covered by a third party. For many visits to the doctor, the health issue is routine. Patients often know the outcome before the visit, but they need the appointment to refill a prescription or get a new one, obtain authorization for physical therapy, or receive a referral to see a specialist. How many times do patients visit the doctor and use only a small part of the physician's extensive training? If the PA or NP faces a more complicated problem, they can call in physicians for consults. A tiered system using PAs and NPs is logical. Adding PAs and NPs as an integral part of the physician network should not only reduce costs, it should allow the network to extend services to those who are currently not receiving care and to reach out and offer more community-based services and clinics.

PAs and NPs would have at least three important jobs:

1. They can work with physicians to leverage their time by handling preliminary assessments and other routine matters. They could give injections, handle follow-up visits from surgeries or other treatment, and correspond with insurers and other third-party payers on medical issues.
2. Second, PAs and NPs could deliver additional capacity by providing services that are normally offered by primary care physicians. PAs must work under the license of physicians, but they can work at a different locations, so speaking practically, they can operate independently. In some states, NPs are not required to practice under a physicians' license.

3. The new emphasis on wellness and prevention provides a third outlet for their abilities. It is conceivable that a multiphysician practice could employ PAs and NPs to monitor and address their patients' need in these important new areas.

A key question is how many PAs and NPs are needed, and the answer is that it depends. It is likely that a large percentage of the physician shortage could be addressed by effectively using PAs and NPs. It is possible over time that the growth in demand for physicians may slow or even decline because PAs and NPs leverage the time and talents of our best physicians and because patients see PAs and NPs as good values, offering high-quality care at a low cost. The number of PAs and NPs would not be determined by central planning or quotas but by demand for their services in a free market.

13.4 Changing Roles of Primary Care Physicians

Two things seem clear about how these changes must be rolled out. First, not every question or problem requires a visit to a primary care physician's office. Many health and wellness questions can be asked and answered using email, text, or other electronic means, and these questions may be answered by nurses, PAs, NPs, or other experts. This communication should be possible because primary care physicians and their staffs are compensated, in part, for having healthy patients through the creation and execution of a personal health plan for each patient. Second, providing additional expertise does not mean that each primary care practice must have a full-time or even part-time expert on location for each area of wellness. Following are some of the mechanisms to consider in providing expertise to enhance wellness:

1. Existing staff could pick up the responsibility: In an office with physicians, registered nurses, PAs, and NPs, anyone could acquire additional training and address these areas.
2. Internet-based assessment tools: Patients who believe they need physical or emotional help could access question-and-answer sessions that provide a basic assessment of their current condition. These would be reviewed by primary care physicians or their staff.
3. Webinars and online videos: These tools can provide the training and education needed to promote wellness and pass along critical expertise to patients such as how to eat better, exercise more effectively, or stop smoking.
4. Use of existing programs: There are a number of programs that are currently available to help people with specific problems, such as Alcoholics Anonymous (AA) to cope with alcohol abuse and hypnosis therapy to control the urge to smoke or overeat. Some of these programs are free, and others have only a modest cost.
5. Specific one-on-one support: In some cases, it is necessary to provide counseling to address a variety of issues, including drug and alcohol abuse as well as eating disorders that impact health.

13.5 Changing Roles of Institutions

As healthcare delivery changes and the emphasis on wellness and prevention increases, it is important to find new ways to collect data and refine the roles of institutions. A focus on wellness and prevention requires ways to collect basic health data, such as blood pressure, pulse, and weight, routinely and inexpensively. These screenings are vital for monitoring fundamental aspects of patient health. There should be fast and easy ways to access routine healthcare, flu shots, and the like. Also, it is important to ensure that emergency rooms are used for serious and debilitating health problems and not for convenience or getting free basic healthcare.

13.5.1 Remote Collection of Routine Health Screening Data

Providing basic health data to primary care physicians typically involves going to their office and having physicians or their staffs do something, such as measuring blood pressure and recording weight. It should be possible to collect these data routinely and make it part of a patient's medical record. It is neither difficult nor expensive to install devices in pharmacies that measure pulse and blood pressure as well as weight. These data could be uploaded to the patient's health records maintained by their primary care physicians. Some may have concerns about privacy, but patients would decide whether to have these assessments knowing that the information becomes part of their health record. This is not different from a typical trip to the physician's office. The first thing nurses usually do is weigh the patient. Next, they measure blood pressure and pulse. When patients leave, they may receive paperwork that lists BMI, blood pressure, and pulse. From the perspective of privacy, there is no difference as long as the electronic link from the pharmacy to the physician's office is secure.

To encourage a focus on health, some employers provide pedometers so that employees can assess how far they walk each day. In some cases, employers offer incentives to employees for using these devices and meeting their health goals. Employers benefit from lower healthcare claims, less sick time, and higher productivity. With permission of the individuals, these data could be uploaded to their medical records.

There are wearable devices, such as Fitbit®, which allows people to monitor important health factors, including activity, exercise, food, weight, and sleep. Fitbit is a small device that is easy to wear, and it records the number of steps taken, distance traveled, and calories burned. At night, it monitors sleep quality, including when you go to bed and how restless you are. Data are downloaded to an online profile, so people can review their status. There are other devices that can measure pulse and assess stress level. In addition, health apps on smartphones and other devices will emerge to provide access to important information and enable data to be uploaded to patients' health records.

Now, primary care physicians, who are responsible for wellness and prevention, have access to baseline information about their patients. It does not take much imagination to look to the future when there is a fast and easy way to measure blood pressure and have it automatically transferred to patients' electronic health records. In fact, someday not far in the future, the Apple watch may be able to make these health assessments and, with the permission of the patients, upload the data.

13.5.2 Pharmacies as Points of Routine Care

Pharmacies are emerging as important points of care. With highly trained pharmacists, they have always been a source of information about which over-the-counter medications to use for ailments such as coughs, colds, and minor aches and pains. They are also helpful in assessing the potential for drug interactions as well as providing a double check on prescriptions, including the dosage and instructions. Most likely, it will never be known how many times pharmacists have kept patients from harm because they caught inadvertent prescription errors. Pharmacists often know more about drugs than physicians because pharmaceuticals are the primary focus of the pharmacist's education.

This role is expanding as pharmacies offer flu shots, vaccinations, and other routine medical procedures. They have an important role to play in providing healthcare information and disease management consultation. In addition to being a place to collect basic health data, such as blood pressure, pulse, and weight, pharmacies can perform routine screenings that are part of the personal health plan. These data can be electronically uploaded to the patients' health record and be accessible by primary care physicians. With a pharmacy seemingly on every corner, they are easily accessible, and pharmacies are usually open seven days a week for up to 12 hours a day and, in a few cases, even more. It is conceivable that some pharmacies could be open 24/7 to meet patients' needs.

The first Minute Clinic was opened by a division of CVS Health in 2000. Since then, CVS has treated millions of patients and achieved a 95% patient satisfaction rating. These clinics are accredited by The Joint Commission, which is a national evaluation and certification agency for nearly 20,000 healthcare organizations in the United States. Typically, Minute Clinics are staffed by PAs and NPs and do not require an appointment. They deal with family health issues and provide care for adults and children. Minute Clinics diagnose, treat, and write prescriptions for common health problems, and they treat minor wounds, cuts, joint pain, and skin conditions. They provide a wide range of wellness services, including sports and camp physicals, and they offer routine lab tests. With the patient's permission, Minute Clinics can share information with primary care physicians. They make it clear that patients with serious problems, such as severe chest pains, difficulty breathing, and suspected poisoning, should not seek care at Minute Clinics.[32] Minute Clinics complement services offered by primary care physicians and can give care to underserved neighborhoods. They can be important alternatives to emergency rooms (ERs) and urgent care facilities.

13.5.3 Defining Roles for Urgent Care Facilities and Emergency Rooms

As shown in Table 13.4, there can be three well-designed and effective mechanisms for care when a problem arises and a quick solution is needed.

1. As described, Minute Clinics provide immediate care for routine healthcare issues when patients want a fast response at a low price.
2. Urgent care centers (UCCs) deal will more complex, but non–life threatening, cases.
3. ERs provide 24/7 care for serious health problems that can lead to death.

ERs cope with life-threatening conditions, such as heart attacks, head trauma, respiratory failure, and injuries from car or industrial accidents. They have sophisticated equipment, and they are staffed by physicians and have access to specialists who can treat problems in depth. ERs have the ability to accept patients who are coming by ambulance or emergency medical services (EMS), and in some cases, they are served by life-flight helicopters. Minute Clinics and ERs are very different facilities with different equipment, staffing, capabilities, and costs. It should be easy to determine when to use one versus the other.

UCCs fit between Minute Clinics and ERs. They are walk-in facilities treating a broad scope of injuries and illnesses requiring immediate care but not serious enough for an ER visit. They have some equipment such as X-rays and can perform minor medical procedures. They must have a licensed physician as the medical director. They are open seven days a week for extensive hours each day, but they are not usually open around the clock.[33]

It should be clear that ERs cost more and can treat more serious medical conditions than UCCs, and UCCs, in turn, cost more and can do more than Minute Clinics. With these three choices, patients must be well educated about the capabilities of each option as well as the substantial cost difference. Patients must understand their medical condition well enough to make the right choice about which facility to use to address their medical problem. When the choice is unclear, pick the option with more capabilities.

Out-of-pocket costs, including the deductible, should motivate patients to make the right decision. There should be a big difference in the deductible cost, which is paid by the patients, with Minute Clinics having minimal costs and ERs having a deductible that is high, say $100, $150, or even more. The deductible amount for UCCs should be between the amounts for Minute Clinics and ERs. When there is an obvious abuse, such as visiting an ER or a UCC for a sports physical, the patient

Table 13.4 Comparing Minute Clinics, Urgent Care Centers, and Emergency Rooms

	Level of Care	Staffing	Equipment	Hours of Operation	Accredited
Minute Clinic	Wellness services, flu shots, and routine healthcare, including colds, minor wounds, and joint pain	Physician assistant or nurse practitioner	Minimal	Variable that depends on the hours of operation for the pharmacy	Yes
Urgent care center	Medical issues requiring immediate care but not serious enough for an ER visit	Licensed physician as medical director plus physician assistant and nurse practitioner	Some, including X-ray and other diagnostic tools	Seven days a week and extensive hours but not usually 24 hours per day	Yes
Emergency room (ER)	Serious and life-threatening problems, including heart attack, head trauma, and respiratory failure	Physicians and access to specialists as needed	Extensive and sophisticated	24 hours a day and seven days a week	Yes

Source: CVS.com. 2015. Minute Clinics. http://www.cvs.com/minuteclinic/services; Urgent Care Association of America. 2015. Urgent Care Centers. http://www.ucaoa.org/.

should be responsible for the entire bill. People would quickly learn to make the right decision.

13.6 Driving Forces for Change

Physicians and physician groups will be opposed to many of these changes. In 2007, the AMA discussed opposition to medical clinics that were opening in pharmacies claiming a potential conflict of interest.[34] The AMA has not been an overwhelming supporter for using PAs and NPs, pointing out in 2010 that most NPs have only two to three years of postgraduate education and less clinical experience than a physician gains in the first year of residency.[35]

To move these ideas forward, it is essential to involve third-party payers who will enjoy the benefits from these changes. Other constituents must be at the table, such as the International Council of Nurses, the American Academy of Physician Assistants, the American Association of Nurse Practitioners, the Urgent Care Association of America, the American Academy of Urgent Care Medicine, and consumer groups. Support from these groups should help to break down barriers and encourage appropriate increases in medical school admission and graduates, expand the number of residencies, and increase the use of PAs and NPs as well as make it possible for Minute Clinics to operate and serve their niche market.

In addition, it is important to overcome resistance from patients who have always had physicians as their primary care physicians or caregivers and want to continue to see physicians. It is important to change their attitudes so that they accept PAs and NPs as their primary healthcare professional. PAs and NPs would help patients to be well, solve problems, have access to physicians as questions arise, and refer them to specialists as needed. Part of this attitude adjustment is an educational process. Another motivator is having lower copayments when PAs and NPs are used. At the same time, it is important to be vigilant about the training, education, and performance of these professionals. When word gets out that PAs and NPs provide high-quality service for less, this barrier will come down.

13.7 Impact of a Rebuilt Provider Network on Healthcare Outcomes

A primary aim of rebuilding the provider network is to address the shortage of physicians that currently exists and will likely grow in the future. But it also provides an opportunity to control costs by offering a mix of medical practitioners, such as PAs and NPs, who are capable of providing high-quality medical care. There are also opportunities to use pharmacies as key players in delivering high-quality health and healthcare services at a competitive price. Following is a summary of the impacts of this issue on the relevant root causes, which are discussed in Chapter 2.

■ Shortage of healthcare professionals: The current shortage of physicians and the shortage that is likely to come can be addressed, at least in part, by employing PAs and NPs in both primary care services and leveraging the time and capabilities of specialists. There are also opportunities to allow enrollments in medical schools and residency programs to be driven by market forces rather than centrally planned (root cause #8).

13.8 Summary of Recommendations

Following is a listing of the key recommendations contained in this chapter:

1. Changing medical school curriculum to be consistent with the solutions offered in this book. This would include enhancing the following:
   a. Education and skill levels of physicians regarding information technology
   b. Knowledge in economics that emphasizes the value of productivity, efficiency, and cost control in the practice of medicine
   c. Understanding of quality and process improvement activities
   d. Ability to work as part of a problem-solving team
   e. Knowledge of primary care physicians and specialists about PCC, wellness, and prevention
2. Using free markets to cope with the physician shortage, including determining the number of medical schools, admissions to medical schools, and the number of residencies
3. Leveraging physician resources by using PAs and NPs
4. Creating an expanded role for pharmacies by becoming a key element in community health and healthcare
   a. Collecting routine health data to support wellness and prevention
   b. Expanding offering of flu shots, vaccinations, and other preventive services
   c. Offering routine care for family health issues, such as minor wounds, joint pain, and skin conditions

References

1. SK&A. 2015. National pharmacy market summary. http://www.skainfo.com/registration .php. http://www.skainfo.com/index.php http://www.nacds.org/ (accessed September 10, 2015).

2. Washington University School of Medicine in St. Louis. 2015. Residency roadmap http://residency.wustl.edu/Residencies/Pages/LengthofResidencies.aspx (accessed February 18, 2015).
3. Study.com. 2015. Educational requirement to become a registered nurse. http://education-portal.com/articles/RN_Educational_Requirements_to_Become_a_Registered_Nurse.html (accessed February 18, 2015).
4. American Association of Colleges of Nursing. 2012. Employment of new nurse graduates and employer preferences for baccalaureate-prepared nurses. http://www.aacn.nche.edu/leading_initiatives_news/news/2012/employment12 (accessed February 18, 2015).
5. Institute of Medicine of the National Academies. 2010. The future of nursing: Leading change, advancing health: Report recommendations. http://www.iom.edu/~/media/Files/Report%20Files/2010/The-Future-of-Nursing/Future%20of%20Nursing%202010%20Recommendations.pdf (accessed June 10, 2015).
6. Pollard, K., and Scommegna, P. 2014. Just how many baby boomers are there? *Population Reference Bureau*, (April). http://www.prb.org/Publications/Articles/2002/JustHowManyBabyBoomersAreThere.aspx (accessed September 14, 2015).
7. American Medical Association. 2015. American Medical Association physicians. http://www.mmslists.com/mailing-lists/physicians/data-cards/ama-physician-list.asp (accessed February 19, 2015).
8. Weigley, S., Hess, A. E. M., and Sauter, M. B. 2012. Doctor shortage could take turn for the worse. *USA Today* (October 20). http://www.usatoday.com/story/money/business/2012/10/20/doctors-shortage-least-most/1644837/ (accessed September 10, 2015); Physician Education and Scholarship Center. 2015. Physician Shortage. http://www.pecmd.org/Physician_Shortage.html (accessed September 10, 2015).
9. Commins, J. 2015. Will there be enough doctors. HealthLeaders Media. http://www.pecmd.org/Physician_Shortage.html (accessed September 10, 2015); Physician Education and Scholarship Center. Physician Shortage. http://www.pecmd.org/Physician_Shortage.html (accessed September 10, 2015).
10. Washington Policy Center. 2011. The looming doctor shortage. http://www.washingtonpolicy.org/publications/notes/looming-doctor-shortage (accessed September 10, 2015).
11. Association of American Medical Colleges. 2014. Total graduates by U.S. medical school and sex, 2010–2014. https://www.aamc.org/download/321532/data/factstable27-2.pdf (accessed February 19, 2015).
12. American Osteopathic Association. 2013. Osteopathic medical report. http://www.osteopathic.org/inside-aoa/about/aoa-annual-statistics/Documents/2013-OMP-report.pdf (accessed February 19, 2015).
13. The Henry J. Kaiser Family Foundation. 2014. State health facts: Total number of medical school graduates. http://kff.org/other/state-indicator/total-medical-school-graduates/ (accessed September 10, 2015.
14. American Osteopathic Association. 2015. http://www.osteopathic.org/Pages/default.aspx (accessed September 10, 2015).
15. Friedman, M., and Friedman, R. D. 1990. *Free to choose: A personal statement*. San Diego: Harcourt Inc.
16. Berlant, J. 1975. *Profession and monopoly: A study of medicine in the United States and Great Britain*. University of California Press.

17. PracticeLink Magazine. 2009. Physician compensation worldwide: From a global perspective, who's earning more—American or foreign physicians? http:// www.practicelink.com/magazine/vital-stats/physician-compensation-worldwide/ (accessed February 23, 2015).

18. Esmail, N. 2011. Canada's Physician Supply. *Fraiser Forum*, (March/April): 12–16. http://www.fraserinstitute.org/sites/default/files/fraserforum-march-april-2011.pdf.

19. Educational Commission for Foreign Medical Graduates. 2011. Definition of an IMG. http://www.ecfmg.org/certification/definition-img.html (accessed February 19, 2015).

20. American Medical Association. 2015. Practicing medicine: Four key steps to practice in the US. http://www.ama-assn.org/ama/pub/about-ama/our-people/member -groups-sections/international-medical-graduates/practicing-medicine.page? (accessed September 10, 2015).

21. American Medical Association. 2015. IMGs in the United States. http://www.ama-assn .org/ama/pub/about-ama/our-people/member-groups-sections/international-medical -graduates/imgs-in-united-states.page? (accessed February 22, 2015).

22. Wikipedia. 2011. International medical graduates. http://en.wikipedia.org/wiki /International_medical_graduate (accessed September 10, 2015).

23. Association of American Medical Colleges. 2014. US medical school applicants and matriculants by school, state of legal residence, and sex 2014. https://www.aamc.org /download/321442/data/factstable1.pdf (accessed February 19, 2015).

24. Association of American Medical Colleges. 2014. Applicants to US medical schools by state and legal residence, 2003–2014 and Matriculants to US medical schools by state of legal residence, 2003–2014. https://www.aamc.org/download/321460/data /factstable3.pdf and https://www.aamc.org/download/321462/data/factstable4.pdf (accessed September 12, 2015).

25. Derry Medical Center. 2015. Definition of primary care. http://www.derrymedical center.com/definitions/#primary-care (accessed September 12, 2015).

26. American Medical Association. 2015. IMGs by specialty. http://www.ama-assn.org /ama/pub/about-ama/our-people/member-groups-sections/international-medical -graduates/imgs-in-united-states/imgs-specialty.page? (accessed February 23, 2015).

27. American Academy of Physician Assistants. 2015. Physician assistants. https://www .aapa.org/ (accessed September 13, 2015).

28. American Association of Nurse Practitioners. 2015. About nurse practitioners. http:// www.aanp.org/index.php (accessed September 13, 2015).

29. PayScale: Human Capital. 2015. Physician assistant salary (United States).http:// www.payscale.com/research/US/Job=Physician_Assistant_(PA)/Salary (accessed September 13, 2015).

30. PayScale: Human Capital. 2015. Nurse practitioner salary (United States). http:// www.payscale.com/research/US/Job=Nurse_Practitioner_(NP)/Salary (accessed September 13, 2015).

31. Japsen, B. 2012. Doctor pay rises to $221K for primary care, $396K for specialists. (June 12). http://www.forbes.com/sites/brucejapsen/2013/06/12/doctor-pay-rises-to -221k-for-primary-care-396k-for-specialists/ (accessed February 29, 2015).

32. CVS.com. 2015. Minute Clinics. http://www.cvs.com/minuteclinic/services (accessed September 13, 2015).

33. Urgent Care Association of America. 2015. Urgent Care Centers http://www.ucaoa .org/ (accessed September 13, 2015).

34. Krisberg, K. 2007. Retail-based health clinics grow in popularity nationwide: Benefits, risks debated by health groups. *Nations Health*, no. 37(7). http://www.medscape.com /viewarticle/567707 (accessed September 13, 2015).

35. American Medical Association. 2010. AMA Responds to IOM Report on Future of Nursing. http://www.ama-assn.org/ama/pub/news/news/nursing-future-workforce .page (accessed September 13, 2015).

Chapter 14

Final Words

Employers are becoming more and more reluctant to pay for health insurance as costs rise faster than the rate of inflation. Medicare is facing trillions of dollars in unfunded liabilities. Medicaid costs are rising. The healthcare issues that have created these problems have evolved over many years. Much of the media attention has focused on costs, but the healthcare delivery system in the United States has less than the best quality, unacceptable delays, limited access, and low patient satisfaction. Attempts to fix healthcare have emphasized lowering costs for third parties, who pay most of the healthcare bills, by doing the following:

1. Shifting costs from payers to their employees and constituents through premium sharing, high deductibles, and copayments for care. Third-party payers include for-profit, not-for-profit, and government employers as well as the federal government, which offers Medicare and Medicaid.
2. Cutting reimbursement levels to physicians, hospitals, and other entities in the healthcare delivery system, so payments for services are lower.
3. Establishing (a) referral systems that require primary care physicians to recommend formally that their patients see specialists, (b) precertification processes that require approval before expensive care can be given, and (c) pathways to care so diagnoses and treatments follow a progression from less expensive to more expensive.

These efforts have been implemented over the past three to four decades and have not been successful in controlling healthcare costs, improving quality, or increasing access.

The Affordable Care Act (ACA) took a different approach. Although its name implies a serious effort to reduce costs, its primary goal is to increase access to care by incentivizing states to increase the number of people eligible for Medicaid, offering subsidies so that people can purchase insurance through state and federal exchanges, and requiring everyone to have health insurance or pay a fine. The goal of increasing access is laudable, but if the ACA does not bend the cost curve lower, how much will this expanded access cost? Can the present system, which is experiencing a physician shortage, cope with higher demand?

These attempts, for the most part, aim to solve the underlying problems with mandates and rules, such as limiting reimbursement amounts and requiring people to buy insurance or pay a penalty rather than focusing on their root causes. On the surface, it seems simple, pass a law or make a rule that fixes the underlying problem. But this approach does not work because mandates and rules do not change the root causes of the problems, and the problems persist.

14.1 Framing the Solution

An effective solution must identify and address the root causes or costs will continue to move higher, quality of care will stagnate or decline, and delays and access limitations will continue and may get worse. That is why this book addresses healthcare by doing the following:

1. Identifying the underlying problems
2. Understanding the root causes and determining how they impact these problems
3. Crafting a comprehensive and integrated solution to resolve the root causes

This pathway is the methodological backbone for creating a comprehensive and integrated solution to the complex and interconnected healthcare problems. Also, implementation should move forward broadly rather than in bits and pieces, in which all parts of the healthcare delivery system, including patients, are involved in creating a better system that has improved outcomes.

The organizing framework for the solution depends on understanding and applying the principles of patient-centered care and resource management. Through this lens, it is possible to understand the following:

1. How patients make decisions about their health and what care to have
2. How third-party payers and insurers make decisions about the kind of coverage to offer and how much they are willing to pay for it
3. How physicians, hospitals, and other healthcare providers acquire, allocate, and manage resources in order to provide care

14.2 Why Is Healthcare Different?

The methodological backbone and the patient-centered, resource management perspective described in this book are important tools and ideas, which are used to develop the solution. But the concept of root cause analysis and the relationships between demand and supply are relevant to many different industries. What makes healthcare different? Part of the answer is that third parties, including government, pay a big chunk of the nation's healthcare bills through premiums paid to insurers or direct payments to healthcare providers, and benefits accrue to patients. As a result, decision making about care is biased toward consumption. Separating payment responsibility from benefits was disastrous as consumption expanded rapidly because the out-of-pocket price for services was low, and cost exploded because the ability for customers or third parties to pay appeared to be unlimited.

This phenomenon also exists in higher education as tuition for students is often paid by parents, scholarships, government loans, states in the form of tuition subsidies, and other third parties. Even though government loans must be paid back, repayment begins after college and extends many years into the future, making it seem less relevant to the borrower when the loan is incurred. Also, in some cases, parents repay these loans. Higher education, like healthcare, has costs that are out of control. Tuition is rising faster than the rate of inflation; many universities have high dropout rates, in part, because of a lack of commitment by students; and graduates have degrees but no job prospects. It is interesting to note that in healthcare and higher education, when customers do not pay all or even most of the bill for services, costs are increasing rapidly and outcomes are less than they should be.

In healthcare, many patients see themselves in a subordinate relationship with physicians who are highly trained experts. Healthcare is a technical, knowledge-rich activity, and many patients feel unqualified to make decisions or contribute in a meaningful way to manage their own care. Plus, society seems to place physicians as the deities of medicine when, in fact, most physicians know all too well that they do not have all of the answers.

Health insurance is also quite different from the other major types of insurance—life, home, and automobile—which seem to have fewer problems, more competitors, and better prices. First, life, home, and automobile insurance policies are capped at a specific amount, so premiums can be set with greater certainty. Under the ACA, there is no lifetime limit on the insurer's liability for healthcare. Payouts for life insurance are listed in the contracts; house insurance payouts are limited to the replacement value of the home; and automobile insurance payouts are based on the market value of the vehicle, which can be found in the Kelley Blue Book or a similar service.

The second reason is that curing an ailment is more difficult and outcomes are more uncertain than resolving claims for life, home, or automobile insurance. Being dead and therefore eligible for a life insurance claim is easy to determine in most cases. It is only difficult when the person is missing and there is no corpse or when the death might be a suicide, which is excluded from coverage. For home and automobile claims, the outcomes are reasonably deterministic. Professional estimators examine the damaged house or automobile, prepare a report, and determine the cost to repair or replace it. If additional damage surfaces during the repair process, which tends to be an infrequent occurrence, the claim can be reopened.

Third, claims for life, home, and automobile insurance policies are fewer and less complex. Over the course of one's life, there is at most one life insurance claim against a policy. People may have a handful of small claims against their house insurance during their lifetime, but the chance of a major claim from fire or other disaster is very small. With automobile insurance, even one claim per year is very unlikely, and having several years between claims is common. With health insurance, the number of claims is much higher, and there is a significant chance of errors, relapses, complications, and other confounding factors. These differences support an assertion that substantial efforts are needed to effectively manage healthcare resources.

14.3 Developing a Patient-Centered, Resource Management Solution

Healthcare is complex with many participants and relationships, and it has impressive and rapidly changing technologies. There are medical professionals, provider organizations, pharmaceutical companies, equipment manufacturers, and other suppliers that must work together and communicate quickly and effectively. There is a vast array of knowledge, equipment, and procedures that are important to know about. As the solution is summarized here, it should be clear that implementation must be across the board rather than piecemeal because the solution is complex, interrelated, and touches all parts of the healthcare delivery system.

The solution begins with patients, the demand side of the marketplace for healthcare. Patients' requests for healthcare services are higher than they should be because patients often make poor lifestyle choices and as a result have more ailments. As described in Chapters 5 and 6, patient-centered care, which focuses on wellness and personal responsibility, should lead to healthier patients, who need less care. It is essential to put patients back in charge, and it is critical to make them decision makers, who are supported by their primary care physicians. Patients must develop and use their personal health plan to become custodians of their health.

In addition, many people with health insurance face biased trade-offs because insurance pays for most of the cost of care, so it is easy to say yes to a diagnostic test or treatment. Rethinking and redesigning health insurance should put patients back in control of their healthcare and allow them to make better choices. As described in Chapters 7 and 8, it is important to put patients in a position in which they are responsible for evaluating trade-offs, considering the benefits and the costs of healthcare, and paying the bills. Because people should have health insurance for catastrophic care, it will not be possible to have patients pay all of their bills. The plan is to give them financial control over their routine care, so they understand how to examine trade-offs and make good decisions about all aspects of their care. Please recall, the proposed solution states that patients would have health savings accounts, and part of the funding for these accounts would come from current third-party payers in lieu of funding insurance for routine care.

The supply side of healthcare is not well organized and managed. Presently, there are too many unoccupied hospital beds, which drive up costs, yet there is a physician shortage. People in rural counties often do not have access to the best care offered by regional and national medical centers. Many administrative and clinical processes are poorly designed and inefficient, leading to errors, oversights, and high costs (Chapter 9). Healthcare has been slow to adopt information technology and is only now embracing electronic health records even though the technology has been available for decades (Chapter 10). Drug costs are higher in the United States than in other developed countries (Chapter 11), and the United States has high legal liabilities and malpractice insurance costs (Chapter 12). The current shortage of physicians is likely to get worse as they retire at a faster rate than new ones can be educated (Chapter 13). It is essential that healthcare entities focus on *assembling, applying, and managing their resources* more effectively in order to deliver high-quality care at a fair price and in a timely manner to all those who need it. A summary of recommendations for improving healthcare is provided in Appendix A.

In addition to focusing on patients and resources, the solution must be comprehensive and integrated. It must be comprehensive because healthcare is a large and multidimensional group of healthcare professionals and organizations who are trying to resolve complex problems. The level of knowledge is high, and the technology tends to be sophisticated. The root causes of the problems are many and interconnected.

The solution must be integrated so that its elements work together to address the root causes, which, in turn, resolve the underlying problems. This is illustrated in Figure 14.1, which is a restatement of Figure 2.1. This figure shows the important roles of Figure 2.2, which describes the links between root causes and underlying problems, and Figure 4.1, which illustrates the points of interaction between the solution and the root causes. These figures also illustrate that each root cause impacts more than one underlying problem and that elements of the solution

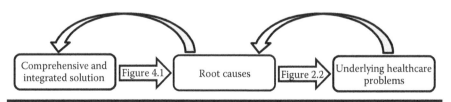

Figure 14.1 Relationships among comprehensive and integrated solutions, root causes, and underlying healthcare problems.

usually affect multiple root causes. There are important relationships among the root causes as well as among the elements of the solution.

From an overall perspective, the solution is comprehensive and integrated, but not every detail of the solution is in place. This book is an attempt to provide a broad framework and a set of ideas to address the problems with healthcare, and the authors understand that additional work is needed before the solution can be implemented. For example, the specific compensation formula for primary care physicians, who will now focus on patient wellness, must be set. The precise description of what is involved in preparing a personal health plan, routine healthcare, and catastrophic healthcare must be written for several reasons, including that some of these activities are covered by insurance and others are not. This book attempts to build consensus about the ideas before deciding specifics that support those ideas. For example, if there is consensus about the notion that people who make poor lifestyle choices, such as smoking cigarettes, should pay higher insurance premiums because they are likely to need more healthcare, then discussions can be held and decisions can be made about how to implement this. Even if the authors had all of the answers to these questions, which they do not, a process must be put in place so U.S. citizens and residents play a role in making these decisions. It is the authors' hope that as much as possible is done through markets rather than by legislation.

The problems with healthcare in the United States are substantial. It is vital that the United States takes actions quickly to address these problems because the changes that are needed will take time to implement and more time to show results. It is not possible to wait until the last minute!

Appendix A: Compilation of the Summary of Recommendations

Chapter 5: Implementing Patient-Centered Care

1. Patient-centered care (PCC) is the centerpiece of the new approach to health-care delivery. It is a partnership between patients and primary care physicians that requires patients to become actively involved and learn about their health and healthcare and to work closely with primary care physicians to make good decisions about lifestyle and treatments. PCC depends on creating an effective personal health plan (PHP).

2. Each patient would have a PHP, which focuses on creating a healthy patient. It has five important components:
   a. The medical history provides an overview of the patients' health and healthcare. It holds useful information about patients' medical conditions and family history. It will be much improved and a far more useful tool once an electronic health records (EHR) system is in place.
   b. The routine health screening plan is a basic set of simple and inexpensive health assessments, such as blood pressure and pulse rate, that provide indications of the patient's health.
   c. The preventive testing plan is a group of tests that are more complex and expensive. They would be different for each patient because they address health problems that may be identified from information in the patient's medical history or results from routine health screenings.

d. The wellness plan is a set of activities that patients do to maintain and improve health. The plan is customized for patients and is based on the medical history, routine health screenings, and preventive testing. The plan would involve various aspects of life, including nutrition, exercise, smoking cessation, and substance abuse.

e. The end-of-life plan addresses the difficult decisions that people face as they age. It outlines how they want to be treated when facing death, and it may include a living will, healthcare power of attorney, and a "do not resuscitate" order. Patients are free to choose any option including full medical treatment to save their lives.

3. Implementing PCC would require changes in the process, that is, how patients and primary care physicians interact, which drives changes in the roles and responsibilities of each party and the measurement and reward system for physicians.

Chapter 6: Emphasizing Wellness and Personal Responsibility

1. Patients must have a wellness plan. The plan is customized and multidimensional, including physical, mental, and emotional health. Wellness is patient-centered and includes a wellness plan, which is based on the following:

   a. A medical history that provides important background information about the patient

   b. A routine health screening plan that provides basic health information to guide decision making and track progress toward the goals in the plan

   c. A preventive testing plan that is designed to catch health problems early

   d. Lifestyle choices that address nutrition and diet, exercise, substance abuse, and mental and emotional health

   e. Preventive treatment that deals with vaccinations, vitamins, and supplements

2. Successfully implementing wellness depends on individuals taking personal responsibility for their health. Implementation depends on education and access to information. This means the following:

   a. Educating and training healthcare professionals with classroom education in medical school, hands-on training in residency, and continuing education during practice

   b. Educating adult patients through public service announcements, knowledge-based websites, and cost–benefit analysis of healthy choices

   c. Educating students in primary and secondary schools so that they are able to make good decisions about health

3. Offering programs that address substance abuse

4. Holding people personally responsible for decisions that impact their health

Chapter 7: Rethinking and Redesigning Health Insurance

1. Create a new approach to health insurance that would put patients in control. This vision requires knowledgeable consumers and would have the following characteristics:
   a. Patients must prepare and execute a PHP, which focuses on improving their health and reducing their need for healthcare. Nearly all of this would be covered by insurance. This would apply to all insurance, including Medicare and Medicaid.
   b. Patients would be responsible for paying for all routine services up to what many would consider to be a high annual deductible. Third-party payers would contribute to a tax-free health savings account to defray part of these costs, and these funds would be under the control of patients. This would not apply to Medicaid because the government pays for everything. Implementation for Medicare would likely come after some experience with the employer-based insurance market.
   c. Catastrophic insurance would pay in full all of the healthcare expenses above the annual deductible. This would be the case in all insurance, including Medicare.
2. There are certain elements of the ACA that would become part of the new approach to health insurance.
   a. Health insurance would come without maximum lifetime limits as legislated in the ACA.
   b. Preexisting conditions would not be a reason to deny coverage provided there is a justifiable reason that a patient does not have insurance. Rules must be in place to prevent people from jumping into health insurance when they are sick and out when they are well.
   c. Extending insurance coverage to adult-aged children would be cut back to 24-year-olds from 26-year-olds.
   d. Efforts would be made to extend health insurance coverage to the uninsured first by improving economic growth and jobs, second by savings that result from reconciling existing programs, and third by offering subsidies for the working poor.
3. Competition would be expanded by
   a. Allowing companies to cross state lines to sell insurance. This would be facilitated by a Website that holds cost and coverage information about all insurance providers.
   b. Providing information about prices for healthcare services so that patients and primary care physicians can shop for the best deal. This would provide access to information on the Internet for easy comparison.

Chapter 8: Viewing Healthcare Trade-Offs Positively

1. The new approach to rationing healthcare would lead to better decision making.
   a. Patient-centered care makes patients, supported by their primary care physicians, key decision makers. Patients would have access to information about diagnostic and treatment options, including their costs. They would understand and consider the risks of having healthcare and be willing to accept a small chance of a negative outcome.
   b. Wellness and prevention become critical elements, so the need to ration care is reduced because demand for healthcare is less.
   c. Improving the effectiveness of the healthcare delivery system enhances patient safety and satisfaction and increases productivity, thereby freeing resources so that access can be extended to those who do not have care.
2. Patients would be incentivized with lower premiums, deductibles, coinsurance, and copayments for providing feedback about care and working effectively with their primary care physicians and insurers.
3. Medicaid patients and their primary care physicians would be incentivized with higher physician reimbursement when there is a long-term relationship between patients and physicians and patients prepare and follow PHPs.
4. Growing the U.S. economy creates high-quality jobs with healthcare benefits and allows the United States to reduce the percentage of the GDP spent on healthcare.
5. To provide lifesaving care for everyone who needs it, the United States must become healthier so that illnesses caused by lifestyle choices are reduced substantially, make its healthcare system more efficient and less wasteful, and grow its economy to provide more resources.

Chapter 9: Improving Healthcare Strategy and Management

1. Several important changes should be made to improve the strategy, structure, and management of healthcare organizations.
   a. Engage in mergers and acquisitions that allow hospitals and hospital groups to share equipment and other resources to build economies of scale and lower costs.
   b. Build strategic and operating partnerships among hospitals so that they can share resources, reducing investment and lowering costs.
   c. Create a tiered system of hospitals that involves electronic information linkages and transport mechanisms so that rural hospitals are linked to regional medical centers and regional medical centers are linked to

national medical centers. This enables people from every corner of the United States to have the finest care.

2. Match capacity and demand so that the number of hospital beds available is in line with the number of beds needed with some safety factor for variation in demand.

3. Address the size and scope of middle management so that there is an appropriate balance between resources devoted to administration and resources for clinical activities. This involves delegating decision-making authority and responsibility to clinicians who do the work and involving them in activities to improve clinical processes.

4. Design and build effective supply chains, including determining what activities to outsource and creating processes to build and manage relationships with suppliers.

5. Identify and use management techniques to redesign clinical process so that quality of care is better and costs are lower.

Chapter 10: Accelerating the Use of Information Technology

1. Ensure the development and implementation of EHR at the hospital or healthcare system level. Hospitals are the key to success as they include the physicians who practice there and the ancillary service providers that support them.

2. Extend EHR beyond a single hospital or system of hospitals to achieve regional and national connectivity so that medical history is portable.

3. Pursue new technology in medical simulation to improve care and lower costs, such as the following:

    a. Sophisticated mannequins that present medical conditions to students and residents so that they can respond to life-and-death questions in a safe learning environment.

    b. 3-D imaging tools to learn about the vascular, nervous, and other systems of the body and to assess their functioning. Also, these are used for surgical planning and other activities.

4. Provide medical professionals with access to the latest knowledge through a medical diagnostic and treatment support system (MDTSS), which could be quickly and easily accessed via the Internet. This would contain diagnosis and treatment information for a wide variety of medical conditions. Development and use of this tool would be incentivized by higher levels of reimbursement from CMS to hospitals that participate.

5. Provide patients with health and healthcare information so that they can improve their wellness, be aware of their current health status, understand

limitations and possible treatments for their health problems, and manage their medical bills to limit overbilling and possible fraud.

6. Address security issues for patients' electronic records by creating strong systems to restrict access, increasing the probability of catching hackers, and having severe penalties for the guilty.

Chapter 11: Making Drug Costs Affordable and Fair

1. Reduce drug development time.
    a. The FDA and the pharmaceutical industry must work together to streamline the drug development process with the dual mandate of reducing time and maintaining safety. Pharmaceutical companies would lead improvements for prediscovery, discovery, and preclinical stages, and the FDA would lead during the clinical trial stage and review and decision stage.
    b. Empower patients with serious health problems, supported by their physicians, to make decisions about taking drugs that are in FDA clinical trials when available treatment options either do not exist or have proven to be ineffective.
2. Reduce drug development costs.
    a. In prior chapters, two important elements are discussed that reduce the consumption of drugs: having patients focus on wellness, leading to less demand, and having patients face a balanced trade-off that considers both the benefits and costs of taking drugs.
    b. Reduce prescription drug fraud by creating a national database and requiring physicians and pharmacists to check prescriptions to verify their appropriateness and check patients' patterns of use.
    c. Reduce the price paid for drugs by reducing the amount of time it takes to develop and win approval for new drugs. This reduces research and development costs and generates revenue more quickly, thereby lowering capital costs.
    d. Reduce marketing and sales costs by cutting back or eliminating direct-to-consumer marketing, direct marketing to physicians, and free drug samples.
    e. Create a prescription drug information clearinghouse (PDIC) that would provide patients and their physicians with a drug's potential uses, side effects, interactions, and costs. This would replace direct-to-consumer advertising and direct marketing to physicians.
3. Currently, drug companies charge a much higher price for drugs sold in the United States compared to those sold in Canada and Western Europe. This discriminates against U.S. consumers and can be resolved by allowing drug reimportation.

Chapter 12: Reducing the Incidence of Malpractice and Reforming the Legal System

1. Several recommendations from prior chapters describe ways to reduce the incidence of medical malpractice. They are the following:
   a. Implementing PCC and emphasizing wellness
   b. Rethinking and redesigning health insurance and viewing trade-offs positively
   c. Improving managerial and clinical processes
   d. Accelerating the use of information technology
2. Create a standard of care that would identify which tests and procedures are appropriate for certain medical conditions and requiring explanations for deviating in order to be reimbursed.
3. Improve CME by providing structure and focus. This involves a five-year plan that sets learning goals and a one-year plan that identifies CME classes taken in the current year. New five-year and one-year plans are created each year. Physicians and other healthcare professionals should do the following:
   a. Link results from regular peer-reviewed assessments to the CME plan
   b. Link periodic reviews of medical errors, as appropriate, to the CME plan
4. Change the legal system to eliminate frivolous lawsuits and balance the playing field between plaintiffs and defendants by
   a. Having penalties or legal liabilities for attorneys who bring lawsuits that lack legal merit, use unreasonable tactics to draw out the process, or ask for extreme remedies
   b. Requiring plaintiffs to have a certificate of merit before proceeding
   c. Capping noneconomic damages
5. Streamline the legal process by
   a. Categorizing and standardizing small and simple lawsuits so that they can be settled quickly and easily, possibly without attorneys
   b. Creating a national, cross-disciplinary group to examine the legal process and simplify it for cases that are too large and too complex to be categorized

Chapter 13: Rebuilding the Provider Network

1. Change medical school curriculum to be consistent with the solutions offered in this book. This would include enhancing the following:
   a. Education and skill levels of physicians regarding information technology
   b. Knowledge in economics that emphasizes the value of productivity, efficiency, and cost control in the practice of medicine
   c. Understanding of quality and process improvement activities
   d. Ability to work as part of a problem-solving team

e. Knowledge of primary care physicians and specialists about PCC, wellness, and prevention

2. Use free markets to cope with the physician shortage, including determining the number of medical schools, admissions to medical schools, and the number of residencies.

3. Leverage physician resources by using PAs and NPs.

4. Create an expanded role for pharmacies by becoming a key element in community health and healthcare.

   a. Collect routine health data to support wellness and prevention.

   b. Expand offering of flu shots, vaccinations, and other preventive services.

   c. Offer routine care for family health issues, such as minor wounds, joint pain, and skin conditions.

Appendix B: Caveats about the Data

The U.S. healthcare cost data used throughout this book are from the Center for Medicare and Medicaid Services for 2012. When the writing process began, these were the most recent data. Also, the worldwide healthcare cost data reported by the Organisation for Economic Co-operation and Development (OECD) were not available beyond 2012. So the decision was made to stick with 2012 data throughout the book and to acquire as much 2012 data as possible so that comparison would be fair.

Readers may be concerned that U.S. healthcare expenditures have changed in a significant way since 2012, but that is not the case as illustrated in Table B1. If anything, the data appear to make the case for change more rather than less compelling. Spending in 2013 and 2014 increased faster than the rate of inflation, and it outpaced the growth in gross domestic product (GDP). Healthcare spending in 2014 was 17.5% of GDP up from 17.2% in 2012. Spending on hospital care, physician and clinical services, and prescriptions drugs continued as the top three categories, totaling 61.8% of the total in 2014 up from 61.1% in 2012.[1]

It should be noted that there are discrepancies in data from different sources. For example, the OECD reported that the United States spent 16.4% of its GDP on healthcare in 2012,[2] and the CMS reported 17.2% for the same period.[3] The OECD reported U.S. healthcare spending per capita was $8,544.412,[2] and healthcare spending reported by the CMS ($2.8 trillion)[3] divided by the U.S. population as reported by the U.S. Census Bureau (314 million)[4] was $8,917. These differences do not significantly alter the point that the United States spends substantially more on healthcare than other countries.

In addition, there are often divergences in cost estimations. For example, one reference listed drug development costs at $43 million, and another listed the costs at $11 billion for each new drug reaching the market.[5] The authors used one to two billion dollars when discussing drug development costs, which is the commonly

Table B.1 Comparison of U.S. Healthcare Spending Data for 2012, 2013, and 2014

U.S. Data	Year		
	2012	*2013*	*2014*
Total Healthcare Spending	$2.80 trillion	$2.88 trillion	$3.03 trillion
Growth Rate over Prior Year	3.7%	2.9%	5.3%
Spending as % of GDP	17.2%	17.3%	17.5%
Hospital Care Spending	$882.3 billion or 31.5% of total spending	$913.2 billion or 31.7% of total spending	$971.8 billion or 32.1% of total spending
Physicians and Clinical Services Spending	$565.0 billion or 20.2% of total spending	$579.1 billion or 20.1% of total spending	$603.7 billion or 19.9% of total spending
Prescription Drugs Spending	$263.3 billion or 9.4% of total spending	$269.6 billion or 9.4% of total spending	$297.7 billion or 9.8% of total spending

Source: Center for Medicare and Medicaid Services. 2014. National health expenditure highlights. http://www.cms.gov/Research-Statistics-Data-and-Systems/Statistics-Trends-and-Reports/NationalHealthExpendData/downloads/highlights.pdf (accessed February 9, 2016).

used range. The intent is to provide the best available, most reasonable data so that readers can fairly judge the underlying problems, root causes, and the solution.

References

1. Center for Medicare and Medicaid Services. 2014. National health expenditure highlights. http://www.cms.gov/Research-Statistics-Data-and-Systems/Statistics-Trends-and-Reports/NationalHealthExpendData/downloads/highlights.pdf (accessed February 9, 2016).
2. Organisation for Economic Co-operation and Development (OECD). 2012. Health resources. https://data.oecd.org/healthres/health-spending.htm (accessed November 27, 2015).
3. Center for Medicare and Medicaid Services. 2012. National health expenditure highlights. http://www.cms.gov/Research-Statistics-Data-and-Systems/Statistics-Trends-and-Reports/NationalHealthExpendData/downloads/highlights.pdf (accessed February 20, 2014).

4. Multpl.com. 2015. US population by year. http://www.multpl.com/united-states -population/table (accessed November 27, 2015); United States Census Bureau. 2015. U.S. census quick facts. http://www.census.gov/quickfacts/table/PST045214/00 (accessed November 27, 2015).

5. Herper, M. 2012. The truly staggering costs of inventing new drugs. (February 10). *Forbes*, http://www.forbes.com/sites/matthewherper/2012/02/10/the-truly-staggering-cost-of -inventing-new-drugs/ (accessed January 9, 2015); PhRMA.org. 2015. Biopharmaceutical research & development: The process behind new medicines. http://www.phrma.org /sites/default/files/pdf/rd_brochure_022307.pdf (accessed November 5, 2015); PLOS Medical Journal's Community Blog. 2012. Pharmaceutical R&D costly myths. (March 7). http://blogs.plos.org/speakingofmedicine/2012/03/07/pharmaceutical-rds -costly-myths/ (accessed January 28, 2015), Morgan, S., Grootendorst, P., Lexchin, J., Cunningham, C., and Greyson, D. 2011. The cost of drug development: A systemic review. *Health Policy*, 100(1) (April) http://www.ncbi.nlm.nih.gov/pubmed/21256615 (accessed January 27, 2015).

Index